A Complete Guide to Careers

Prem P. Bhalla

ATLANTIC

PUBLISHERS & DISTRIBUTORS (P) LTD

Published by

ATLANTIC

PUBLISHERS & DISTRIBUTORS (P) LTD

7/22, Ansari Road, Darya Ganj,
New Delhi-110002
Phones : +91-11-40775252, 23273880, 23275880, 23280451
Fax : +91-11-23285873
Web : www.atlanticbooks.com
E-mail : orders@atlanticbooks.com

Branch Office
5, Nallathambi Street, Wallajah Road,
Chennai-600002
Phones : +91-44-64611085, 32413319
E-mail : chennai@atlanticbooks.com

Printed in India at Glorious Printers, A-13, D.S.I.D.C.,
Jhilmil Industrial Area, Delhi-110095

Preface

Two out of every five people are pursuing vocations that they do not like. Is it then surprising that we see mediocrity in every business and profession? Should this trend continue? Should one be deprived of the happiness one finds in doing something one really likes? It is not necessary particularly when the selection of a vocation is within the means of everyone.

One-third of the adult productive life is spent in pursuing a career. Another one-third is spent in sleep and rest. One does not have much control over this time. The rest of the time is spent in looking after one's personal needs, with the family and friends, and in doing necessary activities like commuting to and from work, waiting for others or just eating our meals. The control one can exert over these activities is also limited.

To find happiness in one's vocation one must do the kind of work one likes. The work must be in harmony with one's personality and circumstances. Since one needs to choose a vocation when one is still in school, and at that stage one is passing through adolescence, most young people lack confidence in making such a vital decision. They often turn to their parents, teachers and friends for advice but are rarely sufficiently confident due to lack of information.

A Complete Guide to Careers is a comprehensive guide that explains how young people need to plan a career of their choice. Beginning from the need to work, it explains how one can evaluate one's feelings and abilities. It also explains how to gauge and understand vocational opportunities. After acquiring the necessary abilities it is equally important to get a reasonable job and get established in life. With greater competition and paucity of jobs, it is necessary for young people to understand and look at self-employment as a means to develop a career. Since manufacturing offers many vocational options, the intricacies of establishing a manufacturing unit are also discussed.

Most young people lack knowledge of the many career options that are open to them. To acquaint them with these, a large number of important vocations have been discussed to provide the information pertaining to the abilities necessary to pursue these careers, the opportunities and educational facilities available, and how one can make a beginning. Self-employment opportunities available in each field are also discussed.

I do hope that young people will find this book useful to find fulfilment in their vocational life.

PREM P. BHALLA

Contents

SECTION TWO: **SOME IMPORTANT CAREERS**

SECTION THREE: **SOME ADDRESSES**

SECTION ONE

Selecting a Career

1 Selecting a Career

The correct selection of a career at an appropriate time can save young people many avoidable frustrations. Several factors are involved in the process of selection and getting established in a career. Every young person is faced with many questions:

- Why do I need to work?
- How is money and work connected?
- Why the emphasis on honesty in work?
- How do I understand my own feelings?
- Where do I look for help?
- How can I be sure as to what career is best for me?
- Aren't opportunities for careers shrinking?
- How does one plan a career?
- Where do I get a good job?
- Can I be the master of my own work?
- What is the scope of manufacturing units?

The chapters that follow answer not only the questions listed above, but also many more that influence the selection of a career by young people. Many practical exercises are included. These must not be ignored. When one wants to benefit completely one must answer the many questions that arise. The answers take one step by step to understand how to choose and succeed in a career.

In the end of this section, a question-answer session is directly reported. It shows the way people think. It also provides ideas how to understand and face the reality. The sooner one starts the selection of a career, the better it is. Young people who are well prepared can be sure of success and satisfaction in the vocations of their choice.

The Need to Work

2

Work is an essential part of everyday life. In fact, almost one-third of active adult life is spent in pursuing a career. Work is important because it is a means of earning a livelihood. It is a way to provide for oneself and the family. At the same time, to many people, it is a medium to express their creative instincts. Very often, it paves a way for people to high positions in the society.

Work for the primitive man was very simple. All he needed to do was to collect berries and fruits in the forests, or sometimes hunt for animals to provide for food. His needs were few. It was not difficult to provide these through personal efforts. With time, as mankind became more organized, no single person could provide all of the needs. There was need for co-operative action.

Each individual began to contribute his labour so that all mankind could live more comfortably and efficiently. The needs of mankind have continued to grow. This has necessitated still greater division of labour. In the present age, the division of labour has grown further. In many of the large assembly lines, the contribution of an individual seems insignificant and trifling. Yet every little effort adds up to ensure that the finished product is cheaper and better. It provides greater satisfaction to the consumer.

Most of the progress has come out of increasing knowledge and experience in every field of work. This encouraged the need for the ever-growing division of labour. The obvious result was the need for specialization in all fields of work. The increasing population, while placing a greater demand on the gifts of nature, has brought about greater competition in everyday life. This is particularly so in the field most important to all mankind—the pursuit of a career.

Work and Money

To an average individual, work means money. When primitive men first began to work to provide each other's needs, the payment for labour was made either through return of labour on another occasion, or in kind. With growing individual needs, this gave way to the barter system. One exchanged the fruits of labour with those of others. However, it was not long before the transactions became too complicated to be practical. A uniform medium of exchange was devised through coins of gold, silver and other metals. These have eventually been replaced by paper money guaranteed by individual governments in different countries. These are freely accepted all over the world.

In its simplest form, money represents human labour. The money we receive for work is for the labour we have done. The word "labour" need not mean only physical labour. It can also mean physical or mental skills and effort. When we save money, it really means that we are putting our labour aside for use later. A person saves his labour as money, for use in old age. This way, a father passes his accumulated efforts to his children. Each generation passes on its savings to the next generation. This ensures that mankind can continue to make steady progress.

Learning Correct Money Values

If we can understand that money represents human labour, we can immediately appreciate the need for developing correct values about money in everyday life. The interest of most young people is restricted to their need for some spending money. They may entertain hopes about earning large sums in their adult life when they are fully involved in their careers. The satisfaction they derive from money will depend upon their attitudes towards it.

Attitudes about money begin to take shape in early childhood. During adolescence, as young people come under the influences of society and environments, money begins to attract their special attention. Money means comfort and security. It fulfils one's personal needs. It is also capable of bringing about great progress and prosperity for many more people. Money is a great source of power. Therefore, people find it particularly attractive. It has great motivating qualities. People are often willing to undergo many sacrifices to attain it. Few realize that money is only as useful as the use you put it to. Possessing it for its own sake may apparently be satisfying but serves no purpose.

The sheer possession of money is no indication that a person is rich or poor. The possession could be deceptive, as the money could be somebody else's. It may have been attained in a dubious manner. A person is rightfully rich not because of the money he may possess, but due to personal qualities, and the attitudes about earning, spending and saving it. Only that person qualifies to be called rich who can confidently meet his everyday needs honourably. Every young person must understand that money is a good slave, but a bad master.

Ethical Standards and Work

In an organized society such as we have, there are certain conventions, which need to be followed when we pursue a career. These are termed ethics. Every business and vocation has its own ethics developed through trial and error. Besides the laws of the country, these must be accepted and followed. These ethics are closely linked with personal morality. Acceptance of high ethical standards in one's work reflects good character formation. Of course, ethical standards vary with each trade and vocation, with education, local conditions, community, etc. High ethical standards are synonymous with virtue, honesty and clean dealings. The ethical code which one accepts and follows in one's career reflects personal attitudes towards money, and what it is capable of doing.

Honesty and Work

Since work means money, and one of money's chief characteristics is that it immediately puts a person's honesty to test, honesty at work has a special significance in everyday life.

Throughout one's career, money continues to exert a very strong motivating force for both good and evil. Depending upon individual attitudes, people undergo great sacrifices to attain it through ethical or unethical means.

The society is especially aware and critical of the unethical advantages some people take to attain wealth. A dishonest person cannot expect to settle down to earn money this way regularly. If one must settle down in a career, be it in a job or even be self-employed, honesty at work is a prerequisite to becoming successful. Through work, one does not earn money only. By providing extra service, one wins human goodwill, which paves the way for a steady progress in one's career and in the community.

A Position in Society

A person pursues a career to earn a livelihood. If this were the only criterion to work, one could do any kind of work and obtain the necessities of life. However, it is not so. A person does not like to do just any kind of work. One makes effort to find work that is in harmony with the personality. This is important because besides being a source of livelihood, work offers the opportunity for self-expression of the creative urge deep within each one. This enables one to enjoy work, and thereby truly achieve success. As the individual discovers the personal self through work, one can contribute more than what is paid for it. This is the beginning of growth in the society. The need for appreciation and acceptance as a worthy individual is inherent in all people. This is possible only through one's contribution to society by way of honest and sincere work.

Points to Ponder

- Everybody needs to work. Work is an important part of adult life.
- Work means money. We earn money for the work we do.
- Money is attractive. It is a great source of power.
- Attitudes about money take shape in early childhood.

- Every vocation has its own ethics. These are closely linked with personal morality.
- Through work one does not only earn money. One earns human goodwill also.
- Through work one makes a position for oneself in society.

3

Personal Evaluation for a Career

Every individual is born unique. Therefore, every individual responds differently to the environment. Brothers born of the same parents, brought up under similar circumstances in the same home, and educated in the same school and college, are often likely to be so very different that few people would be willing to accept this fact easily. There are no two ways about it. Even when it comes to the selection of a career, the same factors continue to operate.

It is only for an individual to decide what one would like to do. Nobody can assess an individual's strengths and weaknesses better. Similarly, no one can truly gauge individual circumstances in the same light as one can personally. It may seem needless to emphasize, but if one is to arrive at a realistic assessment, it is imperative that the individual must do an honest self-analysis. It is not rare when people are carried away by others' opinions and wishful thoughts, rather than by facts.

Factors that Influence Selection of a Career

Several factors influence young people in selecting a career. Many are attracted by the glamour that is a part of some careers. A career in films, television, politics, modelling and games and sports is always attractive to young people because of the great limelight which falls on those who have succeeded in these fields. Despite being aware of the many pitfalls in such careers, the glamour clouds their selection.

Young people are attracted to careers pursued by people who are well-known to them, and have achieved great success in their particular field. Many choose a career as an engineer or a doctor because of the fascination they may have for the field of work, rather than a real understanding of the obligations and responsibilities involved.

In selecting a career, young people are greatly influenced by inadvertent remarks by parents, teachers and others. The subconscious encouragement received by them through these remarks leads them to select a particular career. Addresses on vocational subjects at schools or at social functions also influence the choice of a career.

Another factor that is not easily recognized is the influence young people exert over one another through hearsay, by reading books and magazines for young people, or through discussions with teachers. Vocational counseling is not very popular in our country because of lack of facilities. Even when the young people have the freedom to choose a career themselves, few have the courage and confidence to relate their choice to personal preferences and capabilities. Most of them depend upon elders' guidance and their luck!

Parental Influence

Parental influence is one factor that outweighs all others when the young people consider various careers. This is due to the great dependence of the young people on their parents. However, experience has shown that parents are not always the best people to guide their children on the selection of a career. It is not that they do not know their children well. On the contrary, we can safely admit that invariably always they know them best. While they may understand the strengths and weaknesses of their children better than the teachers, friends or others, they may fail to suggest appropriate careers as their judgement may be biased against certain careers. However, since the parents' opinion may be based upon personal experience, it cannot be easily ignored. We should also not overlook that most parents have little knowledge about careers other than their own. Besides, few people have the insight to understand the employment situation as it really exists.

The Influence of Teachers

Next to parents, we cannot ignore the influence that the teachers, consciously or subconsciously, exert upon all young people in search of a suitable career. Vocational guidance in schools and colleges is still very rare. The influence that the teachers exert comes through stray remarks about a young person's capabilities in certain subjects that lead to a particular career. Most young people are receptive to encouraging remarks in the classroom. Definite inclinations begin to grow in their fertile minds from such encouragement. Many of such selections have proved to be good, but one cannot be certain of success this way. Most teachers in schools have a limited knowledge. Unless one has received training in vocational guidance, or has a reasonable knowledge about various careers, one's suggestions may not always be in the best interests of the young person selecting a career.

The Influence of Friends

Few young people may believe it, but very often it is their own friends who shape their thinking not only about common everyday matters, but sometimes even about a subject as vital as the selection of a career. When young people seek such counsel, they should not overlook that their friends are in a similar position. Young people passing through the trials and tribulations common at the time of adolescence are extremely sensitive emotionally. While they may profess great confidence at one time, they are quite uncertain about their feelings on another occasion. Under such circumstances, it may not at all be advisable to rely upon the counsel of friends who may be facing very similar problems. At best, the friends can help point out personal strengths and weaknesses. This knowledge can be useful when one sets out to analyse personal feelings and attitudes about a particular career. Friend's parents can of course offer some guidance pertaining to the vocations and businesses they are personally pursuing in their everyday life.

Career Counselling

Many colleges and universities have started vocational guidance services. Students can avail of these services to their great personal benefit. Vocational guidance officers are attached to many employment exchanges. They are willing to assist young people who seek their help. Since parents can help in pointing out the areas of strength and weakness in the child, it is always useful if they can accompany a young person seeking the help of a career counselor.

Vocational counselors do not have a magic formula by which they can immediately pinpoint the exact career suitable for a young person. Their role is to guide young people to explore personal feelings and capabilities such as are required to pursue particular careers. They encourage young people to search for answers deep within themselves, rather than be lectured at, as most parents tend to do. Vocational counselors are aware of the occupational trends in the country. To whatever extent possible their advice must receive due consideration.

Personality Traits

Despite one's best efforts, most young people are not able to analyse their feelings and attitudes immediately to be able to draw a clear picture of their personality. They may know how they feel, but may not be able to express their feelings in words, or on paper, so that they may be able to define their personal image. A qualified psychologist can be a great help in assisting a young person to identify areas of strength and weakness, and clearly define personality traits.

Since most young people do not have the services of a psychologist available to them, given below is an elaborate list of words that describe the common personality traits and feelings found in people. The list is fairly exhaustive. Some more traits could be added, but the common ones are there. English has a large vocabulary. You will come across several words that seem to have similar meaning. However, each word has finer meanings. You can choose the ones that describe you best. Tick the ones that describe you. Ignore those that do not relate to you. If you are not sure of the meaning of a word, consult a dictionary. The words are in alphabetic order. They describe both the strengths and weaknesses in people. Irrespective of that tick those that describe you best.

The analysis is for your personal use. Once you have gone through the list, you could note down the words you tick in

Abiding
Absent-minded
Adamant
Adaptable
Adjustable
Aesthetic
Affectionate
Aggressive
Agile
Alert
Ambitious
Amiable
Animated
Anxious
Apathetic
Apprehensive
Arrogant
Artistic
Assertive
Attentive
Attractive
Authoritarian
Autocratic
Aware
Bashful
Beautiful
Bewitching
Biased
Boastful
Boisterous
Bold
Brash
Brave
Broadminded
Brusque
Buoyant
Calm
Candid
Capable
Captivating
Careless
Cautious
Charitable
Charming
Chaste
Cheerful
Chic
Childish
Civil
Close
Clumsy
Colourful
Committed
Companionable
Compassionate
Competent
Complaining
Composed
Compulsive
Conceited
Confident
Conformist
Confused
Connoisseur
Conscientious
Considerate
Conspiring
Contemptible
Contented
Contradicting
Convincing
Coolheaded
Cooperative
Cordial
Courageous
Courteous
Crazy
Creative
Critical
Crude
Cruel
Cultivated
Curt
Cynical
Dabbler
Daring
Deceptive
Decisive
Dependable
Depressed
Detached
Devoted
Devout
Dictatorial
Diffident
Diligent
Diplomatic
Disagreeable
Disapproving
Disciplined
Discouraged
Discreet
Dishonest
Disillusioned
Disinterested
Docile
Dominant
Domineering
Doting
Dramatic
Dreamy
Dull
Dutiful
Eager
Easily-hurt
Easy-going
Edgy
Egoistic
Emotional
Encouraging
Enthusiastic
Erratic
Erudite
Ethical
Evasive
Exacting
Excitable
Exquisite
Failure
Faint-hearted
Fair
Faithful
Far-sighted
Fascinating
Fashionable
Fearful
Feeble
Fervent
Fickle
Firm
Flamboyant
Flexible
Flimsy
Fond

Foolhardy
Foolish
Forgiving
Formal
Frail
Friendly
Frisky
Gaudy
Generous
Genteel
Gentle
Genuine
Good-looking
Gorgeous
Graceful
Greedy
Gullible
Half-hearted
Handicapped
Handsome
Hardboiled
Hard-headed
Hardy
Haughty
Headstrong
Healthy
Heed advice
Helpful
Heroic
Hesitant
Histrionic
Honest
Honourable
Humane
Humble
Humorous
Hypocritical
Idealistic
Ignorant
Imaginative
Immature
Immoral
Impartial
Imperious
Impulsive
Inattentive
Incompetent
Indifferent
Indulgent
Industrious
Inefficient
Ineptitude
Inflexible
Ingenious
Insensitive
Insincere
Intellectual
Interfering
Inventive
Jittery
Just
Knowledgeable
Lavish
Lazy
Lenient
Liberal
Listless
Lively
Lonely
Lonesome
Loud
Loving
Magnanimous
Malicious
Mature
Maudlin
Mean
Meek
Mellow
Merciful
Methodical
Meticulous
Mischievous
Mistrustful
Modernistic
Moody
Motivated
Muscular
Mushy
Negative
Negligent
Nervous
Nice
Novel
Objective
Observant
Obstinate
Offensive
Officious
Orderly
Original
Ostentatious
Outspoken
Partial
Partisan
Patient
Peculiar
Pedantic
Perceptive
Performer
Persevering
Persistent
Persuasive
Pious
Placid
Plain
Plaintive
Playboy
Pleasant
Polite
Positive
Powerful
Precise
Pretty
Procrastinating
Proud
Prudent
Puerile
Punctilious
Pushing
Pushy
Rash
Rational
Reasonable
Refined
Regular
Religious
Reluctant
Reserved
Resilient
Resourceful
Responsible
Reticent
Rigid

Romantic
Rude
Sacrificing
Saucy
Scrupulous
Secure
Self-confident
Self-conscious
Selfish
Sensible
Sensitive
Sentimental
Serene
Servile
Severe
Sharp
Shrewd
Shy
Simpleton
Sincere
Slavish
Sloppy
Slow
Sluggish
Sly
Smart
Smug
Sober
Sociable
Sophisticated
Spirited
Spiteful
Spontaneous
Sporting
Steady
Stern
Straightforward
Strict
Strong-willed
Stupid
Suave
Subjective
Submissive
Subservient
Successful
Superficial
Supportive
Suspicious
Sympathetic
Tactful
Talkative
Tame
Theatrical
Thoughtful
Thoughtless
Timid
Tolerant
Tough
Tranquil
Trendy
Trusting
Truthful
Tyrannical
Unaesthetic
Unassuming
Unattractive
Unbiased
Uncertain
Uncommunicative
Unconcerned
Undisciplined
Undisturbed
Unethical
Unfeigned
Unfit
Unprincipled
Unreasonable
Unruffled
Unscrupulous
Upright
Vague
Vain
Versatile
Vindictive
Virtuous
Vivacious
Volatile
Vulgar
Wary
Wasteful
Weak-willed
Well-behaved
Well-mannered
Whole-hearted
Wile
Wily
Winning
Witty
Worldly
Worrier
Zealous

the list. Do it honestly in privacy. There will be several words that describe you and your feelings. Sort them in two groups. The first one should include words that describe your strengths. The second group should include words that describe your weaknesses. You can differentiate between the two by asking yourself what is the effect of the particular trait. If it contributes to your confidence, it is a positive trait. It adds to your strength. If it robs you of your confidence it is a weakness. Together the two lists will help you understand yourself better.

Using the words in the two groups that describe your strengths and weaknesses, write paragraphs to describe yourself.

You need to identify your strengths so that you could use them to build a career upon. The weaknesses shall guide you about what you need to be careful about. Determined people can always overcome their weaknesses.

Personal Aptitudes

Psychologists have been able to identify certain aptitudes or abilities. With the help of certain tests, these can be measured in individuals. Based on these findings positive suggestions can be made as to what kind of a career would be best suited for a particular person.

There are several interests and aptitudes that have been found to predominate in individuals. These can be measured and identified for individual benefit. However, it is not possible to analyse an individual without specific tests by a qualified psychologist. The only alternative is to go through the lists of the common interests and abilities listed below. Underline those that you feel you possess. It is not necessary that one may excel in only one, two, or three aptitudes or abilities. One may be above average in a few, but may really be capable in as many as eight or nine of them. Underline or tick all those you can identify in yourself. List them on a piece of paper, in the order of importance to you. The first two or three should be the basis of selecting a career. The others could be used to develop avocational interests.

Ability for pitch discrimination
Ability to learn new words
Ability to think in three dimensions
Ability to use small tools
Accounting ability
Aesthetic appreciation
Artistic ability
Business interest
Clerical interest
Cultural conformity

Desire for attention
Desire for diversion
Interest in outdoor work
Interest in self-reliance
Love of adventure
Love of fantasy
Mechanical ability
Resistance to restriction
Scientific interest
Social ability
Social welfare interest

Understanding Abilities Necessary for Success

To succeed in any vocation a certain number of abilities and skills are required. The workers who possess those abilities and skills enjoy the work. Those who do not just drag their way through work. Since every individual is unique, the abilities and skills too vary from one person to another. Some abilities and skills come naturally. Others need to be learnt. This learning too depends upon individual preferences. Listed below are abilities and skills that in general promote success in a variety of careers. Mark the ones that you claim to possess. Later when you get to know the desirable qualities that promote success in particular careers compare your own tally with those. If you are lacking in some field you can take appropriate training and prepare yourself for complete success.

Ability to comfort people
Ability to handle crises
Ability to make decisions
Ability to see in graphic form
Above average creativity
Adaptable to changing circumstances
All-round knowledge
Analytical outlook
Appreciate discipline in life
Appreciate need for secrecy
Appreciate composition and colour
Can face stress and tension
Communication skills
Computer literacy
Enjoy self-confidence
Enjoy working with numbers
Enjoy working with machines
Fond of reading
Fond of upgrading skills
Get along well with people
Good etiquette and manners
Good health and physique
Good imagination
Good knowledge of one's field
Good language skills
Good leadership qualities
Good listening skills
Good memory for names and faces
Good observation
Good speaking skills
Good team member
Good writing skills
Have an eye for unscrupulous people
High intellectual ability
Highly quality conscious
Highly self-motivated
Integrity and honour
Love for adventure and fun
Love for animals
Love for nature and outdoors
Not easily discouraged
Pleasing personality

Possess an aesthetic sense
Possess special artistic skills
Ready to work with own hands
Respect for time
Sense of showmanship
Sensitive to others' problems
Sincere and service-minded
Thorough and methodical
Understands shapes and figures
Vision to see ahead
Willing to take responsibility
Willing to try new ideas
Willing to work in different locations
Willing to work late at odd hours

Personal Feelings

No young person who ignores personal feelings about a career can hope to make a success of it. Each individual must analyse personal preferences, aptitudes and attitudes. One must give due weightage to personal strengths and weaknesses. Nobody can do this better than the individual. Only an individual is aware of the deep-rooted personal hopes and aspirations one may cherish, and what personal limitations hold one back. The process of self-analysis must be ruthlessly realistic. You can be dishonest with somebody else and get away with it. When one's future is involved, one personally suffers for it. Therefore, one must always analyse personal feelings in strict honesty.

Before you set out to analyse your personal feelings about a particular career, it is necessary that you must understand the responsibilities and privileges involved. Your decision must be based on a clear understanding of the career requirements, and not upon the glamour that may be attached to it. It is also important that the work involved is in harmony with your perceptions of dignity of labour.

As you analyse your feelings and attitudes, do not be satisfied by just thinking of them. Note down your reactions. Here are a few questions. As you answer them, there is much that you will learn about yourself.

- Take a look at your family background. Do your family circumstances permit you to take up the career you have in mind?

- How do you rate your personal capabilities? Good—Fair—Tolerable? How do you rate yourself?
- Is your education sufficient? Are you working to acquire the knowledge that would be necessary for the career you have in mind?
- What do you feel about your study habits, keeping in view factors like the time spent for the purpose each day, newspapers and magazines read, number and type of books read each year?
- Is your health good, or are you prone to ailments like coughs and cold, and need to give due importance to this factor in selecting your career?
- Your relationships with people can be an important guide in assessing how well you can get along with others. Do you make friends quickly, or do you have more acquaintances than friends?
- Are you outgoing, or do you prefer relationships with a few, reliable friends? These feelings can have an important bearing, as all careers require a person to deal with people. In some cases, one needs to deal with many people, in others with just a few.
- What are your areas of personal strength? Note these down.
- How can you develop your strengths further, and put them to use in a career?
- Have you any personal limitations? Note these down.
- Can you overcome your limitations? How, and by when?
- Will your hobbies be useful to you in your career?
- Are your personal attitudes in harmony with those required by the career you have in mind?
- Are you mentally capable and prepared to meet the challenges that the career will offer?

Do not answer these questions in a hurry. Take your time over them. Note them with a pencil. Give due thought to every aspect of your personality. Try to match your picture with that of another person who may already be pursuing that career. Subject to a few variations, the two pictures should be similar. Rather, your picture should be brighter as you are setting out with greater knowledge. You will also need to provide for some of those lapses that may have escaped your notice because of inexperience.

Understanding Yourself

The object of personal evaluation in relation to selecting a career is to identify one's strengths and to consider personal sensitivities and shortcomings. If you have been able to appreciate the many unseen influences suggesting a decision to you, and been able to answer pertinent questions about your own feelings and personality traits, interests and abilities, you positively stand in a better position to understand yourself completely.

Assess your personal assets and liabilities to draw an honest picture of you. You will do well to include in your assets, your family status and reputation, your personal appearance and physique, the availability of a personal conveyance, or other similar considerations. On the liability side, you will need to include personal sensitivities like lack of confidence, religious restrictions, secret fears, and other similar shortcomings.

Whatever be the picture that emerges out of this exercise, use it as a stepping stone to a successful career. Do not let areas of weakness discourage you. The very fact that you have been able to identify your shortcomings means that you are aware of them, and can get over them through an effort in the right direction. Having identified your real self, you are beginning from the best point to evaluate the career opportunities open to you. Eventually you will be able to select a career best suited to your personality.

Points to Ponder

- Every individual is born unique. You are the best person to evaluate yourself for a career.
- Several factors influence a person to select a career.

- Parent influence outweighs all other influences. However, few parents understand the vocational situation.
- Teachers influence young people in their own way. Rarely is their judgement complete.
- Friends too exert an influence in career selection. They can only guide about one's strengths and weaknesses.
- Career counselors guide young people to explore and evaluate their personal feelings and capabilities.
- Evaluate yourself by checking your personality traits, aptitude and feelings.
- Get to know the abilities required to succeed at work.
- Every person is the best judge of personal strengths and weaknesses, and of personal hopes and aspirations. Note them down as a personal guide.
- Understand yourself. Your success depends upon you.

Opportunities for Careers 4

Most young people in search of an appropriate career for themselves feel desperate about opportunities for careers. They feel that just as the many gifts of nature are becoming scarce because of the ever-increasing population, so are the opportunities for good careers becoming rare.

It may be all right to say that life is becoming more competitive. However, as far as the opportunities for careers are concerned, they are growing in direct proportion to the population. Newer avenues are opening each day. The unfortunate problem is that most people fail to understand what is a good opportunity. They fail to recognize it. They do not know how an opportunity can be developed into a profitable career.

What is an Opportunity?

What does an opportunity mean to you? Some feel that it is a mysterious force that comes knocking at the doors of a blessed few. Others feel that it is the power to push and pull in life through the recommendations of friends and relatives. To some others, it may mean a tailor-made job, or a running business handed down in the family. When a large number of people feel this way about what opportunities for careers mean to them, it is not surprising to hear them say that opportunities are becoming scarce.

The dictionary defines an opportunity as a favourable combination of circumstances, time and place; as a chance for advancement or progress. From this definition, one thing is very clear. If the circumstances at a particular time and place are not favourable, they can be manipulated through deliberate effort in the right direction. In other words, we can create opportunities for ourselves.

This is exactly what all progressive people set out to do. They create their own opportunities. Like all other things, an opportunity begins with a thought in the mind. This thought becomes a dream. Through it, we visualize a new or better product or service. The dream is turned into reality through sheer hard work. If we can understand how opportunities can be recognized and developed, it becomes simpler to pursue a career, and gradually move towards our goal in life.

Looking for Opportunities

Wherever there are people, there will be needs to be fulfilled. We can also say that there will be opportunities to serve these needs. An opportunity for a career is really no more than being able to recognize human needs, and then setting out to satisfy them for a certain remuneration. This is exactly what every person who is pursuing a career is doing. It is immaterial whether one is doing a salaried job, or is self-employed. It also does not matter whether one is working in a home, or in a factory, field or office. The basic truth is that the remuneration a person gets for his work represents the price for his labour to satisfy a particular human need.

An executive fulfils the need for good management of the resources. The accountant looks after the finances. The office staff provides clerical, record keeping and other similar services just as the workers in the factory keep up the manufacturing schedule. Each individual does his little bit to fulfil the need of producing the final product that is ultimately going to satisfy the need of the consumer. Products and services vary, but the basic truth prevails in all cases. The opportunities for gainful employment begin with human needs.

The need for fulfilling a human need may be observed by only one person. Once he is convinced of the remunerative value of this single human need, he can turn it into an opportunity for gainful employment for himself. By bringing together the many factors that may be involved, he may turn it into opportunities for employment of many more people. These people may contribute their share of labour by doing jobs as varied as extracting the raw material to selling the finished product in retail. Invariably, one human need leads to another. If we can learn to recognize these needs in human beings around us, we can learn how opportunities for gainful employment present themselves in a concrete shape.

Understanding Human Needs

Prehistoric man had few needs like food, clothing and shelter. These too were not in the exact sense as we take them to mean today. Gradually, as mankind gained knowledge and became more organized, other needs grew out of the basic needs. Enterprising men and women utilized the need to fulfil them as opportunities for gainful employment for themselves.

A significant fact is that even after thousands of years of existence of mankind, human needs are continuing to grow. Mankind existed for thousands of years without many of the services and products we enjoy today. Nobody missed anything. Today none of us can think of a life without them. They have become very vital to our existence. Therefore, these needs must find fulfilment.

Many of the human needs are not recognized immediately by an average person. In many cases, the individuals themselves fail to understand their own needs. Only the enterprising people have set forth to study the latent needs of mankind. They have used the knowledge to find gainful employment. For example, the need for clothing is a simple basic human need. However, the enterprising persons observed that wearing any kind of clothes does not satisfy the human need completely. People want comfort and variety. They want to look different from one another. They are in search for better fabrics and designs.

These simple observations about human needs for clothing has given gainful employment to millions of people. They have found work preparing raw materials like cotton, wool, silk and man-made fibres, processing them, creating new designs, fashioning them into attractive garments, and eventually reaching the customers through a network of sales outlets throughout the world. Despite all that is being done, the consumer is becoming more conscious about his need for clothing. The opportunities to produce better fabrics and garments continue to grow.

Even today the basic human needs are only food, clothing and shelter, and providing these keeps millions of people all over the world busy. Many other needs that may not appear to be important have emerged. They are offering gainful employment to millions of people in many spheres of life. Take entertainment, for example. This need has given rise to theatres, circuses, tourism, a huge film and TV industry, sports and a whole lot of other forms of entertainment. Since books need not only be educative, but are entertaining too, a vast publishing network has come up to fulfil one need—it entertains and informs through hundreds of thousands of magazines and books each year.

In the same way, the simple human need to look attractive has given rise to a multi-million cosmetics industry, which has provided gainful employment to millions of people all over the world. Can you estimate the number of men and women who are running a beauty parlour?

Many of the human needs appear insignificant, and without any potential for gainful employment. Yet, enterprising people have used them to build up big business concerns. For instance, man's desire to convey a serious message with a touch of humour has given rise to a huge business of publishing greeting and business cards. These have found ready acceptance for purposes as diverse as requesting a client to remit his dues, or to convey a greeting on a birthday, a wedding anniversary or New Year.

The need to wind one's watch every day did not cause much inconvenience, but the introduction of automatic watches by enterprising manufacturers has found ready acceptance by everyone. A good fountain pen seemed to be serving the purpose well until ball pens were introduced to do away with the need for filling ink in the pens. Already people are shifting over to using felt-tipped and a variety of new pens because they require lesser pressure to write.

Human nature is fickle. At one time man requires one

thing, and at another, the need may be quite different. The more we observe human nature, the better we can understand it. The basic needs for food, clothing and shelter continue to be the same as when mankind first became aware of them. In the present times, innumerable needs have grown out of them, and provided gainful employment to millions of people. To the basic needs of mankind, we can add the needs for health, happiness and security. One can be sure that enterprising young people will continue to use the openings for gainful employment as long as man lives on this planet.

Check Yourself

We have just discussed how several needs have sprung out of the three basic human needs for food, clothing and shelter. Make a list of all the careers that you can think of to provide each of these needs. Make a separate list of careers to fulfil the human need to be healthy. And what about the human needs to avoid boredom? How many careers can you think of to fulfil this need?

Health-related careers:	Boredom-related careers:
1.	1.
2.	2.
3.	3.
4.	4.
5.	5.

Opportunities are Growing

Each time a new discovery is made, an invention perfected, or a new product or service marketed, most young people feel discouraged with the thought that yet another opportunity is exhausted. However, it is just the other way around. In fact, each opportunity used opens up many more opportunities for gainful employment of people. This can easily be confirmed when we look back at the time when some of the most commonly used household products like a fountain pen, a bicycle, radio, the telephone, a record player or other similar articles were first put up in the market. Each one of these products was acclaimed as the ultimate in ingenuity and human endeavour.

Today, when we look at any one of these, we find that the present models resemble the original very slightly, and of course, the efficiency is manifold. Everyone of these items was once new to mankind. However, that single opportunity to present the original idea to mankind opened opportunities for millions of young people. They not only improved the original product or service, but also found out ways to manufacture and market the same at prices more people could afford. Millions of people around the world are busy manufacturing, selling and maintaining these products. A very large number is engaged in improving them still further as we cannot claim that we have reached the stage of perfection.

New human needs are being discovered each day. All these mean growing opportunities for employment. Many of the products and services marketed in one community or country are waiting to be introduced into new areas. Scientific knowledge and experience are growing. The fruits of this labour are waiting to be utilized for the welfare of mankind. The people around the world have a variety of needs and preferences. Each of these continues to offer untold possibilities for fulfilment, and in return providing gainful employment.

Evaluating Opportunities

If ten persons seated in a circle were asked to draw an object placed in the centre of the circle, the drawings of each of the ten persons would be different. Each of them has viewed the same object from a different angle. The same thing happens when different people view opportunities they come across. In fact, the results are even more variable as individual concepts and attitudes about the same thing vary from one person to another.

Personal satisfaction is important if one is to succeed in a career. It is, therefore, important that opportunities for employment must not be evaluated only from the point of view of human needs they fulfil, and the remuneration they offer in return. They must be considered with the view that the efforts required are in harmony with one's concept of dignity of labour and other personal attitudes.

When evaluating opportunities for employment, the need

for a realistic approach cannot be overemphasized. One must look at them with an unbiased mind. Facts must not be tarnished with personal sentiments and prejudices. It is not always possible to be completely original about providing so-called new products and services. You may have heard about them or even seen them elsewhere. If they are new to your community, you should have no guilt about copying an idea from another place. Bringing about improvements has provided an untold amount of opportunities. We cannot overlook that many of the products and services we enjoy today are really based on ideas given to us many, many years ago, and by people who are forgotten today.

While evaluating opportunities, never let competition discourage you. Many young people feel that the opportunity is as good as nothing because they do not have the "pulls and pushes" somebody else may claim to possess. Competition is not an obstacle, but rather a challenge. If life has become more competitive for you so has it for everyone else. In fact, the very situation that life is becoming more competitive is being utilized by thousands of enterprising young people as an opportunity to help and guide other people towards success in many ways.

Points to Ponder

- Career opportunities are not becoming scarce. They grow in direct proportion to the population.
- An opportunity is a favourable combination of circumstances, time and place.
- You can create opportunities.
- Career opportunities aim to serve human needs.
- Look out for human needs.
- Check yourself how well you can recognize opportunities for careers.
- Career opportunities will continue to grow.
- Evaluate opportunities to use them to build a career.

Planning a Career

5

Most young people set out to pursue a career without any planning or serious consideration. To them, these details mean nothing. For all they know, they will reach their destination if they are lucky. Under such circumstances, is it then surprising if hundreds of thousands of young people fail to find useful employment? Those who do, are doing the kind of work they do not like. It is estimated that two-fifth of all people do not find satisfaction from the work they are doing. Can we expect these people to be efficient?

It is not always easy to change vocations in later life. With a large proportion working as misfits in their vocations the general efficiency levels at work are reduced. It eventually results in discontentment and unhappiness in life. This has its own repercussions in the society of which all of us are a part. The planning of a career is essential if we do not want to waste a part of our life in doing things we do not like, or those that do not benefit us. Besides, once we have our goal before us, we know where we have to go and how we can reach there.

Making a Beginning

Have you seen a tall skyscraper or a huge building? It provides the sanctity and security of a happy home to many families. We do know that these buildings did not come up on their own. Behind the strength, security and comfort that these buildings provide, there is immense planning. These buildings must have some day been just a stray thought in the mind of a person. Gradually, this thought must have crystallized, and started a chain of thought-processes.

These thoughts would have been written down on paper, and turned into plans. The experiences of hundreds of people must have gone into preparing the final plans, and turning them into the reality we see today. At every step, we can observe orderly planning and execution of plans. On the other hand, which one of us has not seen the disorder in a slum area where little shacks may have been made of all kinds of materials, and in whatever way a person thought best? Here we can clearly see that there has been no planning.

One may make a home in a hut, a little cottage, or in a flat in a tall skyscraper. Depending upon one's faith in the planning processes in making these structures, one can build a career based upon definite planning, or perhaps just in a haphazard manner. Like a building structure, a career too must begin with a thought. You must know what you would like to do. Let the thought occupy your mind until you feel it is just the thing you would like to pursue. You will want the foundation of your career to be strong. So collect the information you can about it. Talk to people who are already engaged in that particular career. Get information about it from friends and others. Read books about it in the library. Do not be fascinated with the remuneration that may appear very tempting or by the prestige and glamour attached to a particular career. Answer these questions to understand the situation better:

- What are the obligations and responsibilities involved in the career you would like to take up?
- What are the educational requirements?
- Is some work-experience necessary?
- Are jobs regularly advertised in the newspapers?
- Will the career offer any special challenges?

Collect as much information as you can from as many sources as are open to you. Note it down on paper. Since most young people simultaneously consider several careers, the tabulated information is useful to narrow down the choice to two or three careers that can then be studied in still greater detail.

Once you have the details of the careers you are seriously considering, and you have understood the obligations and responsibilities each one of them involves, you can, from your independent point of view, consider which one is in harmony with your personality. You also need to consider whether you have the requisite resources to pursue it. The sooner you can finalize the choice of a career, the better it is for you, because then you know in what direction you need to direct your energies. You can also then begin to equip yourself with the requisite knowledge and the qualifications to meet the challenge of the career needs.

Basic Education

There was a time when one needed a good basic education only for specialized careers. Most people depended upon experience and some physical skill, and rose gradually in their careers through haphazard methods. Today, a good basic education is necessary. For many careers for which eight years of study in school were acceptable even to the government, now the basic requirement has been raised to a minimum of a pass in high school. The advantage of a good basic education may not be readily apparent, particularly when the career involves physical skill. However, the person with a better basic education is given preference when the promotions are due. A good education broadens one's outlook. It is indeed a great asset.

What constitutes a good education is a debatable point. Many young people chase degrees because they feel these will bring them closer to a good job. Girls may pursue higher education just because it may enable them to find a better match in marriage. Much of this education is wasted as is apparent from the fact when young men and women who are graduates and postgraduates apply for jobs for which the requirement is just a pass in high school.

The idea behind a good basic education is to help a young person to learn how to use the latent capabilities. The education should help one to understand life as it is. One should be able to express oneself to find a certain fulfilment in life. In general, a good basic education of the higher secondary level prepares all young people to pursue higher education in the career of their choice. The higher education may be in the form of doing a degree or diploma course, or even learning a practical skill when one is not inclined to pursue a detailed study.

You will do well to answer these questions:

- Have you got definite plans to be well educated for the career you would like to take up? Give an outline of your plans.
- Has your academic work been satisfactory up to the high school level? If not, why?
- Did you deliberately think about and choose the subjects for the +2 level? Was your choice right?
- Have you decided upon the best courses of study beyond the 10+2 level? Will they benefit you in the career of your choice?
- Does the study plan include practical training on the job? Whenever available it is an asset to find early employment.

Vocational Training

Knowledge is power. This is particularly true in one's career. We are passing through an age of specialization where, if you want to rise in life, you must know how to do your job better. If the young people can understand this simple fact, they would not feel shy of acquiring the requisite knowledge in time. If you observe closely, you will find that millions of people all over the world are doing the same jobs which they were doing ten or more years ago. However, there is one important difference. They are doing it a little more efficiently. All human endeavour aims at increasing efficiency. If each generation were to start afresh in each vocation, we would be where we were a few hundred years ago. In reality, each generation takes over where the last one leaves. This is possible only through vocational training and education passed on to people beginning a career.

A young person who has received vocational training has a much better chance of finding employment than one who has not received it. This is simply because all employers are interested in young people who have the basic knowledge about their career. Even when compared to a person, who has some experience, but no training, a trained person has a better chance of not only matching with experience, but also surpassing it in due course of time.

Vocational training is superior even to collecting degrees in arts or science subjects, unless these are specifically needed for a particular career. For instance, young people who have received training in paper technology, hotel management, or some other vocation after their higher secondary, have better prospects of finding employment than those who may have done a degree course in subjects like English, Economics, or Political Science.

Although training in a very wide field of subjects is available in our country, in many cases, facilities for vocational training do not always match demand. Invariably, there is great competition to find admission in these institutions. Very often competitive examinations are held for admission. Even if a person is capable, and has been doing well in the early years of education, it is advisable to plan ahead of time. One must find out the names and addresses of all the institutions offering courses of interest, and write to them to get the prospectus and application forms.

Find out the entrance requirements, periods of study, diploma or degree awarded, job training provided after the course, hostel facilities, the cost of education, and other such pertinent information about the course and the institution which would be helpful to you. Collect the information from as many institutions as possible, although you may prefer a particular institution. This will give you an opportunity to compare the courses and the institutions. You may then select one that offers the maximum benefits to you. Once you have decided on a particular course of study, apply well in time for admission.

Institutions of Higher Education

Most young people who have made up their mind as to the career they would like to take up are at a loss about the details of the preparation required. They are not aware of the educational requirements and what particular institutions in our country offer the right courses which would help them get established in the career of their choice. To overcome this obstacle, several publishers have published directories giving details of the institutions that offer courses in a particular field. Advertisements in the national newspapers, regional newspapers and also the local newspapers can also be very helpful. Many school and college libraries stock these directories. Each one is a handy guide for all young people setting out on a career.

Besides the educational institutions listed in the directories just mentioned, there are many private educational institutions, and those run by government departments to provide vocational training. The details of the institutions nearest to you can be had from the District Industries Officer. There are also state-wise volumes published by the government listing this information in the Handbook on Training Facilities available from booksellers stocking government publications.

There are several voluntary organizations that specialize in providing vocational training. For example, a voluntary organization known as Skills for Progress, at 72 Brigade Road, Bangalore-560025, has as its members over 100 training centres providing technical and vocational education. Many of the private institutions advertise in the national press. Young people who find them offering courses of personal interest can write to them directly.

Financing Higher Education

With the general price rise higher education has become expensive. The cost of education is an important consideration to all young people. Almost no facilities for working and studying together are available in our country except in some special cases. The cost of education has, therefore, to be borne by parents. Young people who are confident of their capabilities can take advantage of the financial help offered by banks at reasonable rates of interest. For the exceptionally brilliant students many charitable trusts offer scholarships and loans.

The government also offers scholarships to brilliant students. The details of most of these can be had from the booklets titled: Scholarships For Study Abroad and At Home, National Loans Scholarship Schemes, Scholarships For Scheduled Castes/ Tribes and Backward Classes, Government of India Scholarships for the Physically Handicapped. These booklets are moderately priced publications issued by the government. They can be purchased from booksellers who stock government publications. The details of scholarships and other aids available at the college level can be had directly from the institutions concerned, or from the District Inspector of Schools.

Making up for Educational Deficiencies

Many young people, pressed by personal circumstances, embark upon a career without sufficient knowledge or training, hoping that they may be able to make up for the deficiency through on-the-job experience. To a certain extent, this experience is helpful, but it really cannot replace formal vocational education and training. It is in the best interest of the person concerned to make up the lack of knowledge whenever convenient. Many times, it may only be theoretical, but formal vocational training provides a person with many details, which may appear rather insignificant, but in actual practice provide the very foundation to practical success in the career. Once the young person is equipped with knowledge steady progress becomes a part of the career.

Many of the educational deficiencies can be made up through short-term courses offered by government agencies, or even by private institutions. Where such facilities are not easily available, one can still understand the theoretical aspects of the subject through postal training. Many correspondence schools are preparing young people for degree courses, and for special examinations conducted by professional organizations. Diploma courses are also offered.

In the larger cities, many private institutions offer part-time refresher courses in some subjects. Many times, special courses which extend over a week or fortnight are also offered by some institutions specially for those already engaged in particular trades, and one can take advantage of such offers. In whatever way one can make up vocational knowledge, it is always worthwhile, and a sure way to success.

Distance Education

Many recognized universities have facilities for education through correspondence. Study through the post has its own advantages in that one can study according to one's personal convenience, making it possible to earn and learn simultaneously. The education imparted is simple and worthwhile. Most employers give due recognition to the degrees and diplomas awarded by universities and important correspondence schools. Choose the course with care after getting details of courses offered by several institutions.

Need for Continued Education

Most young people feel that their educational problems are over once they have secured a good degree or diploma that makes an opening for them in a career. Little do these young people understand that if they depend only upon the knowledge gained through formal education in a college, their knowledge will become obsolete in a few years. They will soon fail to be competitive in their field of work. Knowledge is growing at such a rapid speed that if one does not keep up with the latest developments one is soon left behind in life.

Education today is a continued affair. If one must make success a constant companion, some knowledge must be added each day. This can easily be done through the study of trade journals and magazines. One can also benefit greatly from refresher courses, or by joining trade associations and groups that invite specialists to address them on certain subjects of interest. A little forethought to this aspect keeps the young people steadily on the path to a successful career.

Planning the Career

We are passing through an age when planning is as important as execution. Without it, one can go astray. Governments plan in terms of five-year plans. Companies in terms of production schedules and sales targets they hope to achieve. Individuals need to plan in terms of their personal hopes and aspirations. Planning does not aim only at setting targets. It considers all factors. Accordingly, dates are fixed by when the targets must be achieved. This simplifies the problems. One can organize all available resources to achieve the targets in the best possible manner.

A young person needs to plan a career in the same way. Do not leave matters to chance or luck. Deliberately plan your own destiny. Evaluate your own capabilities and needs. With these as the starting point, decide what career you would like to pursue in life. The very process of making up one's mind gives strength that can be directed to move towards the goal.

Collect all the relevant data about the career you want to pursue. Prepare yourself to meet the challenges it will offer. Your determination will help you shape your thoughts, plans and actions. These will take you in the right direction. Once you have laid a strong foundation the superstructure that you build over it will be strong. You can be certain that despite the many unexpected delays and obstacles which may come your way, you will be well on your way to be established in a career of your choice.

Preparing the Plan

To prepare a plan for a career answer the following questions:

- Have I been able to evaluate my personality traits, abilities and strengths? How do I use these to develop a good career for myself?
- Have I been able to identify my personal weaknesses? How will I get over them? By when can I do it?
- With my capabilities and circumstances what career choices are open to me? Have I short-listed the best of them to 3 choices? What are they?
- Have I collected the necessary details about all the careers that I have short-listed? After studying these details can I prioritize them as first, second and third?
- Have I been able to identify the institutions where I

can be trained for the particular careers I have short-listed? Can I fulfil their admission requirements?

- Am I clear about the financial requirements for training in the institutions of my choice? From where will these requirements be met?
- What are the job prospects after the training? Have I checked up with the old students who have passed out from these institutions? Is there any campus recruitment?

Points to Ponder

- Without advance planning success is uncertain. The same is true for a career.
- Understand career needs. Every career requires a different set of abilities and skills.
- Acquire the basic education for a career. There can be no better foundation for a career than a good education.
- Career prospects are better after vocational training.
- Locate and choose the best institutions of learning.
- Higher education is expensive. Make necessary provisions. Utilize it to the best of your ability.
- Lack of sufficient education can always be made up through distance learning.
- Choose and locate the best institution for distance learning.
- Education is a continuous process. Make a habit to follow up regularly.
- Plan your career in detail. Do not leave things to chance or luck. Plan your own destiny.

Looking for a Job

6

Once the young person has acquired the necessary knowledge to begin a career, the search for a job starts. This can be very trying, full of frustrations and heartbreaks. Good jobs are not immediately available particularly for those just beginning a career. Most employers desire not only the basic academic qualifications for the job, but also some practical experience. Most employers lack the patience to provide the initial on-the-job training, making it difficult for the beginner to find a suitable opening.

Do not let this discourage you. All successful people began their careers this way. There has to be a beginning sometime. There will be one for you too.

A beginning in a career is very much like a big group of people standing at the bottom of the staircase of a tall building, all wanting to reach the top quickly. Of course, not everyone can go up simultaneously. Each one must go up step by step. As the group moves upwards, it will gradually spread out into different floors. Each one will go as far as his personal capabilities can take him. Only the very few capable ones will make it to the top. The maximum rush is at the lowest level. Unless you have the capabilities, and there is an opportunity to show them to the superiors, you will need to be patient and understanding. Progress will come slowly with time and experience.

Planning Ahead

As in all other avenucs of life, it pays to plan when you are looking for a job. You may aim at an important position in life when you set out to pursue a career. However, your journey begins with a single step right at the bottom. You may aim high, but to avoid frustration, take each stride as a part of your journey to the desired goal. Every trial and tribulation provides you with valuable experience that every person must gain on his own. Experience becomes a valuable part of one's personality for a lifetime.

Even before you complete your education or training for a vocation, look out for job opportunities in your line. The more you think of them, the greater the number of opportunities that will come to your notice. This is a natural phenomenon. One attracts what one desires. To be effective, the desire must be realistic. Personal faith and conviction about one's capabilities should be the basis of this desire. Do not be wishful. Wishing for a thing is a definite acceptance of lack of requisite qualities, a clear indication that success is expected through good luck only.

When you come across opportunities that interest you, note them on a notebook. Even if you cannot immediately meet the requisite qualifications, and need additional training, you could make an application for the job with the note that you could join after completing the requisite training. If such action is not possible, you could keep a note of the potential employers in your field of work. This gives you positive knowledge about the potentialities in the particular field of work, qualifications desired, salaries offered, and other similar details. It can help build knowledge about employers in your field. This information is of great use when one needs to move upwards in a career.

Where to Look for Jobs

If you want to know of the entire range of employment opportunities available, you will need to go through all the important newspapers every day. A lot of advertising space, both in the display and the classified sections, is utilized for giving information about job vacancies. Besides the private sector, government departments also advertise their requirements in the national press.

Employment News, a weekly published simultaneously in English, Hindi, Bengali, Urdu, Tamil, Telegu and Assamese by the Directorate of Advertising and Visual Publicity, Samachar

Bhawan, Parliament Street, New Delhi-110001, covers a wide range of employment opportunities. Young people in search for a good opening will do well to read it regularly.

Those who have a specialized career in mind should look out for advertisements in trade journals. Since it is not possible to simultaneously subscribe to many newspapers and magazines which carry the 'situations vacant' advertisements, the best solution lies in keeping in touch with the publications at the local library, and making personal notes when necessary.

It is also useful to get oneself registered at the local employment exchange. They will get in touch with you whenever an opening comes up. Those who have qualified in highly specialized lines, or when it is known that the number of employers in that field are very limited, it is advisable to write directly to the personnel departments of the prospective employers informing them about the availability of one's services. Even if a position is not available immediately, it is customary for the employers to keep such applications on file so that they may refer to them whenever an opening is there. Many such applications have resulted in worthwhile jobs.

Jobs through Competitive Examinations

With a great rush for certain fields of service, entry into many jobs is restricted through competitive examinations. This ensures for everyone an equal opportunity to appear for a written examination, which automatically eliminates weaker candidates, permitting only the best to come up for the final selection through interviews, personality tests, medical check-ups, etc. This form of recruitment has become a regular feature for many fields of service at the national level, as, for example, the administrative services, foreign services, police services, defence services, etc. Recruitment to many jobs at the lower cadre like clerks, inspectors, etc. are also through similar competitive examinations that are duly advertised in the national press.

Many of the competitive examinations are held just once a year. Thousands of candidates sit for the written tests in examination centres spread all over the country. Young people who are interested in jobs offered through competitive examinations should be well prepared in advance. They must apply as soon as the particular examination is advertised in the national press. Besides the important newspapers, the details of these examinations are published in magazines like Employment News, Competition and Success Review, Careers in Science, and other similar publications. Copies of these magazines are available in most college libraries, and sold freely at bookstalls.

There is a well-laid out pattern of examination. The candidate must prepare thoroughly for it. The markets are flooded with model test papers and guides of all descriptions for these examinations. Their huge sale is a clear indication of how the candidates are in search of short cuts to success. Although these test papers and guides have their utility in helping a candidate to understand the pattern of examination and the basic requirements, ultimate success depends upon personal capabilities and efforts. In these examinations, the hardworking young people who have a broad outlook and a good general knowledge of the happenings around them attain success.

Understanding Job Requirements

The purpose of all jobs is the same—to fulfil a human need. In most cases, the fulfilment of a particular need may not result in a financial gain to the employer directly. It may just be one link in a long process where many people are working at a variety of occupations eventually to offer a product or service. In itself, the work of the individual may appear insignificant as compared to the whole set-up. However, we cannot overlook the fact that every link in a chain is important. Unless everyone sets out to do whatever is expected, the whole process is apt to fail. When you look for a job, remember that while it is important to you because your livelihood will depend upon it, it is also very important to the employer. Unless you fulfil your responsibilities to benefit him with your work, his purpose of employing you will be defeated.

When you come across an advertisement offering a job

that you feel you can fill, immediately set out to understand the job requirements. Out of necessity most advertisements need to be brief and to the point. However, they do provide sufficient information for prospective candidates to be able to assess the correct position.

Ask yourself what the advertiser expects to be done. To find out the details, answer these questions:

- Has the employer placed any restrictions on the age of the applicants?
- What basic qualifications does he desire?
- Does he require any working experience?
- Where would you be expected to work?
- Will the job require you to move house, or break present family bonds?
- Are there any problems about securing residential accommodation in the area of work?
- What is the salary offered?

After answering these questions, if you feel that you cannot give the job the best of yourself, it is best to forget about it right away. If you feel that you have understood the job requirements as desired by the advertiser, and you can fulfil them efficiently and conveniently, then go ahead and apply for the job. It is essential that while the employer must get the best you can offer, you must be able to find personal satisfaction out of doing a job well. That ensures continued success.

The Ideal Employer

Every employee has a secret desire of finding the best employer who can offer the maximum benefits and security of service. However, very often the choice is very limited. One can look forward only to mutual benefit where both the employer and the employee find reasonable satisfaction from a particular job.

Employers are generally categorized according to what they offer by way of working conditions, pay scales, security of service, fringe benefits, bonus, etc. In the past the enactment of many laws has made the position of employees secure in the sphere of work, and provided several other benefits. Nevertheless we cannot ignore the human factor, and the presence or absence of a good employer-employee relationship, which helps differentiate good and bad employers. In a congenial relationship, an employee is treated as an individual personality, and not as another machine or piece of equipment in a huge set-up, working from 8 a.m. to 5 p.m.

Government jobs offer the maximum security of service. As compared to other jobs, they have their own advantages and limitations. One needs to weigh them according to one's personal preferences. The entry into these jobs is through competitive examinations, and basic qualifications and merit are very important. The general policy is to streamline the working of government offices and cut down on new jobs.

The larger companies offer better pay scales and benefits to their employees as compared to the smaller ones, but the responsibility shared is much less, and one gains little in experience. In a smaller concern, though the salary is less, a young person is entrusted with greater responsibility. He gets a good on-the-job experience that gives him the confidence to handle responsibility independently. This in itself is a very important qualification that is useful in getting promotions when the right opening shows up.

When special ability is desired of an employee, both the larger and the smaller companies pay similar salaries. The very highly paid jobs are offered only by the larger concerns. These require a very high degree of knowledge and experience, a sense of responsibility, and complete dedication. Only exceptionally qualified young people make it to these positions. Most young people aspire for lower and middle level jobs.

Applying for the Job

When you are mentally convinced that the job advertised is just the right one for you, it is time for you to draft your first communication with the prospective employer. Many employers require the initial application, particularly for subordinate jobs for which there may be many applicants, to be made on a prescribed form that they supply on request, or on payment. In most cases, it is absolutely in order to apply on a plain white sheet of paper, neatly typewritten, or handwritten. If you have a personal letterhead, you can use it for the purpose, but make sure that it is not too fancy or ostentatious. Also, do not use business letterheads or fancy flowery paper.

As you begin to draft your application for the job, remember one thing: the prospective employer, like all other employers, desires to hire somebody who can help him to further his own personal interests. Since his interest in the job is limited to what he can get out of it, your interest of securing the job can be fulfilled only when you can convince him that he will benefit from giving you employment. It is, therefore, necessary that your application must fulfil this need.

There will obviously be many aspirants for the same job. Since it is not practical to meet all prospective employees, scrutinizing the application forms only will do the initial screening. Therefore, another important purpose that your application must fulfil is to convey that you are worthy of being called for an interview. This makes it necessary that your application must be a fair representation of your qualifications and capabilities, with particular reference to the requirements of the job.

While preparing the rough draft, mention details like your academic career, special extra-curricular interests and achievements, jobs held, or experience, if any. Whatever be your achievements, be modest about them. Do not give any information that you know is incorrect or false. You may succeed in cheating a prospective employer temporarily, but when he gets to know the truth as he always will, it will not only create a very bad impression, but you may fall very badly in his personal estimate. Copies of certificates must support the information about your qualifications and achievements. Do not send any originals. They can be shown at the time of the interview. If the employer desires references, you could draw upon your good relations with your family doctor or some of your father's friends, or even the parents of your friends.

Make the application brief and to the point. It is not intended to be a descriptive essay. All that it must convey is that you are qualified for the job, and have the necessary capabilities that can help the prospective employer to pursue his own interests. When the rough draft is ready, do not be satisfied with it. Go through it repeatedly until you are certain that you cannot improve it. Check the facts, the spelling and punctuation marks. Spare no pains about it. Finally, type it neatly on a white sheet of paper, leaving a reasonable margin on all sides.

If you cannot typewrite the application, it would be in order to send it handwritten. Make certain that you do it in your best handwriting, and it is absolutely neat, clear and legible. It must carry a good impression of the person who has written it. If the application is being filed on a prescribed form, fill it neatly. Avoid overwriting or crowding. If the space in any column is less, attach the details on a separate sheet of paper marking each as annexure A, B, C, etc. Do not forget to keep a copy of the application, or of the details mentioned in the application form for your own personal record.

When the application is ready, attach the necessary enclosures as desirable, fold it neatly, and mail by registered post in a neatly addressed envelope. If the prospective employer has specifically mentioned it, do not overlook to mark the envelope with special remarks like "For Management Trainees", "Junior Executives", etc., so that it may reach the appropriate department immediately.

Preparing for the Interview

If the application fulfils the basic requirements as advertised by the prospective employer, the chances are that you will get an interview call. When you are interested in the job advertised, do not wait for the interview letter to prepare for the interview. Get to know all that you can about the employer and the job. The basic purpose of the interview is going to be to assess your personal capabilities, and how the prospective employer can use them to further his personal interests through the job advertised.

Find out all that you can about your prospective employer's company—its set-up, branches, products and services. If you can, then also find out all about the responsibilities and the privileges of the position you have applied for. Such information can be collected from the advertisements in the national press, house journals, the local distributors, and even the local retailers. Information about other companies in the same trade can also be useful. Thus equipped, you will be better able to understand your prospective employer's needs, and will be able to answer important questions at the interview. However, if the interviewer does not show any interest in such questions, do not try to impress him with your knowledge.

It is a simple courtesy to acknowledge an interview call when you receive it. Confirm the place, day and time mentioned in the letter. Have your file containing the original documents in support of your achievements mentioned in the application ready? If you are already working, you may need to apply for leave to be present at the interview. Although all employers do understand that young people are ambitious and desire better positions, they are not always happy about their workers leaving them. Therefore, when you ask for leave, unless it is specifically desired that you have a clearance certificate from your present employer, it is sufficient to mention in your leave application that you require it to attend to personal matters.

The Purpose of the Interview

The purpose of an interview is to afford an opportunity to the prospective employer to gauge the personal capabilities of the candidates who have applied for the job. An employer hires workers directly or indirectly to help him provide a product or service which is a source of income to him. He does understand that an employee is not a machine that can be installed and expected to give the desired performance under given circumstances. Since the human factor is involved, it becomes imperative for the employer to understand the individual's knowledge, performance and efficiency, and how he can use these to his personal advantage.

The prospective employer will use the interview as a

medium to assess the image each candidate projects of oneself. Employers are particularly interested in the general health of the individual, and the personality as exhibited by one's poise, manners, and sense of dress. The employer may also like to confirm the facts you may have mentioned in your application. He will also be interested to gauge your general knowledge, special interests and achievements, the ability to learn new skills, and your attitude towards the kind of job he can offer. The ability to make decisions is vital to many jobs. He may want to judge your ability in this direction also. He may also want to know about past successes and failures, and how you faced them. Your reactions and answers to the interviewer's questions will help him conclude as to what extent you can help him achieve his purpose through the job.

The Interview

You must reach the place of the interview punctually at the appointed time. Be appropriately dressed. Do remember that your sense of dress tells a lot about your personality and your attitude towards the job. The dress should be neither too formal nor too casual. Wear a day suit, or if the weather and the circumstances do not permit it, a white shirt, and a coloured pant with a necktie will be all right. Wear either brown or black shoes to match the pant. Avoid fancy footwear. Make certain that you have had a shave, have clean nails, and the hair is properly groomed. The lady candidates too need to dress modestly, avoiding heavy make up and jewellery. Carry the documents in a neat file. Do not tuck them in an ugly envelope, or stuff them in the pocket.

When you arrive for the interview, do not try to become friendly with the receptionist, or with the other candidates, and start comparing notes and qualifications. Do not overlook the simple fact that they are your competitors. Avoid unnecessary tension. Do not smoke either. You can read the newspaper, or a book, until you are called for the interview. If you prefer to read a book, avoid cheap fiction. Your prospective employer may be reading it too, but when it comes to employees, most employers desire that they should read constructive and useful books.

When you are called for the interview, do remember that first impressions can be very important. Take a deep breath, and enter with a smile. This helps in getting over nervousness. Sit down when asked to. Let the interviewer start the conversation. He will probably begin by asking you questions to which he already knows the answers. This is to put you at your ease. He may ask you to tell him something about yourself—about your achievements and failures. Be brief and to the point.

Gradually he will come to the more pertinent questions. These will be intended to assess your personal capabilities. He will want to hear you rather than speak himself. Do not interrupt him when he is speaking. Hear him carefully, and answer clearly and audibly. Do not use slang, or smoke. If the interviewer offers you a cigarette, even if you smoke, refuse it courteously. If you have mentioned some special interests and achievements in your application, the interviewer may want to know more about them with particular reference to how they affect your own hopes and aspirations. While explaining your special interests, give them only that proportion of your attention as is fair as compared to the interests of the job.

Family circumstances may also crop up in the interview. When the interviewer encourages you to express your opinion about a particular problem, do not take advantage of the situation to discuss personal philosophies, or to show that you are very learned or clever. Answer the questions in simple language to convey a clear meaning. Do not forget that your power of expression is being tested.

The interviewer may want to test your reactions in special circumstances. He may, therefore, ask you provocative questions, or broach controversial subjects. Such situations demand great tact and patience. Do not be provoked under any circumstances. Display complete cool, and discuss your viewpoint with a smile. If the interviewer asks you something you do not know anything about, do not be afraid to admit your ignorance. If it is something vital you do not know about, you can still admit your ignorance, and apologize for it. Your frankness will be appreciated.

All interviewers have an eye for discrepancies. They will positively ask you questions pertaining to your past failures and shortcomings, if any. Under such circumstances, do not try to fool the interviewer. Explain your viewpoint reasonably. If you are changing jobs, explain that reasonably too. Do not be critical of those with whom you work presently, or have worked in the past. It would be more acceptable if you were to say that the circumstances did not suit you, rather than that your present or past employers had made things difficult for you.

Interviewers are like ordinary people, and may have their own whims and fancies. At the same time, they have an eye for people with ability. They will not disclose it to you whether you have been selected or not, but before concluding the interview you may be asked if you would like to ask anything in particular. You can avail yourself of this opportunity to clarify doubts, if any, about the prospects of the job, the fringe benefits, etc. Be brief and specific. Interviewers are busy people. Do not leave behind an impression that you have encroached upon their time.

Intelligence Tests

With the development of psychology and psychological tests to study individual interests, aptitudes, IQ, etc., many employers are using intelligence tests to rate prospective candidates for jobs. These tests aim at gauging an individual's mental agility, power of reasoning, comprehension, memory, etc. These tests are short, require little writing, and must be answered in a limited period. These tests can be useful to a certain degree, but are certainly not conclusive. We cannot overlook that people devise these tests, and therefore, sometimes they can be biased or unfair. It is, therefore, natural that different employers attach varying degrees of importance to the results of these tests.

It would be helpful to understand that the IQ of a person depends upon various factors like family background, education, age, residence, personal problems, the weather, mood, and even the town from where he comes. Women have been found to be as intelligent, but have fewer interests than men. People who spend some time on self-improvement regularly score well in these tests.

Most young people get down to answering these tests as though their life depended upon them, and soon find themselves confused and exhausted. The important thing is to avoid anxiety and tension. Before beginning the test, read the instructions carefully. Go through the test, answering the questions that you can. Do not get anxious if you cannot answer a question. Leave it, and move on to the next one. This way you can go through the test, answering all the questions that you do know, and return to the difficult ones later if the time permits. If there is negative marking, avoid answering the questions you are not confident about. Patience is important and well rewarded.

Negotiating a Salary

While advertising a job, most employers specify the salary and scale of pay offered for the job. Sometimes, the matter is left to negotiation between the employer and the candidate. Under such circumstances, although the employer knows what the job is worth, he may want to test the candidate's ability, and find out about his personal aspirations, and through what stage of development he is passing through presently.

If you are already employed and just changing jobs, it should not be difficult to relate the expected salary to the one you are already receiving. However, if this is to be your first job, you must make reliable inquiries, and find out what the job is worth. This can be done by studying advertisements for similar jobs, or through people already working in similar positions. When asked, demand a salary accordingly. Never show a lack of decision in these matters. If the employer finds you worthy of the amount you have asked for, he will pay it. If you are capable, and the difference is nominal, he will explain his stand to you.

Changing Jobs

In most cases, the first job may not really be the one that offers the maximum amount of opportunity for growth and progress. It is, therefore, natural for young people to desire a change after some time. Do not change just for the sake of changing a job. Employers consider those who change jobs too often as unstable. When you find a better opening, study it thoroughly before taking it up. Consider both the advantages and disadvantages of changing the job. Many times the increase in fringe benefits may only be illusory. To justify a change of jobs, there should be an increased salary, more responsibility, better chances of promotion, and lots of job satisfaction. If you can get these in another job, only then would it be worthwhile to change your present job.

Points to Ponder

- The search for the first job is always the most difficult. Let it not discourage you.
- Plan ahead for a job. Yes, even before you are ready for it.
- Know where to locate a suitable job.
- Competitive exams assure good jobs. That explains their popularity.
- It pays to understand the job requirements precisely.
- All young people seek an ideal employer. Success depends upon being an ideal employee.
- The application for a job must be a fair representative of your personality and skills.
- Prepare ahead to meet your prospective employer.
- An interview is an important meeting with the prospective employer. Be well prepared for it.
- Understand the purpose and technique of solving intelligence tests.
- Negotiate a salary in a businesslike manner.
- Gain valuable experience at your first job. Do not change jobs just for the sake of it.

Self-employment

7

Ever since India became independent, many institutions of higher learning were established in the country. This resulted in a corresponding increase of educated youth. Simultaneously, with more young women now working, there has been a greater pressure on the demand for good jobs. Unfortunately, vacancies have not been able to keep up pace for several reasons. This has disturbed the balance between the need and availability of jobs, in both the public and the private sectors. The obvious outcome of this has been a wide-scale increase of the educated unemployed.

The only solution to the problem lies in wide-scale self-employment by the educated young people. The hesitation on the part of most young people does not stem from the reason that they are not sufficiently educated. Most of them have received specialized training. They are capable in their field of education and interest. However, they lack the confidence to set out on their own. Hidden deep within them are fears of obstacles they may not be able to cross. They are afraid of the defeat and failure they may have to face.

It is true that several factors influence successful self-employment. If young people could understand these, many of their secret fears would be dispelled. They could find satisfying self-employment. Young people who need to set out on a career cannot wait indefinitely for a job. Time is an important factor in life. These young people must equip themselves to meet the challenges they will come across, and set out to employ themselves profitably.

Stepping-stone to Success

Self-employment can be a vital stepping-stone to success in life for young people. It offers not only a great training ground for a lifetime, but opens the door to success and prosperity. It can bring about greater development of human and material resources of the country. Each person who gets self-employed simultaneously opens opportunities for others in his own work, and for those who can follow his example elsewhere.

Self-employment knows no bounds of colour, caste or creed. The richest of people have grown through self-employment in many fields still open to all young people. This form of employment is not restricted to particular fields of work, or to restricted boundaries. It offers ample scope for trying new ideas anywhere and everywhere. Besides, a person is one's own master, working at one's own pace.

Despite many advantages young people have always been shy of self-employment. Very often, they are overtaken by fears of defeat and failure that they may nurture in their minds. Some are afraid of the hard work it involves. Others fear the uncertain or meagre returns in the beginning. Lack of finance and self-confidence is a common problem. Doubts of all descriptions have continued to distract young people from self-employment in favour of the security of a job.

Unless hardworking young people come forward to take the initiative of breaking fresh ground through self-employment, unemployment will continue to haunt young people ready to set out on a career. Provided a young person is educated, and willing to do with small returns against a lot of hard work in the beginning, one is well equipped to open the door to success for all time. One can learn to make up for the other deficiencies as one goes along.

Opportunities for Self-employment

The opportunities for self-employment are almost unlimited. This sounds incredible, but it is true. As long as there are human beings in this world, there will be their personal needs to fulfil—and all these mean opportunities for employment. Of course, not all opportunities can be converted into ideas for gainful employment. The demand for a particular product or service may not be sufficient to ensure a reasonable remuneration.

Enterprise knows no bounds. People have successfully aroused needs in the minds of the public, and then set out to satisfy these to find gainful employment. If you wish to get self-employed, and are looking for products and services that you can supply, study human needs. Ask yourself these simple questions:

- What new products and services can make life more comfortable and efficient in your community?
- Can you manufacture or supply any of these?
- Can you improve upon any of the existing products or services?
- Is there any special service that you can provide?

In answering these questions, you will need to exercise your imagination. The more you meet and observe people, and understand their feelings and problems, the better you will realize how you can provide a product or service to fulfil these needs. You should not be afraid to copy an idea from a product or service being marketed elsewhere. If it has succeeded in another town or city, there are fair chances of success in your area, provided, of course, that the needs of the people are similar.

Personal Evaluation for Success

While it is true that there are many young people looking for jobs when greater rewards await them through self-employment, it would be wrong to say that everyone has the capabilities for successful self-employment. Before you decide to become your own employer, make certain that you have the basic abilities to make success of your work. You will need to be extremely honest with yourself. For your own sake, try to evaluate the position correctly. Eventually, the responsibility of all rights and wrongs is going to rest upon you.

Do remember that starting any new venture is a great uphill task in the beginning. Besides, you will need to be positive that the work you have in mind is in harmony with your perception of dignity of labour. To evaluate your abilities, answer these simple questions:

- Do you have the initiative and drive to try out the new idea?

- Will you enjoy carrying the idea through?
- Do you consider yourself a production man or a salesman?
- Are you technically qualified to undertake the work?
- If not, are you going to rely upon outside technical help?
- Are you willing to put in hard work, very often sacrificing your personal leisure, and even working late hours?
- Do you have the enthusiasm to keep going even when others would be too discouraged to continue?
- Can you get along well with people?

The answers to these questions will give you a good idea of the chances of success of your becoming your own boss. Do not answer the questions in a hurry. Think about them. Note the answers to the questions on a piece of paper. Give the matter further thought. Try to answer the questions again after a few days.

When you are convinced that you have the initiative to start a new venture, are willing to work hard, unmindful of the small returns you may get in the beginning, and know that you are going to face many challenges that the work will offer, then only should you consider going in for self-employment. If you have the basic requirements within you, you should proceed to find out what you would like to do. Keep in view the resources you may have right away. Consider how you can overcome some of the other shortcomings that may create obstacles in your way. This way you can set out gradually to build a business of your own.

Making a Beginning

Many young people are hesitant to think in terms of self-employment. They feel that all that they can offer is plain hard work backed by an average education, and no more. They have no family business or financial aid to support them. Therefore, all they can think of is a job, where they are paid for the personal service they render. Though it may sound surprising, many of the very big business concerns started with almost nothing but an idea for a product or service, backed by hard work. Like anything else, a personal business is built up step by step. There is a wide field of careers built upon self-employment. One can be selected in keeping with personal preferences and circumstances.

Young people who have specialized in particular fields like accountancy, engineering, law, medicine, etc. do not need to consider what they would like to do. They need to change their outlook, to develop greater self-confidence to set out on their own rather than depend upon the security of a job. Some young people have the self-confidence. However, they may hesitate because of lack of financial requirements in the beginning. These can often be conveniently provided if they know where to look for such aid.

Young people with insufficient education, or those who have not specialized in a particular field of work, have certain disadvantages as compared to their better-informed friends. Even then, many young people have set out with almost nothing but sheer determination and hard work, and made a great success of a self-employed career. It is a matter of choosing a work where one finds personal satisfaction. Very often with "hit or miss" methods, or even through specialized education later, young people have built up a very successful self-employed career.

When a person can understand how to recognize human needs, literally dozens of ideas that can be converted into full-time occupations will come to mind. These ideas can briefly be classified into two categories. The first one aims at selling products or services. The second one pertains to manufacturing products of interest to a certain class of people. Since needs vary from one place to another, one will obviously need to assess these from the personal point of view.

Depending upon personal aptitude and interests, look at local requirements for the most feasible ideas for a career. If one has the requisite academic qualifications and knowledge, there is scope for establishing advisory and consultative services as a legal practitioner, an accountant, or a work study or marketing consultant. If one has nothing but one's hard work to offer, one can become a life or general insurance agent. One can start a home delivery service, start a small local newspaper or weekly magazine, get involved in freelance journalism as an author, script writer or translator, take up painting as a commercial venture, or even start a small school. Teaching a group of children can also be remunerative provided you know the curriculum well.

In the larger and middle-class cities, a career as a musician, vocal or instrumental, offers personal satisfaction and growing remuneration with increasing popularity. If you can use a computer, many of the smaller business concerns who cannot afford a full-time data entry employee will be pleased to give you part-time work which you can do at their place of business, or even at your residence. Many a person living in small towns, and even villages, have made good money by acting as a purchasing agent for goods made in that area, or for raw material in abundance nearby, and forwarding the same to large concerns in the cities for processing or sale.

Selling a product always offers interesting possibilities. If you have any local novelties or specialities, you could take the initiative to market them in other towns. You could seek distribution rights of products of reliable companies for sale in your area. Very often exclusive rights can be obtained ensuring one of a steady income that grows with time. Even when such rights are not available on exclusive basis, you could sell on a commission basis until you have proved your worth. If your community can offer products that can be conveniently sent by post, mail order sales can open the entire world to you as a suitable market. This is a growing field of service in our country. Export marketing has developed significantly in recent years. There is a large demand for typical Indian products. For a long time, there would be a continued growth of the trade.

Establishing a retail shop has its own demand for personal discipline, but it offers continued rewards with steady growth. To begin in a humble way, one can start almost on a shoestring budget. Many people who start such ventures have not received much formal education. Provided the retail shopkeeper can establish his creditworthiness, most wholesalers are willing to sell goods to retailers on credit. For those who consider no work too small for them, and are hardworking, a retail shop can be the beginning of a good career.

If one is technically qualified, or has learnt a craft, one can sell personal services as an electrician, plumber, motor or scooter mechanic, watch repairer, air-conditioning mechanic, carpenter, etc. One only needs to be able to understand human needs, and then set out to provide them, and there will be no shortage of ideas of things one can do to find gainful self-employment. Enterprising young people have succeeded to earn by using an idea as simple as loaning magazines and books to families on a daily rental basis, issuing and collecting them personally.

Due to various reasons, the rural area remains untapped as a potential source of business, and therefore offers great possibilities for self-employment. There is a need for many products and services in the fields, and rural homes. Many farmers would like to use special equipment on a rental basis. The need for new and useful products is always there. Re-packing of seeds, chemicals and fertilizers in convenient packs offers a useful outlet for these products to farmers. Millions of rural homes could use many useful products presently available only in towns and cities. The rural market has a great need even for common everyday requirements like soaps, spices, shoes, and such things provided they are a little cheaper and better. There is not much competition in the rural market either.

Young women who would like to combine a career with their responsibilities as housewives can also be self-employed. They could organize cooking classes, teach beauty culture to college girls and busy housewives, start a school for tailoring and embroidery, undertake to design and stitch garments, knit woolens, or do embroidery themselves. Many women have expanded their work to enable them to hire additional help, and run the venture as a full-time career. Free-lancing as a model, dress designer, commercial artist, interior decorator, or something similar offers interesting possibilities for gainful self-employment.

Manufacturing offers both challenges and problems. It interests many qualified young people. It can be the beginning of a big company. Many factors are involved. The subject is discussed separately in detail in the next chapter.

Many ideas for self-employment appear too commonplace, but that should not worry the interested young person as the scope in this field is unlimited. In making a beginning, or selecting an appropriate line, one should not try to be novel, but rather be practical. The emphasis should be on service, and not on novelty. One can go on discussing ideas for self-employment that have stood the test of time.

Many ideas are discussed under individual careers in the second part of the book, and one could go through them. However, one needs to draw a line when one has found an opening of one's choice. Since personal aptitudes and capabilities vary from one individual to another, the choice of a vocation also varies greatly. Consider as many lines as you would like to, but with each consideration go on narrowing the choice until you come to that single line of work on which you can finally set your heart.

50 Ideas for Self-employment

Here is a list of 50 ideas for self-employment. It has been compiled to give you an idea of the kind of things one can do:

Accountancy service.
Article/story writing for magazines.
Bill collection/payment services.
Canteen service in offices.
Car wash service in buildings.
Catering service for students.
Catering service for parties.
Circulating library service.
Cold drinks counter.
Cooking classes for housewives.
Craft classes for children and adults.
Crèche service.
Cyber café.
Door to door marketing service.
Dry-cleaning service.
DTP work for printing houses.
Electrical repairs in housing societies.
Embroidery work.

English speaking classes.
Fast foods stall.
Florist service.
Free lance photography.
Hobby Centre.
Home supplies services.
House painting service.
Ice-cream parlour.
Interior decoration service.
Laundry service.
Local advertising services.
Local courier service.
Magazine service.
Multi-level marketing service.
News reporting for newspapers.
PCO/STD telephone booth.
Photostat service.
Play school for children.
Refrigerator/AC maintenance services.
Retail store.
Scooter repair service.
Selling securities for institutions.
Stationery supplies to offices.
Supply of plants on order.
Supply/maintenance plants in offices.
Tailoring work.
Television maintenance services.
Thesis typescripts for students.
Tourist guide—local/outstation.
Tuitions to school children.
Type writing services in courts.
Video library.

This is by no means an exhaustive list. Many of the ideas are commonplace. They can be seen in every community and in every town. The important thing is not that they are common, but that they are popular. They continue to provide employment opportunities to young people. Young people who are confident can do any of these things, or many more.

Evaluating the Product or Service

When you have selected the product or service you would like to offer you could proceed to the next step that is more important than the first one as your ultimate success depends upon it. Investigate the potential of the product or service you wish to offer. To play safe, do not rely upon personal convictions only. Base your decisions upon bare facts. You will need to be ruthlessly unbiased and honest about your observations and findings. The product or service must offer good value for money. Then only can others be attracted to pay for what you have to offer.

Ask yourself the simple questions that follow:

- Is the product or service that you wish to offer useful?
- Will the product or service be attractive to the consumers you have in mind?
- Can the product or service be marketed at a reasonable price?
- Is the price and quality of the product or service similar to that offered by others in the community and elsewhere?
- Will you be able to get enough sales in the local market?
- Will you need to sell outside as well?
- Are you in any way at an advantage over those who are already offering similar products and services elsewhere?
- Will you be able to hold on until the business catches up?

Answer these questions and any others that may strike you honestly. Do remember that the success of your product or service depends upon a realistic evaluation. Think about every aspect of the product or service. Note down your answers on a paper. You may need to re-evaluate them later.

With your personal evaluation of the product or service completed, ask your parents and friends about it. You do not need to disclose your complete plans at this stage to anyone. Only ask for frank and candid opinions. Listen. Do not argue. Your aim should not be to convince others of your assessment, but to study their viewpoint. If you suspect that their viewpoints are biased on certain grounds, you could discount their views proportionately. Do remember that not everyone can be biased.

After this phase of inquiry is completed, you will do well to contact people through whom you wish to market your product or service, or those who will be interested in it as actual users. If it is a product that is being introduced for the first time, take a sample along to the wholesalers, the retailers and the consumers independently, and ask their opinion about it. Ask them about its utility, and possible demand. Finally, you could ask them what price they could pay for it. If it is a product similar to one already in the market, you could ask them for a comparison. Inquire as to what do the wholesaler and retailer desire as the normal trade discount. Your ultimate sale of the product may depend upon the profit these middlemen can make on it.

Sometimes, the product that a young person has to offer is an improvement of an existing product. Not being able to finance the manufacture one may approach other manufacturers with the hope of earning a royalty on the sales of the product. Young people will do well to remember that many manufacturers are attracted to new ideas, particularly when they can help make money on them. However, many times, they ignore the enterprising young person after they have copied the idea. It is, therefore, imperative that if you have a new product, or have been able to bring about improvements in an existing product, get the idea patented through a trade marks and patents attorney before disclosing it to others.

You could do well to discuss about your product or service with your bank manager, an advertising executive, and a professional accountant. These people have a great insight into various types of trades. They can provide you a lot of useful information about people in similar trades. Marketing consultants feel that if the response to your inquiries is about 80 per cent in your favour, the project is worthwhile. You can go ahead with it.

Preparing the Plan

Once you are convinced that the product or service you have in mind has reasonable potentialities of developing into a business for you, it is time for you to prepare a complete plan of the project on paper. In the plan, clearly define the following:

- What kind of product or service is being offered?
- What will be the place of activity or operation?
- From where is the product or service to be procured?

- How will the product or service be introduced?
- Who will be the potential customers and clients?
- What will be the financial implications?
- How will the financial requirements be met?
- What are the sales targets? Define these month-wise for the first year, and year-wise for the next four years. That is, for five years in total.
- How will you review the progress? Do this at least once in every three months.
- Do you foresee any obstacles? Define them individually.
- How will you handle these obstacles? Suggest options for every obstacle separately.
- Are your plans flexible to make changes? This may be necessary with some working experience.

While preparing the plan, you will need to remember that every business and profession has its own code of ethics. You will have to observe it. In general, many opportunities appear to be more remunerative than others are. Whereas the personal approach to each opportunity does matter, in drafting the plan it is better to be conservative about the estimated demand for the product or service. A variation disheartens many a beginner in trade or profession. You will also need to keep a very tight check on all forms of expenditure. All beginners are guilty of making mistakes like hiring a fancy office, buying furniture, getting a telephone, etc. Let these things wait unless the line you have chosen depends upon this kind of equipment.

Many a large concern today started in a small room in a house, or in a garage. Of course, you will do well to print good business stationery, letterheads, advertising literature, etc. Get the best you can afford because these are your personal messengers to your prospective customers. These will also reflect your personal capabilities and method of working. A tight control on initial expenditure ensures that the individual learns to discipline the activities, and ensures early success.

If you are offering personal services, or starting a selling concern, you will know what margin of profit to expect. In this case, plan out how you intend to attract the maximum clientele. Most people are attracted by good service. List out ways in which you can render this regularly without fail. If you are marketing a product for an existing manufacturer, you will need to confirm that the supply will be enough to meet your demand. Have a reasonable agreement with the suppliers, so that they may not ignore you once you have done the initial spadework for them by creating a demand for their product in the particular area. Many a beginner has suffered on this score.

If you need to advertise your product or service, make a list of local newspapers, national newspapers, magazines and trade journals where you will need to advertise. Find out the cost of advertising, comparing the cost and advantages in each case. Let this be a part of your plans.

Taking into account the various costs and expenses, and a conservative figure to represent the returns in the beginning, find out what you can save for yourself. Will this amount meet your immediate needs? If not, then how do you intend making up the deficiency? You may need to make sacrifices in the beginning. Considering the advantages and the returns later, they may be worthwhile. Young people have lesser liabilities, can work harder, and can wait for results. They have better chances of paving a bright future for them. In preparing the plans, the emphasis must be on strict control on expenditure, and the best quality of the product or service you can offer. The style of working at this stage is unimportant. Ultimate success is not measured by the style you maintain, but the profits you earn.

Financing the Plan

Many young people are hesitant to consider self-employment for the simple reason that there may be no personal funds to execute their plans. However, there are many lines where one can begin with almost nothing. Many of the larger companies today started with small sums of money, and grew gradually. Although it may be necessary to muster some personal resources to make a beginning and give the project some shape, if the planning is sound, it should not be difficult to raise loans and advances for expansion of business. However, a loan should never be raised unless one is certain that it can be repaid within a specified period.

If one enjoys a good personal reputation, a reasonable loan can be raised from friends and relatives. You could also team up with a partner. You will also do well to discuss your plans with your bank manager. If one is technically qualified, and has a good plan, banks offer loan facilities at attractive rates of interest, and convenient modes of repayment. One can also take advantage of credit facilities offered by suppliers, wholesalers and others, provided, of course, one is reputed to have clean business dealings.

The Need to Go Slow

The first two years of all new business ventures are very critical. Experience has shown that many close down the very first year. The most common cause for this is unimaginative and unrealistic planning of the project. Extravagance in spending on unprofitable items has also brought down many a newcomer in business. It is, therefore, imperative that a young person just starting a business venture of his own must go very, very slow in the beginning. This is important even if the returns are meagre. One gets to understand the conditions prevalent in the trade or profession particularly those that are not normally obvious until one is actively involved.

This period must be utilized as an opportunity to observe the entire trade rather than compete with it. You will come across many facts that come to notice only when a person is in the midst of a battle for profits. You will also get to know many people who are unscrupulous, and play on the gullibility and lack of experience of young people just entering the trade. These people use confidence tricks to offer deals that apparently appear sound, but are in reality bogus. One learns slowly.

As one makes steady progress out of small, calculated steps, one builds up a strong foundation for the new business. Under all circumstances, keep the expenses to the barest minimum. Do not hire any expensive factory or office sites. Do not employ assistants or clerks for whom there may be insufficient work. Do as much work as you possibly can do yourself. Only when you are certain that you are standing on firm ground should you take measured steps, making sure that you are going towards your goal of establishing a profitable business for yourself.

Crossing the Hurdles

Self-employment has its own share of hurdles that need to be crossed by everyone. All young people embarking upon a career where they will be their own bosses must understand and anticipate these hurdles to ensure that they have a smooth beginning, and a trouble-free progress and growth with time.

For many trades and professions there are certain restrictions imposed by municipal boards, state governments, or even the Central government. These restrictions should not be taken to represent restrictive forces for discouraging self-employment. They are imposed in the interests of public health and sanitation, or even to collect taxes conveniently. To ensure that you do not infringe any municipal laws, state laws, etc., you will do well to inquire about these restrictions from people already in the trade, or from trade associations who can provide many useful hints to beginners. For taxation problems, it is advisable to consult a taxation practitioner who specializes in the line.

Human nature being what it is, every young person setting out in business on his own will have his moments of frustration and even heartbreak. These are passing phases. Everyone on his way up has passed through them, and others will continue to do so. You must guard against these weaker moments, and not give up the struggle, as many discouraged young people tend to do. Many fail to recognize their goal, and give up the struggle only a few steps short of their target. Perseverance is important. It may be lonely at times to keep working, many times without a fair remuneration for the efforts. You must keep up because eventually you will be amply rewarded through regular and steady gains.

Another important thing that all young people need to remember is that nobody is learned enough to give up further pursuit of knowledge. Trends keep changing. Therefore, it is imperative that you must be well-versed with the latest information through trade journals. Products and services can be outdated in a few years. Keep planning ahead of time. Learn to be observant and creative. The better you can exercise these qualities, the sooner you will be able to rise in your trade. The important thing is to keep giving the people what they want, and not what you think they should have. In this simple truth lies the secret of success.

Expanding Your Work

If you have selected the right product or service as a means for self-employment, and are putting in your best efforts to provide your customers and clients what they really need, it will not be long before you will need to think in terms of expanding your work. In many cases, it will need your attention very soon. In others, you may have to wait a little. Whenever you need to do it, do not get over-enthusiastic, and expand your work overnight. It may appear to be a sensible thing to do to make some quick money, but it may not always be in your best interests to expand quickly or haphazardly.

Plan the growth of your business. Do try to cope up with the increased demand for your product or service. However, the growth must be gradual. Plan a phased expansion so that neither should the investments mount up, nor should the sales lag behind. This is important because many times the increased demand is deceptive, as it may be temporary. Try to keep up only with the genuine and steady increase in demand for your products and services.

Once an expansion has been made with substantial investment, there may be no going back, making the venture a losing concern rather than one which was making a good profit earlier. Once your work is progressing satisfactorily, finances may not be much of a problem as all financing agencies may be willing to help you. However, do not invest short-term loans in long-term investments, a common fault made by many young businessmen causing undue embarrassment later.

Even as your business grows, do not overlook that the demand for a product or service is directly linked to the quality offered. Under no circumstances should you compromise on quality. Rather you should constantly strive to improve upon the quality of your product or service. Never be satisfied that the quality you are offering is at par with the best available elsewhere. Do not compete with others. Compete with yourself. See if you can improve upon your own work. This way you will always be well ahead of competition, and make success your constant companion.

To ensure that your increased output is properly utilized, you may need to advertise locally or even in the national press. Plan your advertising through a good advertising agency. It is always well worth the while to plan your advertising and to get promotional literature prepared and printed by a professional agency. However, if your business cannot afford this expense, and you need to write the advertising copy yourself, make it short, to the point, and be honest in your claims. It must be attractive, but certainly not deceptive. Advertise in the newspapers and magazines read mostly by the people who would be interested in your product or service.

Expansion of a business is a slow and steady process, and will need your attention regularly. It will gradually take you to greater heights of success. Do not try to take shortcuts. All big businesses grew slowly over a period. If you have spared no efforts in planning, and are putting in hard work from day to day, with gradual expansion there is no reason why in a few years from now you should not be the head of a big business concern.

Points to Ponder

- With scarcity of jobs on account of increased competitiveness, self-employment is the best option for vocational success.
- Self-employment can be a vital step to success in life.
- Opportunities for self-employment abound in all communities.

- Self-employment is not for everyone. Evaluate yourself for success.
- Look for opportunities that interest you. Evaluate the product or service you have to offer.
- When ready, do not rush. Move step by step.
- Preparation of an action plan is important.
- Financial implications must be considered in every plan of action.
- Once you start enjoying the work, get entrenched securely before any expansion is planned. Expand cautiously.
- Obstacles are a part of life. Be prepared for them. Review the work periodically.

Establishing a Small Industry 8

One form of self-employment that interests many young people is to establish a small-scale industry. This form of self-employment is of special interest to those who are technically qualified, and understand the technicalities of manufacturing different kinds of products. Very often, even those who are technically not equipped with the necessary knowledge get interested in manufacturing various items. This interest is related to personal aptitude and circumstances. Sometimes, the young people are attracted to such employment because of the glamour of high incomes very often associated with industrialists. Such attitudes must be discouraged. Establishing a small industry involves many sacrifices and heartaches. It is only after much hard work that one can expect to reap good dividends.

The manufacturing of different kinds of goods is a very competitive field. It involves large investments. Unless the person establishing the industry is observant, shrewd, hard working, and understands the many factors that affect his working, success may be no more than a dream. There are changing trends in almost every industry. It is, therefore, imperative that one must keep up with the times. In this field, it is not surprising if a running manufacturing unit sinks to become non-profitable, or become a losing business venture if one cannot keep up with the changing trends.

Opportunities for Establishing Industries

With increasing demand for almost all kinds of products, there are always many opportunities for augmenting the supply with newer and better products. The restrictions on imports from advanced nations had opened fields for technically qualified young people to manufacture substitutes to make up for this shortage. Even in the industrial field, with growing industrial development, new opportunities have opened to supply industrial inputs like machinery, spares and packaging of varied descriptions.

The needs of rural industrialization too offer promising opportunities. The large public sector and private sector undertakings also require many small items. This has made it possible to establish many ancillary industrial units to fulfil this demand. Industrial needs are invariably complex. They keep varying from time to time, but all the same are genuine needs, and must be fulfilled through new industrial units. These add up to offer many opportunities to young people to survey, assess, and if found compatible with personal aptitude, attitudes and circumstances, then to establish useful industries.

Consumer products of all kinds are always in good demand. They will continue to offer opportunities for improvements, and manufacturing newer and better products. In fact, the most elementary industries meet with such common everyday needs of people that must be fulfilled regularly. An industry may be established at the lowest level. The unit may consist of no more than a few indigenous tools, the family members as helping hands, and may be established in a back garage or a vacant room with very little outlay on material and equipment.

At higher levels, there are multi-million companies which produce and market consumer products on a national scale fulfilling the needs of millions of people. With limited technical expertise, experience and capital to be invested, young people will necessarily need to understand their own limitations. They should contemplate only smaller projects where the profits may be low, but so are the risks. Only when valuable experience has been gained in a particular field, expansion may be made in the industry.

Selecting a Small Industry

The selection of a small-scale industry will very much depend upon personal interests and circumstances as linked to local needs, or resources. In making a selection care should be taken to ensure several things.

- The investment must be reasonable.
- Ample raw materials should be available nearby.
- It should not be difficult to market the finished product.
- It would be ideal if the manufacturing process is simple.
- It should not be difficult to maintain quality.
- The gestation period to establish the unit should not be too long.

When these requirements are fulfilled, in due course of time, the returns will be satisfactory.

The smallest form of an industrial unit aims at meeting local needs only. It may do no more than process local produce for immediate consumption locally, or in nearby areas. It could also aim at modifying a local product for further processing by larger units locally, or in the larger cities. A small bakery, an *atta*-grinding unit, a machine tool shop, or stone-breaking units are examples of units that fulfil local needs only. They do not depend upon outside clientele.

Just as many units are established to fulfil local needs, similarly many industries are established to use local resources. Lime units near quarries, disintegrators and pulverizers for powdering deposits from nearby mines, leather industries near large tanneries, timber based industries near forests, sugar mills and mini-sugar mills in sugarcane growing areas are common examples of such industries.

Many industries are based not upon immediate consumer needs or local resources, but upon other kinds of needs. Ancillary units near large public and private undertakings, packaging units near industrial areas, fabricating units for making spares and supplies for other industries are examples of some industries which fulfil these needs.

When you set out to select a suitable small-scale industry in your area, ask yourself if you can manufacture for immediate local consumption. Alternatively, you can set up a unit to use local resources that are not being fully utilized so far. You could perhaps instal a unit to supply special requirements of other industrial units. Provided you can begin in a small way, you can also consider items that can be sold in the national market through retail distributors or wholesalers. The needs are often very complex. It is not possible for young people to decide conclusively about a particular need immediately, but one must observe and assess the need carefully. Selection is very important. A mistake in this direction can prove to be very expensive, as shifting from one item to another is not always practical.

The variety of items that are being manufactured, or could be manufactured, is so large that it is not always possible for a young person to consider the complete range, and arrive at the best decision. Besides, it is also not always possible for a young entrepreneur to be aware of the manufacturing needs and trends. To overcome this problem, and to help prospective young industrialists, the Development Commissioner, Small Scale Industries, Nirman Bhawan, New Delhi, publishes periodically a list of hundreds of industries that can be established by young people. The list also mentions priority industries, and those reserved for the small-scale sector. This list can be obtained directly, or from the District Industries Officer nearest to where you live, or from a Small Scale Industries Service Institute in your area. This will simplify your job of selecting the items that interest you most for a manufacturing unit.

Looking for Help

When you set out to establish an industry, a study of technical books, industrial reports, details furnished by private consultants and publishers, and other such literature is very useful. Established manufacturers can also be a great help as many a young person has taken a cue from them, and set out in the field. Several young people have the requisite knowledge and expertise to establish a particular industry, but not many are so blessed. Even those who are technically qualified may not know all that needs to be known besides the manufacturing process. They may require vital information pertaining to various aspects of establishing the industry. Since such help is not always available locally, or through friends and relatives, a prospective entrepreneur can turn to the Small Industries Service Institute (SISI) in the area.

The purpose of the Small Industries Service Institute is to guide prospective entrepreneurs about prospects of starting different industries at suitable locations, inform them about special assistance available from government and other agencies, guide on purchase of machinery, availability of raw material and sale of finished products. Besides these services, the SISIs have several extension centres spread all over the country where training is imparted in various skills and trades. The SISI also publishes technical reports, model schemes, pamphlets and helpful literature on small-scale industries. Inventions are encouraged, and guidance is given about important government Acts like the Factories Act, 1948, The Trade Marks Act, 1940, etc. The service rendered is very comprehensive, and almost all aspects of establishing a small-scale industry are covered. It would be useful for all prospective entrepreneurs to get in touch with the nearest SISI, or branch thereof for all kinds of problems, and can be sure of getting useful help. You can get in touch with the Small Industries Service Institute in your state at the address given below:

Small Industries Service Institute

Andhra Pradesh
Iftkar Mansion, 79 Azambad,
Hyderabad.

Assam
Industrial Fstate, P.O. Bamunimaidan,
Guahati

Bihar
8, Central Avenue,
Patliputra Housing Colony,
Patna-13.

Goa
Miranda Building,
Margao.

Gujarat
Dudheswar Road,
Opp. Rustom Jahangir Vakil Mills,
Ahmedabad.

Branch:
1/5, Jaganath Plot,
Rajkot.

Jammu & Kashmir
School of Designs Building,
Karan Nagar, Srinagar.
Branch:
Gandhi Nagar,
Jammu.

Kerala
Krishna Vihar,
Verma College Road,
Trichur-4.

Madhya Pradesh
10, Industrial Estate,
Polo Ground, Indore.

Maharashtra
Kurla-Andheri Road,
Saki Naka,
Mumbai-70.

Karnataka
Rajaji Nagar,
Bangalore–10.
Branch:
Bachi Lodge,
Club Road, Hubli.

Orissa
Mahanadi Road,
Tulsi Para, Cuttack.

Punjab
Industrial Area "B"
Ludhiana.

Rajasthan
Mirza Ismail Road,
Jaipur.

Tamil Nadu
65/1, Grand Southern Trunk Road,
Chennai-32.

Uttar Pradesh
107, Industrial Estate,
Kalpi Road, Kanpur.
Branch:
12, Mahatma Gandhi Road,
Agra.
Branch:
E-17/18, Industrial Estate, Naini,
Allahabad.

West Bengal
111 & 112, B.T. Road,
Kolkata-35.

Delhi
Okhla Industrial Estate,
Okhla, New Delhi.

Some Ideas for Setting up a Small Manufacturing Unit

Given below are 50 ideas for setting up a small manufacturing unit. Some of these items can be made at home or in a garage. Others require an elaborate set-up. These will encourage you to think new items.

Atta mill.
Bakery items.
Ball pens/refills.
Bicycle parts.
Carpets and rugs.
Cartons for sweets/confectionery.
CD recording/conversion.
Ceramic-ware.
Colour photo lab.
Computer components.
Computer stationery.
Confectionery making.
Decorative candles.
Decorative glass lights.

Detergents and scouring powders.
Display racks for shops.
Disposable plates, bowls, etc.
Envelopes from newspapers.
Exercise notebooks for schools.
Fabric printing.
Fancy gift items.
Fast food counter.
Food items like papads, vadis, etc.
Food preservation.
Fruit and milk-based cold drinks.
Fruit pulp for big processors.
Greeting and other cards.
Hand bags—leather, cloth, etc.
Handloom items.
Household linen.
Knitted sweaters, pullovers, etc.
Mouth freshners.
Music tapes.
Packaged spices.
Packaging cleaned food items.
Photo albums and frames.
Pickles and jams.
Picture postcards.
Plastic bags.
Printer ribbons/refills.
Printing services.
Printing visiting cards, letter-heads.
Readymade clothes.
School uniforms.
Shoes, chappals, etc.
Socks and stockings.
Steel doors, windows, grills.
Steel furniture.
Wooden doors, windows, etc.
Wooden furniture.

This list is by no means exhaustive. Many of the ideas are to be seen everyday in almost every community and town. The list has been prepared to show you how small items of common everyday interest can be manufactured in every community. The manufacture of many of these items can be started with a low capital outlay. These smaller items lead one to larger volumes and industries. List 10 items that you feel could be manufactured in your community.

1.
2.
3.
4.
5.
6.
7.
8.
9.
10.

Preparing the Plan

It may not be possible for a prospective young entrepreneur to immediately decide what he would like to manufacture in his proposed industry. However, with some consideration he can narrow down his choice to a few items that interest him. He can then set out to prepare the project reports for each of these items. This may seem difficult, but with the help available from the District Industries Officer and the Small Industries Service Institute in you area, it becomes comparatively easy. Chartered accountants also help prepare project reports for prospective entrepreneurs.

In preparing your plan, give due consideration to where you would like to establish the industry. In deciding about a particular site, you will need to make sure that it is connected with the nearby areas, and that the transportation charges on raw materials, or on the finished goods would not be excessive. You may consider if it would be worthwhile to establish it in an industrial area developed by the government or a private promoter. While considering private industrial areas, ascertain that the proposed developments will take place. It is important that the persons promoting the area are above reproach.

In the plan that you prepare, you will need to answer these questions:

- Is a factory shed available to you?
- If not, by when can you have it ready?
- Is a factory shed available on rent?
- What kind of machinery would you require?
- Do you know of dealers from where the machinery can be purchased?
- What are the approximate costs?
- How many workers will you need?
- If they need to be skilled, are they easily available in the area?
- Will you need to train them initially?
- Is raw material available in your area, or will you need to get it from elsewhere?
- How many raw materials will you need to store to keep the industry going without any interruptions?

- Is there any government restrictions on the raw materials?
- If so, will enough stocks be made available to you?
- Alternatively, will you have to make do by working your unit part-time until the position of the raw material eases a little?
- Where will you sell the finished products?
- Is the demand good, or fluctuating?
- Will the quality of your products be as good as that of those already in the market, or even better?
- Are your prices competitive as compared to other manufacturers?
- What method will you follow to sell your products?
- Have you discussed the subject with a party already dealing in similar products?
- Will the industry require electrical power, and is the same available easily?

Answer these questions in detail. Write the answers on paper. Work out individual costs. Do keep in view the interest on capital, wastage, and unforeseen obstacles. Consider the investment required on the project. Work out the possible profitability. Once you have figures worked out, also seek the advice of your friends, or others in the trade. You need not disclose your plans, but others' opinions can be valuable in guiding you about the accuracy of your own estimates and plans. You can also discuss your plans with a bank manager and a professional accountant both of whom can offer valuable suggestions.

The District Industries Officer and the Small Industries Service Institute can also help you make plans. The Development Commissioner, Small Scale Industries, under whose supervision the SISIs function, can offer model schemes, impact schemes, industry prospects sheets, analysis and planning reports, and pamphlets on the theme "Towards Better Techniques". These publications are prepared on a general pattern, but can be adapted to suit local conditions and circumstances.

Professional business consultants also offer readymade plans for some industries. They can also prepare special reports on a particular industry, but considering the labour involved, their charges may be high and beyond those of a young entrepreneur. Consider your plans from every angle you can think of. Personal interest, raw material availability, financial implications, and market possibilities are all very important. You should go ahead only when you feel convinced that you have good prospects of early success.

Getting the Proposed Unit Registered

Once you have finalized your plans to establish a particular industry, keeping in view personal resources and the financial implications, you will need to decide whether you would like to do it all alone. You could get into a partnership with a relative or friend, or perhaps even start a company. A professional accountant could guide you best as to what you should do. This matter decided, give an appropriate name to the unit, and get the letterheads printed.

Since the development of small industries is a state subject, you will do well to get your unit registered with the Directorate of Industries in your state. The application for the registration should be forwarded through the District Industries Officer. When your unit is registered you will be eligible to several facilities offered by the government to establish small-scale industries like availability of building material for the factory shed, electricity connection, making raw materials available, purchase of machinery, etc. This will also help you keep in touch with the latest regulations affecting the industries.

Government Controls and Restrictions

No licence is required from the Central or State Governments to establish a small-scale industry. However, there are certain controls and restrictions imposed by the government on the establishment of certain industries. It is best to get in touch with the District Industries Officer who can guide you in this direction. You will also need to take note of the provisions of the Factories Act, the Commercial

Establishments Act, and of local municipal rules and regulations pertaining to your kind of industry.

The manufacture of certain items attracts excise duty. If such is the case with your products, you will need to get your unit registered with the excise authorities in your area. Most items are liable to sales tax, or trade tax, and a tax practitioner is the best person to guide you about getting your firm registered with the local Sales Tax office. Invariably, the details pertaining to controls and restrictions imposed by the government can be ascertained from existing units or from those in similar trades. You could also consult legal practitioners practising in the field, or visit particular government offices yourself.

Looking for a Collaborator

With restrictions on certain imports during the past several years, it is obvious that many new industries would be established to fill the void created by the imposition of these restrictions. The technical expertise for some of these is available. However, there are several industries, for which sufficient expertise is lacking, and may have to be imported by way of foreign collaboration. The government always favourably considers proposals for foreign collaboration where technical expertise is not indigenously available, or where an industry can result in huge savings in imports, or can encourage exports.

When working out an agreement with a foreign collaborator, an effort should be made that the agreement is for a fixed period—say for 5 to 10 years. During this period, it should be agreed to develop local expertise. The royalty should be on a percentage basis, and not based on a minimum guarantee. An effort should be made to pay a minimum royalty. It should certainly not be more than 5 per cent. The agreement must aim at progressively developing indigenous inputs. The foreign dependence should be got over in the shortest possible period. It is also advisable that the agreement must provide for some exports. If the collaborator is not willing to give you a free hand to export anywhere in the world, you must insist upon some countries where in due course of time you can develop the market gradually.

Before you finalize collaboration, you will need to seek the permission of the Government of India to do so. Apply to the Secretary, Ministry of Industry, Government of India, Udyog Bhawan, New Delhi, through the Director of Industries in your state. You will need to enclose a draft agreement with the collaborator, a complete scheme giving the details of "recurring" and "non-recurring" requirements of foreign exchange, and an estimate of the expected savings in foreign exchange, along with your application for collaboration. The approval of your scheme will depend upon how well you can project your scheme, and convince the officials of its success.

Ancillary Industrial Units

An ancillary industrial unit is one that produces parts, components, sub-assemblies and tooling for supply against known or anticipated demand of one or more large units manufacturing or assembling complete products. These units are owned and controlled independently of the larger unit, or units, producing the final product. Units which manufacture tools, dies, jigs and fixtures fall within the definition of ancillary industrial units.

The Small Scale Industries Board has expressed special interest in ancillary industrial units, and appointed an Ancillary Industries Committee at the national level, and sub-committees in several states. The development of ancillary industrial units for many industries like bicycles, industrial machinery, machine tools, automobiles, air-conditioning, radio and electronic equipment, has been recommended. Many concessions are allowed for the development of ancillary industrial units, and a complete list of suggested industries could be obtained from the District Industries Officer, or the Small Industries Service Institute.

Financing the Project

Financing the industrial unit is the most important aspect of the project. Nothing can be achieved without finance. At one time, an entrepreneur had to depend upon his own personal resources, or those of his immediate friends and others from whom he could borrow money. Presently, a large number of agencies are willing to finance the projects of entrepreneurs at reasonable rates of interest. The Government of India, the state governments, and nationalized and other banks have introduced a number of schemes.

Loans are granted to small-scale units under the State Aid to Industries Act by the State Directors of Industries in every state against security or mortgage which may include land, buildings, machinery, equipment, stocks, etc. The loan can be conveniently repaid in instalments over a period of 10 years.

The State Financial Corporations are functioning in almost all states, and advance loans to meet long-, medium- and short-term requirements. They are available against 50 per cent to 75 per cent value of assets offered as security. The addresses of the State Financial Corporations are as follows:

Andhra Pradesh State Financial Corporation,
Chapel Road, Gun Foundry,
Hyderabad-4.

Assam State Financial Corporation,
Glener Quart House, Shillong.

Bihar State Financial Corporation,
Fraser Road, Patna.

Delhi State Financial Corporation,
Saraswati House, Connaught Place,
New Delhi-110001.

Gujarat State Financial Corporation,
Gujarat State Co-op. Marketing Society Building, 5th Floor,
Opp. Relief Cinema, Relief Road, Ahmedabad-1.

Haryana State Financial Corporation,
72/73 Bank Square, Sector 17-B, P.O. Box no: 74,
Chandigarh.

Jammu & Kashmir State Financial Corporation,
P.W.D. Building, Nehru Market,
Jammu.

Karnataka State FinancialCorporation,
7, First Main Road, Gandhi Nagar,
Bangalore-9.

Kerala State Financial Corporation,
Yellayabalam, Trivandrum-1.

Madhya Pradesh State Financial Corporation,
Shiv Vilas Place, Rajwada Chowk,
Indore.

Maharashtra State Financial Corporation,
United India Building,
Sir P.M. Road, Mumbai–400001.

Orissa State Financial Corporation,
Killa Maidan, Cuttack.

Punjab State Financial Corporation,
Bank Square, Sector 17-B,
Chandigarh.

Rajasthan State Financial Corporation,
Surya Niwas, C-18,
Bhagwan Das Road, Jaipur City.

Tamil Nadu State Financial Corporation,
Madras Industrial Investment Corporation,
38, White Road,
Royapettah,
Chennai.

U.P. State Financial Corporation,
7/154 Swaroop Nagar,
Kanpur.

West Bengal State Financial Corporation,
23, Rajendra Nath Mukherjee Road,
Kolkata.

The National Small Industries Corporation with its head office in New Delhi, and branches in Mumbai, Kolkata and Chennai, helps entrepreneurs to purchase machinery on hire-purchase basis. The application for loan must be made on a prescribed form, and forwarded through the Director of Industries. You can contact the National Small Industries Corporation for details at the following addresses:

The National Small Industries Corporation Ltd.,
Rani Jhansi Road,
New Delhi.

The National Small Industries Corporation Ltd.,
116-A, Lower Circular Road,
Kolkata.

The National Small Industries Corporation Ltd.,
5th floor, Janmabhoomi Chambers,
Fort Street, Mumbai.

The National Small Industries Corporation Ltd.
Khivraj Mansion,
150-A, Mount Road,
Chennai.

The State Bank of India and other banks offer credit assistance to small-scale industries against the pledge of raw materials, semi-finished and finished products. Loans for longer periods are also available for establishing small-scale industries if the entrepreneur is technically qualified, is a person of integrity, has the ability to work diligently, and has a worthwhile project. You can discuss the details with any bank manager in your area. He will be pleased to discuss your project with you.

If you are interested in obtaining financial help for your industry just as many other entrepreneurs are, you should get in touch with the District Industries Officer. He can give you the details of all the available help schemes. You could also discuss the matter with your bank manager who will be pleased to assist and guide you to meet your requirements conveniently.

Establishing the Unit

Once you have all the details worked out on paper, and are convinced that you have a worthy project, you are ready to turn your dream into a reality. It will be in your interest to get the unit into production as soon as possible. Delays can be expensive in terms of mounting interest, changing market trends, and similar problems. It is important that you go through the entire process very carefully to avoid unnecessary expense.

At every step, consider what economies can be exercised. Consider if it would be better to hire a factory shed rather than build one. If you are making your own shed, consult an architect about it. He may have good suggestions to offer. A collapsible shed can be conveniently built, altered, or moved. While planning the size, you will do well to make provision for future expansion also. The general layout should be such as to permit comfortable movement in handling of raw material and finished products. Safety at work is just as important as good ventilation and ease in working. The stores must be located at a convenient distance only. Do not go in for any luxuries until the unit is paying for everything.

As regards machinery and equipment, get the best you can afford, but do look around before you buy. Many of the smaller manufacturers can supply machine tools at very competitive prices. Inquire about spares. Buy suitable quantities with the machinery. The capacity of the machinery must meet your requirements. Idle machinery can rob you of your profits.

The layout of the machinery must permit easy operation. It must be as foolproof against accidents, as is possible. In some industries, you can bring about very useful economies by not doing the entire job of manufacturing yourself. You could get some of the work done by others so that you may cut down on investment in machinery or processes which cannot be fully utilized, and instead concentrate on the final product.

In the beginning, you should not employ excessive staff. Even those you employ will need to be supervised carefully. It is important that every investment must bring back proportionate returns. There should be no wastage.

Arrangements for the raw materials must be made well in time. The machinery must not remain idle. This way you can get the returns at an early date. Marketing of the products must be planned well in advance. It is important that you keep your marketing outlets well informed about your production plans. They should get the goods in time. This way you will keep your money in rotation, and get the best of what it can offer.

As you get the machinery going, you will find that you are playing many roles simultaneously. You will not only be entrepreneur/proprietor, but will also be the industry's purchase officer, production supervisor, the sales manager and financial controller. Each role entails much responsibility. One broken link can mean a broken chain of activity, and loss to the industry.

You must also remember that the first two years of an industry's existence are perhaps the most critical as miscalculations in planning are bound to show up and affect the industry adversely. You must be cautious with expenditure. However, do not overplay this role as it can stifle normal working. At all times keep a tight check on finances. As you find the work well within your personal capabilities, you will gradually build-up the industry. You are bound to come across tight corners, moments of loneliness and frustration, but sacrifices made initially pave the way towards a brighter future.

Marketing your Product

Many young people meticulously go to great lengths to plan the layout and production of their industry. However, they fail to understand the market for their product. When their product moves out of the factory, the market fails to pick it up, causing great anxiety and frustration. It is, therefore, important that before you establish your industry, or go into production, you must understand the characteristics of your market, its changing trends, consumer preferences, competition from the competitors, pricing, packaging and other similar details. This way you can be certain of success when you put out your product in the market. Those people who give due importance to marketing always do well. We have all seen how marketing men succeed when they set out to manufacture products for which they know their markets well.

When you plan your marketing, do not wait to contact your potential customers, retailers and dealers until your production is ready. Get in touch with them at the planning stage. Inquire about their requirements, the selling commission desired, and competition from other brands. You can also get in touch with the consumers, and get to know their reactions about existing brands and prices. The Small Industries Service Institute can also guide you about the marketing potentialities, and for a nominal fee will conduct market research for you. Keep your marketing techniques ahead of the production methods. You will have smooth sailing in your industry.

Expanding the Industry

Young people become ambitious too soon. The moment they feel that their industry is on a strong foundation, they become anxious to expand it. Industries must expand with time, but do not become over-anxious about it, or go about it too soon. Expansion entails heavy outlay on additional buildings, machinery, raw materials and finished products.

An increased demand for a product can be deceptive. It may be temporary. Expansion carried out indiscriminately may immediately increase financial liability. If returns do not increase proportionately, as very often they do not, the additional burden can offset the profits being made earlier. Before planning the expansion, let the industry be fully established.

Always ensure that the demand for your product is more than the supply. Try to fulfil this additional demand through working over-time, or through help from other industrial units. When you are convinced of a continued demand and profitability of making long-range investments in machinery and equipment you should plan a phased programme to expand the industry gradually.

Points to Ponder

- Many young people with good organizational skills get interested in manufacturing products as a form of self-employment.
- Manufacturing is a competitive field. It requires many skills and big investments.
- Opportunities for establishing manufacturing units exist every where. They will continue to be so in the future.
- When selecting a line of manufacturing, select one that benefits from the point of its location.
- To a certain degree one can avail of government support for establishing an industry. Check on what support is available.
- It is important to prepare a project report before starting an industry. The report will spell out the plan of action.
- It is useful to get the unit registered with the District Industries Officer.
- Do not overlook the statutory requirements laid down by the government for establishing manufacturing units.
- If the field of your choice involves special technology, it may be useful to collaborate with a foreign partner.
- Those who are weak in marketing skills may find it useful to establish ancillary units.
- The financial aspects must be considered in detail.

They can make all the difference between success and failure.

- The manufacturing unit must be established as expeditiously and meticulously as possible. Delays can be costly.
- Marketing is an important part of the business process. Ignoring it can result in wasted production.
- Expand with caution. Do it slowly.

9 Your Questions Answered

Q. How soon should young people start thinking in terms of selecting a career?

A. The sooner one can decide the better it is. By the time a student reaches class 10, one should be thinking in terms of selecting a career. This is important because one needs to choose subjects for class 11 and 12. The choice of the subjects will indicate the career options that one can take up.

Q. When choosing subjects in class 11 most of us select ones that we are comfortable with. Our immediate aim is to score well in class 12. Most of us do not think in terms of linking the subjects with a career that might interest us. Besides, we are not aware of the field of careers that are open to us, or what subjects lead us to a particular field of careers. Could you guide us on this?

A. I appreciate what you have said. What has been going on is wrong. The young people need to change their attitude. They need to be proactive. They need to understand which way they would like to go. They can discuss the issue with their parents, and plan educational activities accordingly.

I am aware that most young people do not know enough about the career options available to them. They are also not aware of what subjects lead one to particular careers. In general, at this level there are four definite subject groups that a person can select—Arts, Commerce, Science (Physics and Chemistry) with Maths, and Science with Biology. Listed below are some important careers. The foundation study group that leads to the career is marked 'Y'. You will notice that for some careers the study range is wider and better.

S.No.	Career	Arts	Com.	PCM	PCB
1.	Accountancy	-	Y	Y	-
2.	Advertising	Y	Y	Y	-
3.	Agriculture	-	-	Y	Y
4.	Alternative Medicine	-	-	Y	Y
5.	Animal Husbandry	-	-	-	Y
6.	Architecture	Y	-	Y	-
7.	Art	Y	-	Y	-
8.	Astrology	-	-	Y	Y
9.	Banking	Y	Y	Y	Y
10.	Biotechnology	-	-	Y	Y
11.	Business Process Outsourcing	Y	Y	Y	Y
12.	Call Centres	Y	Y	Y	Y
13.	Catering and Hotel Management	-	-	Y	Y
14.	Civil Aviation	-	-	Y	-
15.	Commerce	Y	Y	-	-
16.	Company Secretary	Y	Y	Y	-
17.	Cooking	Y	-	Y	Y
18.	Cottage Crafts	Y	Y	Y	-
19.	Courier Service	Y	Y	Y	-
20.	Dairy Science	-	-	Y	Y
21.	Dancing and Dramatics	Y	Y	Y	Y
22.	Defence Services	Y	Y	Y	Y
23.	Dentistry	-	-	-	Y
24.	Dress Making	Y	-	Y	-
25.	Engineering and Technology	-	-	Y	-
26.	Entertainment	Y	Y	Y	Y
27.	Event Management	Y	Y	Y	Y
28.	Fashion and Design	Y	Y	Y	Y
29.	Film and Serial Making	Y	Y	Y	Y
30.	Fitness and Beauty Business	Y	Y	Y	Y
31.	Forensic Science	-	-	Y	Y

Contd...

S.No.	Career	Arts	Com.	PCM	PCB
32.	Forestry	-	-	Y	Y
33.	Franchising	Y	Y	Y	Y
34.	Games and Sports	Y	Y	Y	Y
35.	Gemology	Y	-	Y	-
36.	Government Service	Y	Y	Y	Y
37.	Homoeopathy	-	-	Y	Y
38.	Horticulture and Floriculture	-	-	Y	Y
39.	I.A.S. and Allied Services	Y	Y	Y	Y
40.	Information Technology	Y	Y	Y	Y
41.	Insurance	Y	Y	Y	Y
42.	International Trade	Y	Y	Y	Y
43.	Investigation Services	Y	-	Y	-
44.	Journalism	Y	Y	Y	Y
45.	Languages	Y	-	-	-
46.	Law	Y	-	Y	-
47.	Librarian	Y	-	Y	-
48.	Management	Y	Y	Y	Y
49.	Medical Transcription	-	-	-	Y
50.	Medicine	-	-	-	Y
51.	Merchant Navy	Y	Y	Y	Y
52.	Multi-level Marketing	Y	Y	Y	Y
53.	Nursing	-	-	-	Y
54.	Ophthalmology	-	-	-	Y
55.	Pharmacy	-	-	-	Y
56.	Photography	Y	-	Y	-
57.	Police Service	Y	Y	Y	-
58.	Printing	Y	-	Y	-
59.	Public Relations	Y	Y	Y	-
60.	Publishing	Y	Y	Y	Y
61.	Railways	Y	Y	Y	Y
62.	Real Estate	Y	Y	Y	-

Contd...

S.No.	Career	Arts	Com.	PCM	PCB
63.	Religious Services	Y	-	Y	-
64.	Retail Selling	Y	Y	Y	Y
65.	Selling	Y	Y	Y	Y
66.	Service Providing	Y	Y	Y	Y
67.	Social Service	Y	Y	Y	Y
68.	Teaching	Y	Y	Y	Y
69.	Telecommunications	-	Y	Y	-
70.	Transportation	Y	Y	Y	-
71.	Travel and Tourism	Y	Y	Y	Y
72.	Veterinary Science	-	-	-	Y

Q. You have listed many careers. What careers out of these would you rate most popular?

A. Individuals have a personal choice. There are always the traditional careers like engineering and medicine. Looking at the current trend, we could list the popular careers as follows:

1. Information Technology and Telecommunications.
2. Banking/Finance/Insurance.
3. Entertainment/Media.

At lower levels we have Advertising, Consumer Goods, Manufacturing Industries, Fashion and Medical Services.

Q. What is your view about careers through competitive examinations?

A. They have always been popular. Their popularity will continue. The careers at the top level are for brilliant students. Although many try for these positions, but only a few make to them. When opting for one of the many competitive exams, a person must try to evaluate one's capabilities, and then only apply for appropriate positions.

Q. In every town there are coaching institutes that promise you success in the competitive exams. Must one study in these institutions? Is education in schools and colleges not sufficient?

A. There are two reasons for the popularity of coaching institutes. Firstly, through advertising they have created an image of their importance. Secondly, most students are not sufficiently motivated to study on their own. Although eventually the success of every individual depends upon the effort one puts into study, but the competitive spirit generated at these institutions motivates people. They are exposed to a variety of situations. The students are compelled to put in intensive effort because of the goading by the parents who have paid the coaching fees, and by the coaches who know that their existence depends upon the success of the students.

Q. What should be the criteria for selecting the best coaching institute?

A. The best test lies in the taste of the pudding. Look at the success rate of the institute. If a large number from the institute are selected each year, the coaching must be good. Talk to the students who are studying there. Is the atmosphere in the institute congenial? Does it motivate you? What have the students to say about the teaching staff? Join only when you feel that you will benefit from the coaching provided in the institute.

Q. When appearing for competitive exams to enter into prestigious institutions many young people are discouraged when they do not get admission into an institution of their choice. Is there any justification in their getting discouraged? Has their vocational success been cut off even before they have really begun?

A. No. It is natural to desire admission into the best institutions. These institutions are labeled 'best' because besides providing technical instruction they offer an atmosphere where students get mentally prepared to make success a part of their professional life. Let us not overlook that the lesser-acclaimed institutions follow the same curriculum, and offer the same degree. The ultimate professional success depends upon the individual. Success comes from thorough knowledge and practical skills. These can easily be attained at any good institution even though it is not labeled 'best'. I have seen many successful people who have come from poor homes, studied in ordinary schools and colleges. Through dedicated effort they have attained great heights.

Q. **Vocational trends keep changing. How can young people cope with these?**

A. To cope with changing trends in any field one needs to be proactive. People who have a high level of awareness can always foresee the changing trends. Success comes from adapting oneself with the changing trends.

Q. **My son wants to become a doctor. He has been an above-average student, but looking at his performance I am not confident that he will qualify in the competitive exam to enter a medical college. What do you suggest?**

A. This is a common problem. There are many young people who want to become doctors and engineers. There are others who want to become big industrialists. You will agree that the top places are for the best in any field. However, what I would like to emphasize is that if one cannot become a doctor, one can still get into the medical field. There are a large number of options from being a medical attendant to being a top specialist. One can do whatever is in harmony with one's personal capabilities. This is true in every field of work.

Q. **Are there any fields of work that are gender-based?**

A. Only a few decades back many fields were divided on the basis of gender. Whereas most vocations were strictly for men, there were some for women. The situation is totally changed now. We see women in almost all fields of work. They have reached top positions just like men. We see women in top positions in Police, in Banks and in Business. We see women in the Defence Services. Only in very special cases, employers specifically ask for applications for men or women.

Q. **What is the reason for this change in the workplace?**

A. Education! Women are doing better than men in pursuing

higher education. When you look at the exam results, girls are outdoing boys at school level. This is because boys have more diversions than girls. Even at higher levels the women are more dedicated to learn, and are finding good positions in every field of work. In the near future we should not be surprised if more women enter the workplace.

Q. **Earlier we had the conventional schools and colleges that were managed either by the government agencies or by trusts and societies interested in community development. In the recent past many schools and colleges have been established by closely held societies. The courses offered by these institutions are recognised by the government. They claim to offer more facilities. The fees charged are on the higher side. Besides better hostel facilities do these institutions provide better education?**

A. In the recent past there has been a big swing from studying in conventional colleges to studying in vocational institutions. Since the government was unable to cope with this change mostly because of financial constraints, private enterprise has established schools and colleges, pushing the fees to the higher side to cope with the expenses. This has made it possible to spread vocational training to almost every town in the country without any expense to the government. However, it has made education expensive. It has been possible to provide employment to a lot of people. It would not be right to say that all the institutions are doing a fine job, but since their existence is need-based, they will fulfil the changing needs of education. Considering the need they fulfil, they are here to stay.

Q. **A large number of foreign institutions have opened branches in India, offering a part of the study here, and the rest abroad. Does studying in these institutions offer any special advantage over studying in Indian institutions?**

A. These institutions are a step ahead of the private educational institutions we have just discussed. These institutions woo those students who have the capacity to pay high fees and study abroad. Some of the courses are not recognised by

Indian universities. Private employers, who look for certain abilities rather than particular degrees in their employees, accept many courses. Many countries regularly promote their educational institutions. In the first place this helps enroll more students in these institutions, making them financially better. Secondly, once these students qualify to their way of education, these people are a good source of additional trained personnel for the development of the country.

Q. **What is the status of private universities?**

A. All universities that are incorporated through the Act of State Legislature are valid and legal. The degrees and diplomas that are offered by these universities too are legal.

Q. **What is the most important thing to get a job?**

A. The most important thing is academic achievement followed by the personality and family background of the person applying for the job.

Q. **What should one look for in an employer when applying for a job?**

A. Most people look for an appropriate salary. However, it is equally important to look for the opportunity to grow within the company and in the field, the security provided by job conditions and the image of the company.

Q. **How long do most first-time employees stay with an employer?**

A. Most stay on for at least two years. In five years most first-timers change jobs.

Q. **Is it useful to have postgraduate qualifications before one takes up a job for the first time?**

A. It is not always necessary to have postgraduate qualifications when one takes up a job. However, these additional qualifications always help one to grow in the future.

Q. Are job opportunities better in big cities rather than the smaller cities?

A. Yes, they are. However, the better opportunities are not because of a higher population in a big city. The general working environment in the city is equally important. Many surveys have described Mumbai, Bangalore and New Delhi as the best cities to work in. Surprisingly, Pune and Hyderabad rate better than cities like Kolkata and Chennai.

Q. How do most companies hire their employees?

A. Companies have several criteria for hiring their employees. It is common for big companies to employ people through campus enrolment or through agencies. A large chunk of the applicants are employed on the basis of advertisements in the newspapers and also through personal direct applications.

Q. What final advice would you give to a person taking up his first job?

A. Try to understand what your employee expects of you and provide the best service.

SECTION TWO

Some Important Careers

Some Important Careers 10

In the chapters that follow, some of the important careers open to young people are discussed. Each career is considered under various headings such as desirable personal qualities, the opportunities available in the field, how one can make a beginning in the career, the scope for self-employment, and other details as necessary. The names and addresses of educational and professional institutions have also been included in some cases to enable a person to get the details directly from the institution concerned. In other cases the addresses are given in Section 3.

All young people are interested in the earning potential of different careers. It is not possible to provide this information in exact terms because of the changing pattern of the circumstances. Income from the same job varies from one place to another because of several reasons. In most jobs where a person has vocational ability, one can hope to start with a salary of Rs. 5,000 and above. For better qualifications and some experience it could be Rs. 10,000 and above. For responsible positions where a person has gone through competitions and has received specialised training, the salaries can be very attractive. Foreign assignments offer the highest salaries. Study current advertisements to get the correct idea of what to expect in a particular field of work.

The basic purpose of discussing the various careers is not to analyse any particular career. It is also not intended to make any comparisons. The idea is to present details of the responsibilities and privileges that are a part of the various careers. In many cases the fields of specialisation and the different possibilities offered are considered. Since jobs are not always readily available, the opportunities for self-employment are also discussed. Through the details provided a young person can understand the many opportunities available, and after a fair appraisal, be able to decide which career would suit him best.

Accountancy

11

Accountancy as a specialized subject is of recent origin as compared to other occupations. Large-scale production in every sphere of work has necessitated purchasing, manufacturing and selling on a large scale, often making the transactions complicated. Therefore, there is the need for qualified accountants in different positions to keep track of various transactions.

Even in small-scale and medium-scale business operations, the profession of accountancy has an important role to play. Accounts can be very revealing. Positive guidance can help the business organizations to grow quickly by laying greater emphasis on items of income, and eliminating those that entail wastage and losses.

The taxation structure too has so grown that assessees need to get their accounts audited, and presented by professional accountants in a form acceptable to the authorities. The field of accountancy is growing fast. With increased development in every sphere of life, excellent opportunities for careers in accountancy will continue to dominate the vocational field.

Desirable Personal Qualities

To be successful in this field, a person must:

- be of high integrity and honour. People like to keep their account secret.
- have an analytical outlook. One can learn a lot about the business through proper analysis of accounts.
- have good observation and an eye for discrepancies. Detecting deliberate errors is important.
- enjoy working with figures. This is not a common trait amongst people.

- be a stickler for accuracy in calculations. Unless there is accuracy, accounts have no meaning.
- have a good all-round knowledge of people and things. One needs to deal with varied situations and all kinds of people.
- be computer literate with working knowledge of accounting software. Good accounting software has made accountancy easier and more accurate.
- be able to get along well with people. Unless one can do this, it becomes difficult to collect information from people.
- be willing to work away from home for long periods. Auditing jobs require one to keep away from home for long periods.

Opportunities in Accountancy

Accountancy is a growing field of service. With its application to all kinds of businesses and professions, and its need in both government and private organizations, opportunities for employment exist at all levels in this profession. At the lower levels there are positions for accounts clerks, bookkeepers, ledger-clerks, audit clerks, cost and works clerks, and similar positions in business and government organizations.

At upper levels, there are positions of greater responsibility as accountants, auditors, financial advisors, taxation experts, company secretaries, administrators and receivers, company directors, consultants and even general managers. Accounting is the heart of all business transactions. Those who are well-versed in accounts always have their finger on the pulse of the business. There are good opportunities for capable young people to rise to top positions in all kinds of organizations.

Although the responsibilities at all levels of the profession pertain to maintenance and analysis of accounts, the higher positions carry more responsibility, particularly as one is expected to analyse and present accounts to convey a definite meaning.

In senior positions, accountants look after more complicated financial transactions, and coordinate the work of the subordinate staff. Cost accountants are responsible for keeping a check on various factors that affect production costs, and therefore help promote profitability. Auditors examine account books and financial records, and certify that they were correctly maintained, and reflect a true financial picture of the organization. Chartered accountants fulfil varied responsibilities like auditing, preparing of accounts, filing tax returns, and even act as financial consultants and executors of wills. With their wide outlook and knowledge, chartered accountants often rise to high positions in different kinds of organizations.

Educational Facilities

To qualify as a cost accountant one must pass the examination of the Institute of Cost and Works Accountants of India. To become a chartered accountant, one needs to pass the examinations conducted by the Institute of Chartered Accountants of India. Those working in banks can qualify for better positions by appearing in examinations conducted by the Indian Institute of Bankers, and the Indian Merchants' Chamber, both in Mumbai.

Those employed in clerical positions in banking institutions can become members of the Indian Institute of Bankers by appearing for the Associate and Certificate examination of the Institute. Diploma courses in Specialized Accountancy and Income Tax, Specialized Costing, Specialized Banking, Specialized Company Secretarial Work, and also a Senior Grade Certificate in commercial subjects are offered by the Indian Merchants' Chamber.

The British Institutes offer facilities for study through post for these examinations, and also offer courses in accountancy, cost accountancy and management accountancy. Useful postal courses in accountancy and auditing, and in cost accountancy are offered by the International Correspondence Schools.

To qualify as a cost accountant one needs to be a member of the Institute of Cost and Works Accountants of India. The membership of the Institute is of two types. To qualify as an Associate, one must be 21 years of age, must be working as a cost accountant, have three years' practical experience, and must have passed the final examination of the Institute. An Associate is designated as A.I.C.W.A. To qualify as a Fellow, designated as F.I.C.W.A., one must be 26 years of age, and must have held the position of a Chief Cost Accountant for at least five years. To qualify for the examination of the Institute, one must be 18 years of age, and must have passed the 10+2 examination. All registered students are required to undergo postal and oral tuition for 18 months each before becoming eligible to appear for the Intermediate and Final examinations of the Institute. Postal tuition is conducted directly by the Directorate of Coaching Administration of the Institute. For imparting oral tuition some educational institutions and colleges have been recognized by the Institute.

To qualify as a chartered accountant, one needs to become a member of the Institute of Chartered Accountants of India. Membership of the Institute is granted to those who have served as 'articled clerks' for four years or as 'audit clerks' for six years, and passed the Intermediate and Final examinations of the Institute.

Articled clerks and audit clerks are apprentices attached to qualified chartered accountants who are practising their profession, and are entitled to train apprentices. To qualify as an articled clerk or an audit clerk, one must have passed the 10+2 examination, or its equivalent. Graduates and others who have studied accountancy and auditing as a part of their study are entitled to one year's remission in the training period before appearing for the Institute's examinations. An articled clerk is different from an audit clerk in that he must work full time without any remuneration and without engaging himself in any other work or study without the permission of the Institute. An audit clerk is not so bound. He must, therefore, work as an apprentice for a longer period.

Articled clerks and audit clerks gain valuable experience while working as apprentices for their principal. They do personal study during off time. Postal tuition imparted by the Institute is necessary to qualify for the examination of the Institute. It may extend from 9 to 12 months for the

Intermediate examination, and 9 months for the Final examination for those appearing in one group at a time, and 15 months for those appearing in both groups at one time.

On passing the examinations one qualifies for the membership of the Institute, and is called a chartered accountant. There are two categories of membership—Associates and Fellows. Associate members who have been practising continuously for five years are entitled to apply for becoming Fellows of the Institute. Whereas an Associate member is entitled to use the letters G.C.A. after his name, a Fellow of the Institute can use the letters F.C.A. after his name.

Some Important Addresses

Institute of Chartered Accountants of India,
New Delhi.

Indian Merchants' Chamber,
76, Veer Nariman Road,
Churchgate, Mumbai-400020.

Institute of Cost & Work Accountants of India,
Kolkata-700016.

The British Institutes,
359-D, Naoroji Road,
P.O. Box 1025, Mumbai-400023.

Indian Institute of Bankers,
State Bank of India Building,
Apollo Street, Fort, Mumbai-400001.

International Correspondence School,
P.O. Box 1023, Mumbai-400023.

Making a Beginning

One can make a beginning in a career in accountancy at the lower levels by seeking employment after passing the 10+2 examination. Some seek employment after a degree in Arts or Commerce subjects, and gradually learn the work by working in an established organization.

At the lower level an account clerk is responsible for recording everyday financial transactions under appropriate heads of accounts in the books. A bookkeeper maintains account books as prescribed. A ledger clerk is responsible for making postings in ledgers. Audit clerks examine and compare vouchers with entries in account books. Cashiers are responsible for cash transactions. In banks, a teller is responsible for making small payments to customers. Costs and works clerks help to calculate production costs.

One cannot reach higher positions in a career in accountancy just through working experience. One will need to pass certain examinations within the organization in which one is working, or by passing certain professional examinations, which qualify one for higher positions in the career. The responsibilities at all levels of the profession pertain to maintenance and analysis of accounts. The higher positions involve more responsibility. It is necessary to analyse and present accounts in a standard form.

One can also find self-employment as a part-time accountant to small business organizations, or as a taxation advisor after graduating in law after a B.A. or B.Com. and gaining some practical experience by working with an established tax consultant for some time.

Income from Accountancy

Since greater responsibility is involved in careers in accountancy, jobs at different levels are better paid as compared to similar positions in other fields of work. The salaries offered by banks, the Life Insurance Corporation of India, the general insurance companies in both the private and public sectors, and other similar organizations are good. The salaries for jobs at lower levels vary with the kind of work and responsibility involved. Those at higher levels are good. Cost accountants and chartered accountants draw very handsome salaries when employed by the larger organizations. The salaries offered by the government departments are not very attractive comparatively. Practising chartered accountants enjoy both a good income and prestige in the society. Therefore, many prefer to work on their own rather than seek a job.

Opportunities for Self-employment

There are opportunities for self-employment at all levels for young people interested in careers in accountancy. At lower levels, many people earn a steady income from writing accounts on part-time basis for several small firms and business houses. Besides writing the account books, preparing bills, filing vouchers, helping to prepare statements for purposes of filing sales tax and income tax returns provides useful work.

Cost accountants can work as consultants to several small industries simultaneously helping them to plan their production schedules, and making a good career out of it for themselves. Good chartered accountants are always in great demand for purposes of audit, consultancy services, filing tax returns, and other similar assignments. There is a good demand for qualified accountancy personnel. Those who know the job well can earn a steady income through self-employment.

Advertising

12

Advertising plays an important role in everyday life. For established products, it helps to sustain demand; for new products, it helps create it. Advertising has helped generate demand for many products. That has made it possible to produce on large scale, and pass the benefits by way of lower prices to millions of people all over the world. This has helped raise the standard of living all-around. Besides promotion of commercial products and services, advertising plays a vital role to help make announcements, develop and influence public relations, help people meet, and other similar things.

An important role of the advertising business is to study and understand market trends. This helps design better products. Designing of packaging and promotional literature, organizing sales campaigns, suggesting the correct advertising media to the clients, and looking after other such details comes within the scope of this vocation. With electronic media playing an essential role in the lives of people all over the world, advertising as a career has become very important. It is a growing field of employment. It has grown 500 per cent in the last decade. Young people can look forward to a satisfying career that offers both excitement and money.

Desirable Personal Qualities

To be successful in this field a person must:

- be creative. Creativity plays an important part in advertising products and services in new ways.
- have a good imagination. One must be able to imagine appropriate situations to project new products and services.
- be observant of people and situations. That is where the best ideas come from.

- be willing to take initiative and try new ideas. A new idea is useless unless one has the initiative to try it.
- understand human psychology well. Good market promotion aims at appealing to the human mind.
- possess the ability to play with words. Words play a crucial part in conveying advertising messages.
- be able to create good visual displays. A good picture is worth a thousand words.
- get along well with other people. This can mean additional work.
- be willing to work as a team. An advertising campaign is a united team effort. No one can handle it individually.
- appreciate the need to keep to time schedule. There is no scope for procrastination.

Opportunities in Advertising

All businessmen agree: advertise or perish. Wherever action is important, advertising steps in. The field of advertising encompasses every aspect of our everyday life. Besides the electronic media, which depends wholly on advertising, there are thousands of local and regional newspapers and magazines we see everywhere. Each one of these requires advertisements for its existence. The larger companies that have an interest in the international market are interested in advertising in other countries also.

To fulfil the need for advertising in all kinds of media, the advertising business first needs to get in touch with prospective customers, creating opportunities for accounts executives. Next, it is necessary to prepare advertisements for the clients. The clients expect that the advertisements will be designed with catchy slogans, and illustrated with attractive visuals. This need opens many opportunities for young people who have the imagination and creativity to promote products and services.

Besides the print and electronic media, advertisers are aware of the impact of hoarding boards, kiosk signs, neon lights, boards on buses and trains, messages on match boxes, inland letters, gift items, exhibitions, road shows and other such methods create on the public. Each of these media has opened opportunities for young people to build a career in advertising.

Designing of labels, packaging and promotional literature for all kinds of products opens yet another field of advertising. With many responsibilities involved in creating the advertising needs of a developing nation, at both government and public level, one can look forward with optimism to a variety of fields of specialisation in advertising. Career opportunities will grow with increasing needs for all kinds of advertising activities.

Responsibilities Involved

People that handle different kinds of responsibilities staff an advertising agency. For instance, a copywriter must have the knack to use words that win immediate attention, and create an interest in the product or service. Art assistants design the artwork. Layout artists put together the final copy. Besides, there are part-time or full-time models, artists and photographers. Market research assistants help collect and compile facts and figures about products and markets. Typographers help select the correct kinds of type for different kinds of presentations.

For radio and television advertising, scriptwriters who see in terms of sound and visual balance prepare the scripts. The newspaper circulation, radio and TV audiences, and a good knowledge of people, their income and buying habits are of special interest to the media executive in the advertising agency. The link with the clients is through the account executive. He must understand the client's background and needs. Accordingly, he coordinates the advertising campaign as developed by the different departments. He is also responsible for allocating the advertising to various media, and to keep the client updated about the progress in each field of work.

Educational Facilities

Since a variety of skills are used in this field, people come trained in different fields like writing, photography, art, marketing, etc. Courses in advertising are offered by several institutions. The field has a vast potential. At the same time it is very competitive. Many join in senior positions after a master's degree in Management.

Making a Beginning

In view of the fact that there are many different fields in a career in advertising, most young people are attracted to specific responsibilities. These depend upon personal aptitudes and capabilities. Some are interested in cinema slides, or in hoarding boards, or kiosk signs. Others may have inclination towards radio and TV advertising.

Keeping in view their personal interest, young people begin a career in an advertising agency in one of the departments of their choice. At the lower levels there are no minimum educational qualifications prescribed for various responsibilities, but interest and proficiency in the field of choice along with a good general education are desirable. Young people with a photogenic face and an attractive figure can do well as part-time models.

A bachelor's degree is desirable for rising to senior positions. However, many times even those with lesser formal education have done well. A diploma in advertising is always a useful asset to understand the responsibilities well, and to rise to higher positions. Many of the larger companies have their own advertising departments. These may perform all the functions of an advertising agency, or partly take support from large established agencies. Many young people begin their careers in these advertising departments. After gaining some experience, they move to better positions in big agencies.

Income from Careers in Advertising

Many of the advertising agencies prefer to get certain jobs done on piecework basis, paying for each job as mutually negotiated. Several others maintain their own staff. There are no rules about what the salary should be. Depending upon the kind of work, they are mostly negotiated. At lower levels they are similar to those in other careers. Good work brings about fast promotions and increments in salary. The prospects for imaginative and creative young people are good with swiftly rising incomes. The top executives in advertising agencies draw handsome salaries, and enjoy many benefits.

Opportunities for Self-employment

Like many other fields of work, advertising too offers good opportunities for self-employment. These include canvassing advertisements for the local or national press and blocking of hoarding sites to be rented to advertising agencies or to companies. Making of promotional presentations and advertising movies for business concerns offers good opportunities. Many specialize in the making of different kinds of neon and light signs.

Preparing promotional literature for business organizations, drawing out master mailing lists for various trades and businesses, conducting publicity campaigns for business houses, or publishing a directory of interest to business also offer opportunities for self-employment. Starting an advertising agency after some experience is also possible. These opportunities are used repeatedly by young people to find profitable self-employment in a career in advertising.

Agriculture

13

Agriculture continues to be the oldest and most popular of all occupations in our country. It is not because we depend upon it for food and clothing, but 70 per cent of our population lives in the rural areas. They know no better than to depend upon agriculture for a livelihood. We do not really need as many people as are working to carry out farming operations. Those that are engaged in such work are underemployed. They have little to do besides the seasonal agricultural operations unless they have other things to keep them busy round the year.

Some benefits of research and modernization have trickled into the agricultural operations. The country has become self-sufficient in food requirements. In the present context, there is a need to bring about further improvements in concepts and techniques in agriculture. With improvements, the released excess manpower will need to be absorbed in rural industries.

The administrative structure of the Department of Agriculture in various states has not been as effective as it could be. There is scope for improvement. Despite the overcrowding in this field of work, opportunities that aim at improved techniques and greater productivity continue to be available to young people interested in careers in this field. There is a need for a slow and steady revolution to develop agriculture in the country.

Desirable Personal Qualities

To be successful in this field, a person must:

- have a love for nature. Without this one cannot succeed in agriculture.
- be willing to accept the vagaries of nature. Man has no

control over nature. It should not become a source of unnecessary tension.

- not be shy to work with one's hands. When a work has to be done, one cannot wait for help. The work must be done.
- appreciate the need to work within a tight time schedule. Nature has its own pattern. We need to work in harmony with it.
- be willing to try new ideas. All progress has come about because of trying new ideas.
- be healthy and possess stamina to work hard when required. It can be difficult at times.
- be adaptable to changing circumstances. Wherever there is life, there will be changes. One must necessarily adapt to them.

Opportunities in Agriculture

The field of agriculture is overcrowded. Too many are employed in this sphere though they are underemployed. Nevertheless, considering the need for taking the fruits of science and research to the farmer to increase productivity, there exist many useful opportunities for careers in this field of work.

Besides opportunities for self-employment of running one's farm, every state has a vast administrative set-up with a District Agriculture Officer at the district level. Subordinate staff at different levels assists him. Block Development Officers operate at the level of blocks constituted of several groups of villages. Subordinate staff also assists them. Gram Sewaks and Sewikas work at the lowest level. They are in direct touch with the farmers and women in the villages.

The need for more organized selling of agricultural produce has created many opportunities for semi-governmental marketing co-operatives. Many young people have found useful employment with them. The success that some of these co-operatives have achieved is being adapted by other states. The methods used can be tried in other fields of agriculture.

Government seed and fertilizer stores and purchasing centres offer useful opportunities for employment.

In the private business sector, there are opportunities for the marketing of good seeds, chemicals, fertilizers and other agricultural inputs. At many centres there are purchasing points established by the Food Corporation of India and the state governments. Many people are involved in direct purchasing from the farmers. Products through these purchases may find way directly to consumers or to the wholesale and retail markets.

Opportunities for research in a wide variety of subjects connected with agriculture will always provide employment to young people interested in such work. Teaching these subjects in institutions spread around the country also offers employment opportunities. Contrary to what many believe, agriculture is not a simple subject of study. With growth of science and knowledge, it is no longer restricted to major subjects like Agronomy, Agricultural Botany, Entomology, Plant Pathology, Agricultural Engineering or Agricultural Chemistry. It has gone into finer lines of specialization in different subjects related to individual crops, diseases and pests. Subjects like Plant Breeding, Genetics, and Microbiology are common place.

Practical agriculture too is becoming specialized with farmers growing particular crops, with the special purpose of seed production, plant propagation, maintaining nurseries and similar operations. The development of Horticulture has helped people to establish orchards. Packaging and export of quality fruit has opened the world as a market to many in this field. The need for flowers has seen growth in Floriculture, particularly near cities, or places from where they can be exported. (See Horticulture and Floriculture)

With the message of better techniques to be communicated to farmers in all parts of the country, the field of agricultural journalism also offers many opportunities for useful employment. The needs of agriculture will continue to offer challenging opportunities for young people who are interested in this field of work.

Educational Facilities

There are agricultural colleges offering graduate and post-graduate courses in agriculture and allied subjects spread all over the country. Many states have also established agricultural universities that offer comprehensive courses in a wide variety of subjects connected with agriculture. The details of the universities and the colleges offering these courses nearest you can be had from the District Agriculture Officer, or from the local Employment Exchange.

The Indian Council of Agricultural Research, New Delhi, supervises research in agricultural subjects. The foremost research institute in India is the Indian Agricultural Research Institute, Pusa, New Delhi-110012. There are several other research institutes such as the Rice Research Institute in Cuttack, the Dairy Research Institute in Bangalore and Karnal, the Indian Potato Research Institute in Shimla, the Indian Sugarcane Research Institute in Coimbatore. These institutions have subsidiary institutions in various parts of the country.

Making a Beginning

In the practical field of agriculture, past experience indicates that most young people joined more out of necessity than choice. Family circumstances, and knowledge and experience passed on by the elders has played a significant role. However, young people are beginning to understand the need for training. Many study agriculture at the 10+2 or Intermediate level. Some prefer to pursue the Bachelor's degree in agriculture. Those interested in working at the lowest levels as Gram Sewaks or Sewikas can join soon after completing school. They should have a rural background.

Most young people who pursue higher education in agriculture and allied fields do not have a career in practical agriculture in view. They think more in terms of serving in a private firm, or in a government department to pursue a full time job. The jobs offered by the Departments of Agriculture in different states and other employers are advertised. One can join after a Bachelor's degree in agriculture. Most young people find it useful to acquire a Master's degree in a field of choice. Many go in for a doctorate in a specialized field, particularly as higher qualifications are essential for research jobs.

Private business houses employ graduates in agriculture or veterinary science, depending upon their specific need. Besides the technical knowledge, they prefer young people with a pleasing personality, and those who can speak effectively.

Income from Agriculture

The income from practical agriculture varies from place to place, depending upon the condition of the land, the cattle, and state of development in the area. Whereas progressive farmers have shown that a good steady income is possible from agriculture and allied lines, farmers who are against trying new methods are just able to make their ends meet. Many factors are involved. The incomes are liable to vary from time to time.

Jobs in the government departments fetch similar incomes as those from other technical lines. The private business houses that deal in agricultural products pay their staff salaries similar to those paid to other staff in the sales department.

Opportunities for Self-employment

All people other than those engaged by private business houses, Departments of Agriculture, or those involved in research work, will need to think in terms of self-employment if they are interested in careers in agriculture. All farmers are self-employed. However, since farming offers seasonal employment, and unless one owns substantial land, most farmers are underemployed. Therefore, it is necessary that those interested in agriculture must think in terms of additional work to provide full-time employment throughout the year.

Self-employed farmers can specialize in seed production, operating a nursery, in floriculture, vegetable growing, dairy management, poultry farming, rearing pigs, rabbits, goats, etc. Those who specialize in fruit growing, or live in fruit growing belts, can specialize in preservation of fruits and other products. Co-operative milk centres offer many opportunities for useful employment, and development of dairy resources of the country.

Alternative Medicine

14

It is natural for all human beings to fall sick sometimes. There is nothing new about it. This has been going on since times immemorial. Over a period man learnt how to conquer sickness. Through trial and error methods mankind learnt a lot about sickness. Several systems of treatment emerged. As man conquered sickness, many successes were recorded to benefit future mankind.

With science and technology developing rapidly, the twentieth century witnessed great progress for the medical science. At the same time it was realised that no system of treatment was perfect. Whereas many new drugs were formulated to cure serious illnesses, there were side effects to cope with. Many of these even proved fatal. It is, therefore, natural for people not to depend wholly on conventional medicine and to look for alternative methods of treatment.

In the immediate past there has been a strong swing in favour of alternative methods of treatment against the conventional medical treatment. This includes Ayurveda, Homoeopathy, Unani, Reiki, Pranic Healing, Acupuncture, Acupressure, Magneto-therapy, Nature cure, Aroma-therapy and Music-therapy. Meditation in its various forms has also been used for treatment of ailments.

Desirable Personal Qualities

To be successful in this field, a person must:

- have a pleasing personality. The personality must inspire confidence in the patient.
- be a person of good etiquette and manners. This enhances the response to a pleasing personality.

- have a good knowledge of the subject and its limitations. No system is complete.
- be sensitive and service-minded. Without sensitivity one cannot appreciate individual suffering.
- have a good knowledge of human nature. Much suffering comes from human imagination and not from other causes.
- have an interest in updating his knowledge. Knowledge is growing in every field. One can easily be left behind.
- have knowledge of Sanskrit for some fields. Many ancient books on therapies are in Sanskrit.

Opportunities in Alternative Medicine

With wide-scale fear of strong medication often used in conventional medicine, people are looking forward to treatment through alternative ways. Just as in other fields where opportunities abound, many unscrupulous people take advantage of the situation. However, with greater awareness and better facilities for organised learning of various subjects, one can look forward to a happy co-existence of different systems of treatment.

Many hospitals now have sections in Alternative Medicine. With international acknowledgement of Ayurveda and Homoeopathy great respect is now accorded to these systems of treatment. The education and research is getting better attention. There is greater standardization in preparation of medicines. People from all over the world are pooling in their resources to streamline the systems.

The Department of Indian System of Medicine and Homoeopathy in the Ministry of Health and Family Welfare maintains two separate bodies. The Central Council of Indian Medicine deals with Ayurveda, Unani and Siddha. The Central Council for Homoeopathy deals with Homoeopathy. The government controls activities pertaining to treatment through these systems through these bodies.

Ayurveda, Homoeopathy, Unani and Siddha systems are widely acknowledged. The other systems in practice are gradually gaining importance as they record more successes in treatment of sickness. Massage as a part of Acupressure and Ayurveda is gaining great popularity and widely advertised to attract foreign tourists who find it beneficial. The usefulness of meditation is already accepted. Other systems like Reiki and Pranic Healing are gaining popularity in the hands of able practitioners.

Educational Facilities

Almost 25,000 persons are taking undergraduate and postgraduate training in these alternative systems of medical treatment. Colleges offering courses at different levels of study are spread all over the country. For the bachelor's degree admission is through competitive examinations conducted at state and national level. To take these exams one must be 10+2 with Physics, Chemistry and Biology. Courses are similar to those for conventional medicine. Only the treatment part is different. In the integrated system use of conventional medicines is also taught. The course is for five and half years ending with internship for one year. Postgraduate courses run for 2 to 3 years.

Reiki, Pranic Healing, Acupressure and similar techniques are taught individually through personal training. Since there are a variety of courses, it is advisable that before taking admission one must verify the complete details pertaining to the institution, the courses it offers, and whether they are recognised by government bodies. It may also be advisable to meet and talk to some of the students that have passed out from the institution. Their experience may be a good guide in helping one select an appropriate institution for study.

Making a Beginning

After qualifying for practice most people either join a hospital, nursing home, or an established practitioner. This enables one to gain valuable experience before one can set out on one's own. Very rarely some prefer to set out on personal practice. Those who are eager to specialise go on for higher studies in the field.

Few people practising Reiki, Pranic Healing or Acupressure techniques practice full time. They begin practice beginning with friends and relatives and gradually by publicity through word of mouth outsiders begin to visit them by appointment. It is a slow process. However, once their credentials are established, patients visit them regularly.

Income in Alternative Medicine

Those who have undergone complete training in a college qualify to become practising doctors, and often earn as well as those qualified in conventional medicine. They may begin at a slightly lower level, but those who are endowed with healing skills do well and rise swiftly. Private practitioners are known to earn well.

Opportunities for Self-employment

Just as in conventional medicine there are ample opportunities for self-employment in all forms of alternative medicine. In fact, most of the practitioners are loners, and work individually.

Animal Husbandry

15

Almost 70 per cent of the population live on small plots of land in rural India and depend upon agriculture. The vast majority is underemployed. The usual additional income comes from animal husbandry. While most depend upon keeping a cow or a buffalo, many rear camels, goats, pigs and sheep.

The recent past has seen a rapid growth in animal husbandry. People are beginning to realise the need for specialisation in fields like poultry keeping, running a piggery, or maintaining a dairy. The demand for both eggs and poultry is continuously rising. The need for milk and milk products was always there. With greater emphasis on specialisation a white revolution has ensured the availability of a variety of milk products. Considering the consumption in developed countries, we have still a long way to go.

With the availability of better refrigeration and preservation facilities, the demand for other animal products is also rising. The field was initially restricted to a few animals, but with growing needs and enterprise, it has seen wide scale expansion including a variety of animals.

Desirable Personal Qualities

To be successful in this field, a person must:

- have a love for animals. One cannot succeed in animal husbandry without it.
- not be shy to work with one's hands. When a work has to be done, it must be done. One cannot wait for help. It might be too late.
- appreciate the need to work within a tight time schedule. Nature has its own pattern. We need to work in harmony with it.

- be willing to try new ideas. All progress has come about because of trying new ideas.
- be healthy and possess stamina to work hard when required. It can be very trying and difficult at times.
- be adaptable to changing circumstances. Wherever there is life, there will be changes. One must necessarily adapt to them.

Opportunities in Animal Husbandry

Opportunities in animal husbandry always existed, but there was lack of effort and specialisation that restrained its growth. Most farmers reared animals only for some additional income. They never gave it the importance it deserved.

With specialisation in every field, large scale poultry farms, dairy farms and piggeries have come up all over the country, opening many opportunities for work for young people. The supplies have become comfortable. However, there is need for better organisation and marketing. That will ensure better returns to the producers. Dairy co-operatives need to be developed on a much larger scale in every state in the country. Considering the consumption in developed countries, we have still a long way to go.

India has many ponds, lakes, rivers and a vast coastline along the sea, which offers many opportunities in fishery and seafood. Pisciculture, or rearing of fish, offers great opportunities wherever water bodies are available.

The rearing of silk worms wherever the necessary facilities are available also has a great potential. This is a specialised field called sericulture. Many young people can find useful occupation in this field.

Bee keeping, or apiculture, is yet another field that has a great potential in areas where there is abundance of flowers such as in places where sunflower, mustard, or other flowering plants are grown or there are orchards nearby. Honey is always in great demand.

The breeding of camels, horses and mules is necessary in certain areas. The breeding of dogs and other animals as pets also offers some opportunities. The rearing of sheep and angora rabbits for wool in cooler regions also offers opportunities in this field.

With better handling techniques, preservation and refrigeration facilities, there are opportunities in the field of packaging fish, poultry and other items both for the local market and for export.

Educational Facilities

Young people interested in animal husbandry as a career will do well to get a degree in Veterinary Science rather than in a field connected with agriculture. A degree in agriculture with dairy management as a special subject can be useful. There are many Veterinary colleges spread all over the country. For a Bachelor's degree in Veterinary Science, one must have passed the 10+2 exam with Physics, Chemistry and Biology. Admission procedures vary in different areas and can be verified from the institution. A Master's degree in the field of specialisation is useful.

Making a Beginning

In the past, most young people entered the field more out of a personal interest in the field than for any other reason. With experience they gradually grew. In the present context young people are taking to this field, as one would join an industry. The larger operators are hiring fresh graduates and training them on the job. The details must be planned and executed precisely. The investments can be very high. Those who would like to set out on their own do so at a smaller level to begin with, and then expand as they get to know their market and are able to perfect production techniques.

Income from Animal Husbandry

Just as with any other field of activity one has to start at the lowest level and come up through hard work and experience. Most young people join a larger operator, and after gaining some experience set out on their own. The income is similar to other jobs at the lower level. The work has its own risks. At higher levels when well managed it can be very remunerative.

Opportunities for Self-employment

Most young people who take up careers in this field do so for the pleasure of working on their own. One can start part-time with a few animals, or do so on a large scale. Some people have grown to the extent of converting the work to the scale of large-scale companies.

Architecture

16

An architect is a combination of an artist and an engineer. While as an engineer an architect ensures that the building is strong and meets the safety requirements of a house, as an artist he makes it beautiful, more of a home than a house. The responsibilities of an architect include the planning, designing, supervision and construction of building structures.

With growing population, urbanisation is rapidly growing. There is need for more buildings in lesser space. Communities are spreading horizontally and vertically. With land prices soaring there is need for better utilisation of space. There is need for good architects who are innovative and can design better homes. People know what they want in a home, but do not know how their needs can be efficiently met. Only professional architects can help provide this need.

Desirable Personal Qualities

To be successful in this field, a person must:

- have a good imagination and be creative. Every person likes the home to be unique.
- think like an artist. This ability helps one to think in terms of art forms.
- possess artistic skills. Much of the work is done on paper before being converted to reality.
- be able to visualise the clients' needs. Individuals are unique. So are their needs. The architect must understand them.
- possess good engineering skills. The strength of the building structure is as important as its appearance.
- be able to lead a team of artisans. Many groups of people together help to construct a building.

- be able to get along well with people. Unless one can do this, one cannot provide the best service.
- be well acquainted with building regulations. Laws that may be enacted at the local, state or national level govern every place.
- be computer literate. Designing work has become easier with computers and other peripheral devices.
- work to strict time schedules. Delays can often be very expensive.
- be willing to work hard till late hours. There is no substitution for hard work.
- be willing to work in difficult situations. The situations may not be congenial most of the time.

Opportunities in Architecture

With rapid expansion of communities, there is greater need for good houses, commercial areas and industrial estates in the country. There is need for good architects to make this possible. Land is becoming scarce. There is great pressure in every field. People are beginning to appreciate that an architect's cost is well covered through better utilisation of the resources, greater comfort and a better looking building.

Every day new colonies are emerging, shopping malls are replacing the old shops, specialised commercial areas are being preferred, industrial estates are being planned to look ahead at the future business potential. All these will be possible only through good architects. One can therefore well appreciate the opportunities that exist for architects.

India has a vast rural area housing almost 70 per cent of the population. The influence of architecture has yet to touch this vast potential for future work. Some individuals may avail of the professional skills of architects. Many may not. However, there is greater scope due to the need of public buildings like schools, colleges, hospitals and government buildings even in rural areas.

India has a big heritage of ancient buildings of great tourist interest. These buildings are spread out throughout the country and need expert maintenance expertise to exploit the tourist potential. This field can provide many opportunities to dedicated young people.

Specialised Fields

Architecture is a vast field. Individuals have their own strengths and weaknesses. Most prefer to move into areas of personal efficiency. Many people gradually specialise in distinct areas and services. Some of the common lines of specialisation include residential buildings, commercial buildings, urban planning, industrial designing, interior designing, furniture designing, architectural journalism and teaching. Those connected with insurance companies opt for valuation services.

Educational Facilities

Many engineering colleges that offer a bachelor's degree in Architecture are spread all over the country. It is a five-year course after 10+2. Admission is on the basis of a written test usually divided into two portions, the first to test a candidate's knowledge in Physics, Chemistry and Maths, and the second in general awareness, creativity and drawing skills. Some institutions may finalise the admission list after an interview. It is a difficult test, but those who have done well in 10+2 can easily take it. Some institutions give preference to those who have done well at the 10+2 level.

Making a Beginning

As in all other careers one will necessarily need to start at the lowest level as an assistant to an established architect. Many prefer to join a firm of architects where they can get good insight into all kinds of activities involved in planning and execution of a variety of buildings. After a good academic foundation this additional experience can be very useful in helping an individual to develop his own skills and set out as an individual architect.

Some individuals decide to start on their own soon after they qualify. They pick up smaller jobs for individuals, and execute them through local contractors. Their personal relationships help them succeed and rise gradually in the field.

Many young people also go on to specialise in evaluation work, assessing building values for individuals and firms. They also get connected to insurance companies and banks that have special interest in this field.

Income in Architecture

The income from careers at the lowest level may be like those in other professions. However, those who are capable rise quickly. Those at the higher levels earn substantially. As assistants to established architects one draws a fixed salary, but later when one is involved individually the remuneration for the services is in the form of a commission on the total value of the work. The commission is paid in portions depending upon the quantum of work done. The income is in harmony with those in other fields of engineering.

Opportunities for Self-employment

Opportunities for self-employment abound in this field of careers. One needs to possess good skills and self-confidence to set out on one's own. A few people decide to become self-employed soon after qualifying to become an architect. Others opt to become self-employed after they have gained valuable experience through work with established architects.

Art

17

Young people who study art in schools feel that they do so more for personal recreation and pleasure rather than building a foundation for a career. There is a big field of occupations for those interested in taking art for a full-time career. As a pastime or hobby, art is both recreating and stimulating. It provides a healthy outlet to one's personal creative energy.

There is a great need for good artwork in various spheres of life. Our country has a rich history in art. With the worldwide growth of photography, computerization, and techniques of reproduction of artwork, there has been a rapid expansion in the field of art. There is a great need for good artists. This need is growing. With it, the opportunities for satisfying careers in art will also increase.

Desirable Personal Qualities

To be successful in this field, a person must:

- be able to see people and things in graphic form. That is what an artist is primarily expected to do.
- be able to visualise things in three dimensions. That adds to the reality of work.
- have an interest in drawing and painting. The foundation of a career is built upon this interest.
- possess an aesthetic sense. The work must be appealing to others.
- have an appreciation for composition and colours.
- have a good imagination. This factor adds to the reality of work.
- have a creative urge and be original. These help one make progress.

- be able to work as a team. Very often the cooperation of others is important.
- have a thorough knowledge of one's field of work. The work is becoming more specialised each day.

Opportunities in Art

Opportunities for artists exist in many spheres of life. Not all artists are endowed with qualities that enable one to produce the kind of work that would fetch large sums of money. However, there is a steady demand for good artwork particularly in the larger cities. Many artists are regularly marketing medium-priced paintings suitable for average homes.

On the commercial side, there has always been need for attractive nameplates, boards for commercial establishments, hoardings, etc. Besides painting new boards, the need for repainting existing boards periodically ensures painters a steady business.

Advertising agencies have a definite place for commercial artists. They help plan the designs on advertisements, labels and packaging. Making of cinema slides, preparing attractive sales promotion literature, booklets, brochures and similar work also comes within the scope of the commercial artist. Many business houses have their own advertising and publicity departments. They employ artists for all creative artistic work.

There has been a growth in the number of good magazines that maintain their own art departments, or get artwork done on a regular basis. The artists do all the creative work. They help illustrate the articles and stories published by them.

There is a very big publishing trade in India. All publishers need artists to illustrate written work. An important need is that of producing attractive designs for book covers. These must help draw the immediate attention of the reader. A prospective reader should feel like picking up the book, browse through it, and eventually buy it. Good artwork is particularly important for children's books as both the textbooks and storybooks need to be illustrated. Some publishers have their own art departments to meet their requirements. Many get their covers designed by free lance artists.

Almost all newspapers carry cartoons. They are a favourite with all readers. Magazines devote a substantial amount of space to this form of reading. Some magazines fill most of the space with cartoons. Besides these magazines, comics in themselves are good business. We do not have enough artists to fulfil this need for cartoons and comics for both the young and the old. These offer an excellent medium of communication particularly amongst the illiterate sections in our rural areas.

Designing and printing of cards is big business. The business of printing cards for weddings, birthday greetings, for Dewali, Christmas, and New Year, and a whole lot of other occasions need innumerable designs each year. Our artists just do not seem to cope up with this demand fully. Designs for pictures for display, picture postcards and calendars too are in constant demand.

Let us not overlook the need for commercial artists by government organizations. The State Directorate of Advertising and Visual Publicity, the Publications Division, the Directorate of Commercial Publicity and Directorate of Exhibitions in the Ministry of Foreign Trade and Supply are some of the government departments which need good artists. The field of television has its own need for artists. TV stations all over the country require artists to prepare artwork, and help stage shows and commercials.

There is a huge textile industry in our country. One thing that adds beauty to fabrics is the design and prints on them. This is the work of artists. We have a rich heritage of Indian designs. If we can use them on the many kinds of fabrics, furnishing materials, carpets, etc., artists can help generate an additional demand for Indian goods in the export market.

Photography has added new dimensions to the field of art. In every town, it has given employment to many people. Besides the huge market for general work, good photographers are in good demand by newspapers, magazines, TV and the film world. Opportunities abound for all kinds of photographic work, both in black and white and in colour. All newspapers, magazines, calendar manufacturers, and publishers of picture postcards and tourist guides are on the lookout for good work by freelance photographers. The subject is discussed in greater detail in the chapter on Photography.

Besides the many opportunities open to all young people interested in art as a full-time career, there is always the need for good art teachers who can help young people bring out the very best in them. There are many distinct branches in the field of art available to young people for specialization. One can select one, which is of personal interest to ensure steady success in the career.

Educational Facilities

Many artists have learned their work the hard way, not bothering about high academic qualifications. Considering that we are passing through an age of specialization, one must qualify to face the competition that is present in every sphere of life. It is desirable that young people interested in taking up a career in art must go through formal training in art. This can be done in many art schools spread all over the country, followed by specialization in their field of interest.

Many schools and colleges all over the country offer diploma and degree courses in drawing and painting. Post-graduate courses are offered in some colleges. For details of institutions offering these courses, get in touch with the Inspector of Schools, or consult a directory of institutions offering these courses. Many private schools offer useful courses for those interested in becoming artists.

Some of the important institutions are also recognized by the Lalit Kala Akademi, which has its centres in important cities. The British Institutes and the International Correspondence Schools, Mumbai, offer commercial art and painting courses in fine art and cartooning, for postal study.

Making a Beginning

Earlier, most young people who took up a career in art entered this vocation in a small way by joining as an assistant to a person already working in this field. Things are different now. Prospective employers look for talent and ability, and a willingness to learn because this way they know that the artist can quickly understand their requirements, and produce the kind of work they want. Openings in government departments are always advertised in the press. They are also communicated to the employment exchanges. Private employers may also look for their requirements through the employment exchanges. Many times, they employ artists directly through personal contacts.

Artists desirous of working as freelancers can begin by getting in touch with art galleries, advertising agencies, publishers, greeting card and calendar manufacturers, and mutually negotiate to provide their needs. Cartoons and comic strips can be directly submitted to newspapers and magazines. They accept them on merit, and pay according to prevalent rates. Many young people who produce good work regularly have succeeded in finding a permanent market for their work.

Photography in itself is a very specialized art with several sub-divisions of specialization within itself. Considering its importance as a specialised career, it is discussed separately.

Income from Art

A young person interested in a career in art may begin his career in a small way as an assistant. Depending upon the kind of work, the charges are often negotiated. Increments depend upon personal capabilities. Young people with some business ability and creative interests have every chance of rising very swiftly in the career. Income from teaching art is equivalent to that from teaching other subjects. At the upper levels, artists earn very good salaries. Many self-employed artists are earning large sums every month.

Opportunities for Self-employment

Perhaps few careers offer as much scope for self-employment as a career in art. As free-lancers, artists can earn a steady income through selling paintings, taking up special art assignments, running an art gallery, designing greeting cards, painting pictures for calendars, designing book covers, labels and packaging, and undertaking similar work. Many young people who have the ability, initiative and drive have built up satisfying and profitable careers in art.

Astrology

18

Astrology is the study of the influence of stars and planets on human affairs. In the developed countries, it may not be considered to provide opportunities for careers. At most people would look at it as a hobby. However, in India the situation is different. Hindus believe that the *Navgrah* or the nine planets influence their lives. All religious offerings include prayers to *Navgrah*. In the Western world human lives are said to be influenced by the 12 signs of the Zodiac.

From birth until death, rites, rituals and customs influence Hindus. They are obsessed by auspicious and inauspicious times. Everyone searches for an auspicious time to start a new work, to get the children married or for building or shifting to a new home. Many get the horoscopes of their children made at birth. Some get an annual horoscope reading prepared. At the time of marriage the horoscopes of the prospective bride and groom are tallied. Astrologers conduct this work. Since this sphere of work has not received the attention it deserved, Hindu priests have been providing these services on the basis of whatever they learnt through self-study or through a personal guru.

Desirable Personal Qualities

To be successful in this field a person must:

- know the subject well. Success depends upon one's knowledge.
- know the basis of other systems of forecasting. It is helpful at work.
- have analytical abilities. These are necessary to analyse planetary influences.
- have good communication skills. One will need to

listen carefully and also communicate one's personal analysis of a situation.

- be willing to keep studying. There is no end to learning in this field.
- be proficient in geography. Calculations are based upon individual positions in towns and countries.
- be a stickler for accuracy. There is no scope for approximation in calculations.
- be computer literate. Computers have made calculations accurate and swift.
- be able to get along well with others. One needs to build a clientele gradually.

Opportunities in Astrology

With the Hindu belief that the *Navgrah* or the nine planets influence the lives of all people, Astrology has an important role to play in our country. Once a year the astrologers from all over the country get together and finalise the details to be published in the *Panchang* or the almanac that gives details of the planetary positions of the planets. The dates for religious festivals and important auspicious dates are also fixed on the occasion. It is on the basis of the *Panchang* that Hindu priests make horoscopes, or fix dates for marriages and other auspicious occasions.

At the birth of a child every Hindu desires to get a horoscope made if the facilities are available. The horoscope gives details of planetary positions and influences through life. Many adults like to get their annual horoscopes made. These forecast good and bad periods throughout the year. These are made for an individual based upon the planetary positions at birth. Even otherwise, one can appreciate this need when one sees the general forecasts for all the 12 signs of the Zodiac as sold in the market, not only in English or Hindi, but also in the regional languages.

One can also appreciate the demand for astrological forecasts when we see that almost every newspaper carries a column on daily forecasts for all the signs of the Zodiac. The

Sunday editions carry a forecast for the whole week. Even the general magazines cover fortnightly or monthly forecasts. There are several magazines totally devoted to the field of Astrology. Astrological journalism too offers opportunities for work.

An important aspect of astrological forecasts is to recommend and carry out prayers to propitiate the malefic effects of some planets. Making of charms and recommending the use of stones too is common.

A certain amount of uncertainty is involved in matrimonial alliances. To put their minds to rest many parents like to compare horoscopes for the prospective bride and groom. On many occasions total incompatibility is forecast and the proposed match is dropped. Astrological forecasts have prevented possible tragedies.

It is commonplace to fix dates for auspicious occasions after consultation with astrologers. The starting of a new work or project, entry into a new home, building a new home, going out on a special assignment or pilgrimage or special things pertaining to children and the family members provide occasions to consult an astrologer for an auspicious date and time.

Astrological calculations are difficult and take time. However, computers have made the work easy. Calculations are made swiftly. With a variety of software now available, the astrological charts and the findings are printed swiftly and neatly on the printers connected to the computers. The interpretations given in the software are generalized. However, a capable astrologer can use the charts to give accurate forecasts.

Irrespective of one being a simple worker or a person in high position, it is human nature to seek which way one's destiny will sway. Palmistry, Numerology, Tarot cards, body language, handwriting and other similar ways to forecast the future enjoy great popularity. Astrology leads them all. It offers opportunities for a variety of careers.

Educational Facilities

Earlier, people learnt Astrology along with Hindu rites and rituals by serving as an assistant to an established Hindu priest-cum-astrologer. One picked up knowledge gradually. The only formal training was by way of learning Hindi and Sanskrit. Even now Hindu priests are being trained this way. Those interested in Astrology can take it up as a subject in college. Several institutions are offering courses. Since many of the teachings are based upon old Hindu texts, knowledge of Sanskrit is necessary.

Making a Beginning

Most people make a beginning in this field by joining an established astrologer. After some time one can work independently. It is not possible to set out alone even though one may know the subject well. Many people are not immediately convinced. When one has learnt Hindu rites and rituals and is working as a priest, it becomes easier to practice astrological skills and build up clientele.

Income from Astrology

In the earlier stages astrologers do not work on the basis of fixed charges. Very often their professional charges are covered up through making or obtaining charms or precious stones for the clients. Most accept whatever money the clientele offers. At later stages established astrologers charge fees on the basis of time and work involved. They negotiate the charges. Many are well established with good incomes.

Opportunities for Self-employment

In the initial stages the opportunities for self-employment are very limited. One may be knowledgeable but not be able to inspire confidence. With time and experience when one is accepted one can work independently.

19

Banking

Many young people are attracted to careers in banking. There has been a rapid expansion of banking services all over the country. This has been particularly so after the nationalization of important banks. Reserve Bank of India has placed controls on banking institutions. Many branches have opened in the rural areas. Large-scale deposits have been mobilized, and credit facilities are extended to people who, only a few years ago, could not even think of such benefits being offered to them.

The expansion of banking services has obviously resulted in an increase of banking staff. There has been large-scale enlistment both at the clerical level and at the managerial level. With computerization and the entry of international banks, and growth of trade, there is greater emphasis on quality service. The banks are now offering a wide range of services. With such growth opportunities for careers in banking will continue to be available to young people interested in careers in this field.

Desirable Personal Qualities

To be successful in this field, a person must:

- be honest in word and deed. The work requires handling large sums of money.
- enjoy high integrity and honour. People must have trust without any doubt.
- be fond of working with figures. The work involves working with figures the whole day.
- be a stickler for accuracy. There is no scope for carelessness. Other people's money is involved.

- not talk about one client to another. Secrecy is mandatory in banking.
- be able to get along well with people. The public can be very demanding most of the time.
- be service-minded. The work is competitive. People go where they get the best service.
- not shirk from taking responsibility. With work revolving around money, one must be ready to accept responsibility.
- have an eye for unscrupulous people. Just as there are good people, there are others who are not. One has to be careful.
- be computer literate. Like other professions, banks are now depending upon computers to do the work swiftly and accurately.
- have a good knowledge about businesses. Bankers need to have a wide knowledge and understanding of business trends in general.

Opportunities in Banking

Almost one new branch of a bank opens somewhere in India everyday. However, this is not all by way of opportunities in banking open to young people interested in banking as a career. There are thousands of branches all over, which are not only expanding their business, but also offering additional services through extension counters, evening service, Sunday service, ATMs, and similar facilities.

There has been a rapid growth of banking services in the recent past. Nevertheless, with 70 per cent of the population living in the villages, it is still a long way before banking facilities can reach the people all over the country. Even in the urban areas where people are beginning to feel that there are too many banks, in reality they are not enough in terms of population figures. Many people are still shy of going to the banks. They are not even aware of the facilities available to them. Even in the existing branches, until the recent past, the business transacted was restricted, and fulfilled the needs of a limited few.

As people are becoming aware of the benefits they can derive from banking institutions, newer opportunities are taking concrete shape. There are many branches of specialization in banking. Those with interest and initiative can specialize in subjects like deposits, foreign exchange, agricultural financing, industrial financing, general advances, etc. Banks play a vital role in the development of a country. They will continue to offer many opportunities for careers in this field.

Educational Facilities

With the emergence of the Indian Banking Service cadre, entry into careers in banking will be through a competitive examination open to graduates. Training in banking is through a bank's own training centres. Even the officers are required to undergo special refresher courses in certain subjects from time to time according to need. The Indian Institute of Bankers, Mumbai, conducts an examination, which qualifies one for an Associate Certificate of the Institute, designated as Cert. A.I.I.B. All banks in India recognize this. It is important for bank employees interested in higher positions in a banking career. The Indian Merchants' Chamber, Mumbai-400020, also conducts an examination in Specialized Banking, and offers the D.Com. (I.M.C.) Diploma. The British Institutes, Mumbai-400023 offer correspondence courses to appear for these examinations. Details can be had from them directly, or from the organizations conducting the examinations.

Some Important Addresses

Indian Institute of Bankers,
State Bank of India Building,
Apollo Street, Fort,
Mumbai-400001.

Indian Merchants' Chamber,
76 Veer Nariman Road,
Churchgate,
Mumbai-400020.

Making a Beginning

Careers in banking can be divided into two categories—clerical jobs and officer grades. For clerical positions, the minimum requirement is a pass in 10+2, but proficiency in English and arithmetic is important. However, the competition for jobs is very acute. Even graduates and post-graduates apply for and hold clerical positions. It is estimated that almost one thousand young people apply for every single job available.

To make a beginning in the career, although some people get employed directly, one needs to pass an entrance test followed by an interview by a panel of bank executives. For officer grades, the minimum qualification is graduation. Once selected, the recruits are sent for training for a few weeks where they are thoroughly groomed about the organization of the bank, how to maintain books, everyday procedures, responsibilities, etc. This provides the foundation of the career. It is of interest to note that people who have risen from clerical jobs fill 75 to 80 per cent of the posts of officers. Young people with interest and initiative can rise swiftly in the career.

With specialised needs many banks are picking up brilliant students directly from important management institutions. The salaries offered are excellent. For those who work hard promotions are swift with good perks.

Income from Banking

Jobs in banking are well paid. Even at the lower levels, the salaries are very attractive. Besides a good salary, there are other facilities like bonus, medical benefits, house allowance, travel allowance, loans for building a home, buying a vehicle, etc. Capable persons rise swiftly in the career.

Opportunities for Self-employment

The nature of work of people working in banks is such that there are no opportunities for self-employment for them. On retirement, people prefer to invest their savings in stocks or shares to enjoy a retirement income. Some people with initiative and confidence may use their experience and contacts to start a small business where they can work part-time for a retirement income.

Biotechnology

20

Biotechnology is a new field of vocations that is developing very rapidly. Its phenomenal growth is second only to that of Information Technology. What is particularly significant is that India is a leading player in this field, way ahead of some of the developed countries in the world. It is expected that a very large number of opportunities for vocations will emerge in this field in the near future.

Biotechnology aims at the use of living organisms to manufacture foods, drugs and other products. We are already aware of the use of yeast in brewing and baking industries, or the use of bacteria in the dairy industry to make yoghurt and several kinds of processed cheese. In the allied field of Biochemistry one is concerned with the chemistry of living things, leading us to a greater understanding of the life processes. Another allied field, Bioengineering, pertains to the application of engineering to biology and medicine, making it possible to use artificial tissues or organs in the body or the use of biological processes in industry.

Modern Biotechnology is directed at processes like genetic engineering, cloning of plant and animal tissues, and production of useful drugs and vaccines at low costs. The developments will greatly benefit the fields of public health and agriculture. Openings at all levels will provide useful work in this field.

Desirable Personal Qualities

To be successful in this field a person must:

- be well-versed with biological processes and their chemistry. One may have to coordinate between different fields of study.

- possess more than normal intelligence. One should be able to see what others normally oversee.
- have an inquiring mind ready to study details. New experiences will emerge at the workplace.
- be able to concentrate for long periods until the finest details are within understanding.
- be willing to study continuously. There is no end to learning. Perseverance is important.
- be creative with a good imagination. What may appear a fantasy may be real.
- be willing to work as a team. One will need to cooperate with each other to share research and findings.
- be a stickler for accuracy. There is no scope for approximation.

Opportunities in Biotechnology

It is difficult to trace back the beginning of processes like the use of starters to make yoghurt or the use of bacteria and fungi to make cheese, or even the use of yeast for baking or brewing of alcoholic drinks. The products date back to ancient times. There are references to their use even in the scriptures that date back thousands of years.

However, the scientific application of these processes has been better understood through fields like Biochemistry and Bioengineering that are comparatively new as compared to the earlier processes used by man. Earlier uses were limited to the food industry or manufacturing of enzymes from natural products. It has now gone on to making live-saving products like statins that are used to prevent heart attacks through lowering of the blood cholesterol level. Another new use is to manufacture recombinant human insulin. These products are required by millions of people around the world and will revolutionize the treatment of heart disease and diabetes.

Another area in which Biotechnology has made great progress is the field of manufacturing vaccines. Only a few years ago, the Hepatitis-B vaccine was imported and was beyond the use by a common man. It is now available through indigenous effort at 5 per cent the earlier price.

Biotechnology is a research-oriented field. Although it touches many fields, in India its use in the medical field is significant. In the recent times it has attracted thousands of scientists who are busy with a variety of projects. It is expected that in the future bio-drugs will replace most of the conventional drugs. The treatment would be directed at the individual rather than the use of a general drug for a problem. It will be possible to have an anti-cancer drug. The process of aging and death too would be slowed down.

Biotechnology has not only made it possible to produce and bring down prices of many important drugs, but with 60 per cent of the products being exported — a big foreign exchange earner. Few looked at this field earlier, but now large sums of money are being invested in this field. Biotechnology aims at innovation. With India having some of the most capable trained scientists who are willing to work on reasonable salaries, and also a huge population, the developed nations have an eye on India to revolutionize the development of Biotechnology. It is a field for the intelligent young men and women. Many opportunities await them.

Educational Facilities

One can begin the study of Biotechnology after 10+2 with science subjects by opting for a Bachelor's degree in one of the IITs or other institutions that offer the course. Entrance is through an engineering entrance examination. Graduates with science subjects can proceed for M.Sc. (Biotechnology). Jawaharlal Nehru University, New Delhi, conducts an All India Combined Entrance Examination in Biotechnology every year. Several Indian universities offer courses in Biotechnology. Since a large number of scientists are involved in research and development activities, many prefer to specialise and pursue a doctorate in a field of choice.

Making a Beginning

This field requires educated intelligent young people. It is a rapidly growing field and young people join companies in different positions immediately after completing the formal education. Continued study and research are necessary in this field of vocations. Studious individuals grow rapidly. There is a good demand for qualified personnel in this field in the developed countries also.

Income from Biotechnology

Since this is essentially a field for well-educated people, those joining the work do so at very good salaries. Intelligent hardworking individuals make rapid progress. Those who entered the field as entrepreneurs have made great fortunes.

Opportunities for Self-employment

Work in this field of vocations requires teamwork rather than individual effort. It is, therefore, not practical to find self-employment unless one is willing to set out as an entrepreneur.

Business Process Outsourcing 21

Business Process Outsourcing or BPO in short is an opportunity that can provide work to a large workforce. Only a few years ago nothing like it could be even imagined. The availability of educated computer literate persons in large numbers owning a personal computer and their willingness to work for a reasonable amount through the Internet services have made this possible. The difference in national time has helped make the service efficient.

In the Western developed countries there is a vast amount of data that needs to be correctly formatted and shaped before it can be used. This data may be in the shape of old books, documents, legal or medical data. Through Internet facilities this data is received, distributed amongst individual workers, corrected, checked and returned in a very short time.

Since there is a time difference of 10 hours between India and U.S.A., it becomes possible to collect the data in the day in U.S.A., send it to India in the evening when it is morning here. The data is processed in the day when it is night in U.S.A., and returned. Practically, the data sent from U.S.A. in the evening is received back the next morning. What could be more efficient? And it is at a fraction of the cost of doing it locally?

Medical Transcription and Call Centres do similar work. This really means that some of the work that was being done locally there is now being done through BPO because of cheaper English-knowing computer literate Indian personnel. Besides U.S.A. other developed nations are also availing of these services. This has faced political problems because this reduces the work for local personnel, but economies are important to business, and BPO will continue to provide vocational opportunities to a lot of people.

Desirable Personal Qualities

To be successful in this field a person must:

- have good English speaking and writing skills.
- be computer literate. All work will need to be done on the computer.
- be responsible to handle data. It is to be processed and returned.
- be particular about time. Some data must be returned immediately.
- be a stickler for detail. Very often the payment is made on the basis of accuracy.
- be willing to work as a team. Many times it is necessary to work together.
- be willing to work long hours to complete the work at hand.

Opportunities in BPO

Earlier, the BPO work was restricted to specialised work like one company asking another to provide software solutions, etc. But with better telecommunications, good Internet facilities and a vast computer literate workforce BPO is an important source of work at lower levels. Medical Transcription and Call Centres were the first to receive attention. It gradually spread to other fields like legal documents, old manuscripts and publishing.

Now the larger companies have entrusted work to smaller companies that get the work done at their level, or even hire computer literate persons who own computers to do the work on piecework basis. The workforce works from their residences at their own time and convenience. The workers are explained what is expected of them. The work is sent to them through the Internet. They do the necessary work and return it through the Internet. The work is checked for accuracy, and the amount for the work credited to the individuals. The payment for the work is done on monthly basis. This kind of work has provided employment to young people, to housewives and even retired personnel.

Although BPO has given rise to political issues, but with

businessmen finding an opportunity to get the work done at competitive prices, even when restrictions may be imposed, people will find ways to utilise the facilities that are available.

Educational Facilities

The basic necessity for this kind of work is to be computer literate and know English. The common word and data processing software is used. The exact details of what the client desires to be done are explained to the workforce. When necessary training in new software is provided. Most clarifications can be done online. Very often the work can be done at home on one's personal computer working 4 to 5 hours daily.

Making a Beginning

Those interested in this kind of work can get in touch with the companies involved in BPO. Most companies charge refundable registration fees. They explain the details of the work that needs to be done, and allot an identification number that is used to access the website of the company and to download the work to be done. The company staff normally does urgent work that needs to be returned daily. Freelance workers submit the work of lesser importance weekly. It is checked by the company staff and returned to the principals.

Income from BPO

The income from jobs in this work is equivalent to those from other similar jobs. Where a sense of urgency is involved the salaries are higher. The income from freelance work is good. To receive regular work and generate a steady income it is necessary that the person must work diligently ensuring swift accurate work.

Opportunities for Self-employment

Rather than be bound with a big workforce most companies prefer to get their work done through freelance workers who own a personal computer. The more enterprising workers sometimes team together to earn higher incomes. The major workforce in this field is self-employed and can look out for better opportunities whenever they are there.

22 Call Centres

Literally, a Call Centre is an office in which large number of telephone calls are handled for an organization. This work has been greatly facilitated with the growth in Information Technology. Information can now be swiftly accessed in a computer. The purpose of the modern Call Centres is to provide information support to customers in a variety of fields including travel and tourism, banking and finance and also in the field of technical support.

It is estimated that there are more than 400 Call Centres in India. The number is growing. The principal reason for this growth is the availability of English speaking young people who are computer literate. They are willing to work for a fraction of what their counterpart charge in developed countries. Many of these Centres are dedicated to a particular clientele. For instance those that are dedicated to the American clientele operate at night to coincide with the daytime there. It is expected that this field will continue to grow and offer opportunities to young people for useful vocations.

Desirable Personal Qualities

To be successful in this field a person must:

- have clarity of speech. One must be easily understood when talking to different people.
- have a good knowledge of the language. One must understand the client's language, and be able to respond.
- be proficient in the field of one's speciality. This is important if the Centre specializes in a particular field.
- have courteous speaking habits. The customer is king. One must give the best service.

- possess computer skills. Swift access of information is important.
- be willing to work long hours at odd times. Working in night shifts is common.

Opportunities in Call Centres

It is expected that the number of Call Centres will rise manifold in the coming years. Many people will be requiring information about several subjects including technical information. To provide such information large number of technical personnel having good communication skills will be required for these Centres.

Another important aspect is that at present these Centres are located in or nearby the larger cities. They are likely to spread out to smaller cities. Good telecommunication facilities are available everywhere. Trained personnel too are now available in these cities.

Training of personnel for Call Centres is an important area for providing work opportunities. With expansion in this field it will be necessary to train people to fill different positions.

Educational Facilities

This is a new area of vocational activity. Most of the Call Centres provide the initial training to the employees. The basic requirements for work in this field are the ability to speak good English and be computer literate. All that is required is graduation from a college with English as one of the subjects coupled with the ability to use a computer.

With the growth of opportunities in this field several training and enrolment centres have come up all over the principal cities of the country. Many of these institutions charge high fees and promise jobs. One must check on the facilities available, make comparisons, meet students who have passed out from a particular institution and ensure that the claims of the institution are genuine.

Making a Beginning

Initially those who were selected for work were given some training and put on the job. There is far greater awareness now. People take the necessary training before being selected for the job. Depending upon the kind of services offered at the Call Centre, appropriate training is imparted for a short period on the job and then one works as a part of the team.

These jobs do not offer the opportunity for individuals to display a sense of greater responsibility. The work involves receiving an inquiry for information, and providing the same to the satisfaction of the client. The promotions are slow. Over a period the more responsible persons head a team of workers. In due course a person can become the manager of the Centre.

Income from Call Centres

The starting levels in this field of careers are similar to those for office assistants. To make the job interesting special care is taken to have the Call Centre well furnished with an ambience that does not permit boredom to set in. Since the working times may require commuting at odd hours, transportation facilities are provided. Tea and meals may also be provided depending upon the working hours. Promotions are slow.

Opportunities for Self-employment

The nature of the services provided does not permit an individual with the opportunity to be self-employed. The only option for self-employment is to set up a Call Centre.

Catering and Hotel Management

23

With tourism growing within the country and with increasing tourist traffic from other countries, careers in catering and hotel management have a special significance. Despite the opening of many good restaurants and hotels in the more important cities in the recent past, the gap between the supply and the demand is still very wide. There is still a great demand for good hotels everywhere.

To this, we can add the need for smaller hotels and lodging houses providing moderately comfortable rooms in the smaller towns and places of tourist interest. It is a very big need that cannot be immediately fulfilled. It will continue to provide untold number of opportunities for young people not only to build these hotels, but also to manage them on efficient and modern lines to provide the best service at competitive prices.

Desirable Personal Qualities

To be successful in this field, a person must:

- have a pleasing personality with a smile on the face. This inspires confidence. It also makes hotel guests feel welcome.
- observe good etiquette and manners. This enhances the role of an attractive personality.
- be service-minded. Good service makes people feel important. Guests want to feel important.
- enjoy meeting and looking after people. One will meet a variety of people every day.

- be disciplined to follow up assignments. Itineraries need to be followed in every detail.
- believe in good time management. There is no scope for carelessness. In work every minute matters.
- be willing to work for long hours at odd times. Schedules can involve late night or early morning services.
- have managerial abilities. With many factors involved good managerial skills help smooth working.
- be willing to work as a team. The work involves many people working together to serve the guests.
- be able to get along with a variety of people. They are the purpose of the work.
- have good communication skills. Just as it is important to appreciate what the guests desire, it is equally necessary that one should be able to communicate effectively.

Opportunities in Catering and Hotel Management

Catering and hotel management are no longer simple things to do. At one time, managing a hotel meant letting out rooms to guests on a daily basis, and providing whatever other facilities that can be provided conveniently. Presently, hotel management has become a specialized subject. It requires special knowledge about several things.

There is need for on-the-job training and all the experience one can possibly get. The large five-star hotels operate almost like a mini-city. They offer residential accommodation, food from several restaurants, the comforts of room service, a round-the-clock coffee bar, a shopping arcade, a swimming pool, a health club, taxi and sightseeing service, travel agents, banking facilities, etc. Managing a hotel of this kind is not a small job.

It requires hundreds of men and women each one of whom knows his or her responsibility, and fulfils it well. Many of the positions like pages, bell boys, receptionists, account assistants, telephone operators, waiters, cooks, helpers, lift operators, room attendants, housekeepers, stewards, restaurant managers, etc. are filled by young people setting out on a career. There are many kinds of jobs to be done in a hotel. Each job means an opportunity for a career.

Opportunities in a career in catering are no less. Good food is a human weakness. Even where the tourist traffic is small, there is still a need for eating places, or restaurants. With a growing interest of the local people not to be restricted to conventional home food only, and to try specialities of other states and places, opportunities have opened to cater to these specialized needs. It is not necessary that such needs can be catered to only in restaurants.

Many young people with initiative and drive have made a small beginning by establishing refreshment corners or snack bars. Some have made the very best of the available opportunities by building a mobile snack bar or an ice cream counter, making it possible to bring food specialities at the doorsteps of those living far away.

Although the Departments of Tourism in some states have made a bold beginning by establishing restaurants, motels, and other such facilities on major highways, there is still a great scope for extending these facilities to other places. Even in the private sector, many enterprising young people have ventured into this field. This can provide useful opportunities in catering and hotel management to young people.

In India where cooking is comparatively a lengthy affair, preparing and marketing of semi-cooked or pre-cooked food holds good opportunities for employment. Preparing of syrups, squashes, jams, pickles and chutneys holds good possibilities. Making of biscuits, cakes, pastries, sweets and baked specialities has a vast potential, particularly in the larger cities where the educated elite demands such goodies.

Catering at parties in general, and at marriages in particular, holds many possibilities where such assignments can be sought conveniently and regularly to ensure a steady income from it. Specialists in dietetics are in good demand by hospitals, nursing homes, public schools and such other places where it is necessary to plan special diets for children and patients. Food will continue to be a weakness with everyone. Varying tastes will continue to provide opportunities in careers in catering.

Educational Facilities

Institutions offering courses in catering and hotel management have come up all over the country. Admission is on the basis of a competitive examination after 10+2. Many people are also taking training in foreign institutions. It is difficult to say whether they are at any special advantage over those who have been trained in the country. Most hotel chains have their own training centres where they provide additional training periodically. In the hospitality industry everyone desires to do a little better than the others.

Four major institutions in India offer courses in catering and hotel management after passing the higher secondary or an equivalent examination. They are:

Institute of Catering Technology & Applied Nutrition,
Veer Savarkar Road,
Dadar, Mumbai-400028.

Institute of Catering Technology & Applied Nutrition,
21, Convent Road,
Kolkata-700014.

Institute of Catering Technology & Applied Nutrition,
Adyar, Chennai-20.

Institute of Hotel Management, Catering & Nutrition,
Library Avenue, Pusa,
New Delhi-110012.

Some of these institutions also offer short-term courses in baking and confectionery, hotel reception, and similar subjects for housewives and others. The details can be had directly from the institution nearest to your place of living.

Several private individuals and institutions are offering courses in cookery, bakery and confectionery, canning and food preservation, restaurant and counter service. The following institutes offer some of the best courses:

Foodcraft Institute (Lucknow) Society,
18-B, Ashoka Marg,
Lucknow (U.P.)

Foodcraft Institute (Mysore) Society,
S.I. Polytechnic Buildings,
Seshadri Road, Bangalore.

Foodcraft Institute (Kerala) Society,
Government Polytechnic Building, Kalammassery,
Alwaye-4 (Kerala)

Foodcraft Institute (Maharashtra) Society,
Government Polytechnic Campus,
Sadar, Nagpur.

Foodcraft Institute,
Chandigarh.

Foodcraft Institute (Goa) Society,
P.O. Betim (Bardez),
Goa.

Foodcraft Institute Society,
Kamla Nehru Polytechnic for Women,
Hyderabad.

The All India Institute of Hygiene & Public Health, Kolkata, and the Institute of Catering Technology & Applied Nutrition, Mumbai, offer postgraduate courses in Dietetics for graduates. Courses in Nutrition are offered by most of the colleges that offer courses in Home Science.

Making a Beginning

Many young people have had a humble beginning in a career in catering or hotel management by joining as an assistant in some department, and gradually learning the art. Many have joined out of necessity. They worked and studied simultaneously to advance to important positions.

Young people who have received specialized training have better prospects, and readily find openings in good hotels. Many of the good hotels prefer to provide some additional on-the-job training to all new entrants in the profession. They appoint them in departments where they feel they can work best. Promotions for young people who can show their capabilities are rapid. In due course of time, one can expect to reach a comfortable, though responsible, position.

Young people beginning on their own cannot expect to establish a good hotel right away. Many have started in a small way by opening a snack bar, a cafeteria, or a small restaurant alone, or in partnership with a friend, and made a good business out of it. Expansion in business comes with increased knowledge and experience. Some young people have also set out to establish small hotels on leased buildings after making some improvements in them, and furnishing them to meet the requirements of guests. Starting a small guesthouse has also paved the way to bigger things for some people. However, small the beginning, but if one has the interest and desire to learn and gain valuable experience, promotions come with time.

Income from Catering and Hotel Management

Income from careers in catering and hotel management is invariably always good. The salaries for jobs with private employers owning small restaurants and hotels vary greatly. They are negotiable according to circumstances. Jobs with large restaurants and hotels are well paid. Young people with initiative and drive can look forward to rapid promotions. Besides good salaries, hotels offer allowances for uniforms, and heavily subsidizes the food and beverages served in the workers' canteens.

Income from personal ventures varies from one place to another. A well-planned project can hope to begin earning right away. When service and quality of food are maintained, people have amassed fortunes even out of small snack bars and restaurants. Income from small hotels picks up gradually as the establishment earns a name for service, good food and respectability.

Opportunities for Self-employment

There are many opportunities for self-employment in a career in catering and hotel management. Depending upon the type of town one is living in, one can establish a refreshment corner, ice cream booth, snack bar, fresh fruit juice bar, restaurant, etc. Those with special talents can specialize in selling items like fish and chips, *kababs,* hamburgers, *masala dosa, chaat, chhole bhature*, sandwiches, etc. Those living close to a national highway, and owning a point, which can be developed as a resting point, one can start a snack bar or a restaurant for tourists. Catering for boarding schools and colleges, for special functions like marriage parties, government canteens, and school cafeterias offers useful opportunities for self-employment in a career in catering.

Many of the smaller hotels are either owned by a single person, or developed on a leased property hired on a long-term basis. One can build a small guesthouse, a motel, or even rent or buy an old building and renovate it to develop a complete business in itself. Offering paying guest accommodation has good possibilities. One can begin in a small way, and gradually build one's way up. The Departments of Tourism in many states are encouraging the building of small hotels, and offering loan facilities for the purpose. Hotel business is a growing business, and one can look forward to a happy future in it.

Civil Aviation

24

Careers in aviation are amongst those glamorous vocations that all young people look forward to. Earlier, young men looked forward to becoming pilots and women wanted to serve as hostesses. However, now both the avenues are open to men and women. Whereas there are lady commanders flying some of the largest airplanes, there are men stewards helping hostesses to look after the passengers.

Since there are a limited number of airlines flying a limited number of airplanes the opportunities in this field are necessarily limited. However, by the very nature of the work, the opportunities are not restricted within the country. In this field one can work anywhere in the world. Opportunities for careers are limited, but are extremely attractive.

Desirable Personal Qualities

To be successful in this field, a person must:

- not be afraid of heights. The work will involve flying at great heights in a variety of aircraft and conditions.
- be in excellent health. Health requirements are stringent.
- have perfect eyesight. This is a very important requirement particularly for the flying staff.
- be disciplined. There is no scope for any kind of irregularity in this field.
- be a stickler for procedures. Nothing should be taken for granted. The procedures are clearly defined to ensure safety of the passengers and the aircraft.
- be willing to work and rest at odd hours. Flying schedules begin very early in the morning, and extend till late hours.
- have swift reflexes and the ability to make fast decisions.

There is every chance of a difficult situation. One has to be ready for it.

- be willing to learn regularly. Periodic training is a part of work in this field.
- be service-minded. Passenger comfort and safety are important.
- appreciate the need to work as a team. Many people are employed to give the best service to the passengers. One should fulfil one's responsibility as a team-mate.
- know how to cope with tension that is a part of this work. This is important if one does not want the tension to have a bad effect upon health.

Opportunities in Civil Aviation

Unlike in the past when we only had Indian Airlines operating within the country and Air India flying overseas, we have several airlines flying around the country. Even the two national air carriers have expanded their services to new destinations within the country and abroad. Besides these, opportunities exist overseas also. Several business houses own private planes. Flying clubs spread around the country need trainers. The airlines have requirements for pilots, airhostesses, stewards, pursers, and a large ground staff, which looks after aircraft maintenance and ground services to passengers. The expansion in this field is very restricted. The growth in opportunities too is restricted.

Educational Facilities

To become a pilot one needs to first get a Student Pilot Licence (SPL). One needs to clear an oral examination covering air regulation, air navigation, air meteorology, and technical details. One must be medically fit.

After the SPL one needs to qualify for a Private Pilot Licence (PPL) for which one needs to log 60 flying hours of which 20 hours are solo inclusive of 5 hours of cross country flying. This licence is basically for those doing hobby flying.

To qualify for a Commercial Pilot Licence (CPL) one needs to log 250 hours of flying. For the Senior Commercial

Pilot Licence (SCPL) another 500 hours of flying is necessary. After completing 1500 hours of flying one can apply for the Airline Transport Pilot Licence (ATPL).

There are several Flying Clubs spread around the country where one can get the SPL and PPL. Some training schools being operated by senior pilots provide training for the CPL. Since the flying costs are high, training is expensive. Some complete the training in two years, but many take 3 to 4 years. It may cost several lakhs of rupees. Before joining any training school one must check up with Director General of Civil Aviation, New Delhi, that the training school is duly recognised to provide training. After getting employed by an airline, additional flying experience is gained on the job. To fly different kinds of planes one needs to be trained on them. Airlines have their own training facilities to upgrade their staff.

There are several institutions preparing young people to be air hostesses, stewards and pursers.

Indira Gandhi Uran Academy, Rae Bareilly, offers an 18-month course for CPL for 20 aspirants every year.

Making a Beginning

Air hostesses, pursers, stewards, etc., required by airlines are employed as and when necessary by calling applications through advertisements in the national press. To be an air hostess, one must be unmarried, smart and attractive, and must have done her 10+2. The ability to converse fluently in English/Hindi and other languages is important. One can learn the work at some of the private institutions that have come up recently. Those who are selected for such work are also trained by the airlines before being assigned responsibilities on a flight.

The demand for pilots is very restricted. To qualify for recruitment, one must possess a valid Commercial Pilot Licence. Further training on different kinds of planes is provided by the airline. Indian Airlines have their Central Training Establishment at Begumpet, Hyderabad, and train pilots according to need and qualifications. The ground maintenance staff is employed from amongst technically qualified young people for various responsibilities.

Medical Requirements

The medical requirements for pilots are very stringent. They are tested for medical fitness once every year. After the age of 40, they need to be tested every six months.

Income from Civil Aviation

The income from careers in aviation is very good. Besides the salary the perks by way of additional allowances and free tickets are very attractive. The income and the glamour attached to careers in this field leave one with the impression that the people in this field are indeed a privileged class.

Opportunities for Self-employment

By the very nature of the work there are no opportunities for self-employment in this field.

Commerce

25

The word 'commerce' refers to business and trade in general. Many kinds of occupations can be included. Many of these, like careers in accountancy, management and selling are discussed in separate chapters. Several occupations do not come within a specified category of vocations. They are discussed in general in this chapter.

The large variety of businesses and trades depend upon a very large workforce that does varying kinds of jobs. Many of these functions may appear small and insignificant. Together, they push business and trade to great heights. These jobs do not lead to top positions unless one continues to study and specialize in a particular field. Nevertheless, the opportunities for such jobs are so large that many young people can look forward to begin a career in a small way through one of these vocations. A significant section of the office staff comes within this category of workers. With expanding business and trade, the opportunities continue to grow. Young people can find many openings in this category of work.

Desirable Personal Qualities

To be successful in this field, a person must:

- possess clerical ability. One needs to do a lot of writing work.
- be able to communicate well through the written word. Unless one can express well in writing, several problems can arise.
- have good language skills. Besides English a good knowledge of the local language is important.
- appreciate that knowledge of English is an advantage. It can be useful all over the country and abroad.

- be computer literate. Most offices are now using computers, or planning to do so in the near future.
- be well acquainted with use of office machines. Much communication is now done through fax machines, scanners, printers, etc.
- be able to work as a team. In offices one needs to cooperate with each other to promote greater efficiency.
- be disciplined and follow office rules. It is not possible to make progress without basic discipline.

Opportunities in Commerce

Besides the opportunities for the executive positions in various fields of commerce, most of the opportunities exist at lower levels. They are for work as receptionists, as clerks in filing, record keeping and accounts sections, as bookkeepers, typists, stenographers, steno-typists, and personal assistants.

In the larger business houses there are positions for telephone operators, computer operators, and those that operate other equipment. At higher levels, there are responsible positions in the fields of accountancy, public relations, management and marketing. These are discussed in detail in relevant chapters.

In the larger companies, a Company Secretary supervises the general administration in the office. The details are discussed in a separate chapter: Company Secretary.

Educational Facilities

Depending upon the need, one can join clerical positions after passing the Higher Secondary, or the 10+2 examinations. Those aspiring for higher positions prefer to graduate with commerce subjects. Specialized courses in shorthand/typing and operating of computers and other equipment are available in almost all towns with many private commercial schools. Some institutions provide tuition in commerce subjects through correspondence courses also.

Training for operating small telephone exchanges and other office equipment is also provided by several vendors, or small private schools. Many polytechnics offer courses in secretarial practice and other similar work. Institutions that offer courses in accountancy, management and marketing are discussed in appropriate chapters.

The institute of Company Secretaries of India, New Delhi, offers A.C.S. (India) examination in three parts. On qualifying, one is entitled to work in a senior position as a Company Secretary. The details of the examination can be had directly from the Institute. The Commercial Examination Board of the Indian Merchants' Chamber, Bombay, also conducts examinations leading to senior positions in the field of commerce.

Some Important Addresses

Institute of Company Secretaries of India,
A1/111, Safdarjang Enclave,
New Delhi-110016.

Indian Merchants' Chamber,
76, Veer Nariman Road,
Churchgate,
Mumbai-400020.

Making a Beginning

Most of the positions are filled through advertisements in the press, or through employment exchanges in the area. Direct recruitment is also common. One starts at the lowest level putting personal skills to best use. The employer attaches the person to another employee who acquaints one with the responsibilities, and also provides the initial training. Keeping the employer satisfied with one's work is important. Promotions are slow. However, those who perform well can look forward to steady work.

Income from Commerce

The income from careers in commerce varies with the amount of responsibility handled by an individual. The lower levels are overcrowded. The initial salary may be small, but with experience and a definite show of dependability, steady increments can be expected. Promotions are slow. At each stage, one needs to convince the employer of one's ability and loyalty. Promotions are swift in the higher levels if one is capable of handling the work well.

Opportunities for Self-employment

The opportunities for self-employment are restricted to those who can write in shorthand, do typewriting, operate computers and other office machines, or are good in accounts. Such people can offer private services to the smaller firms, or even run a typing pool to offer such services on piecework basis. Those working at the higher levels can consider going into business on their own.

Company Secretary

26

The position of a Company Secretary in a company carries prestige, but this is not a career for everyone. The Company Secretary is an important link between the Board of Directors, the company shareholders and staff, the government and other bodies that control business. The Company Secretary is a likely candidate to become a director in the company.

With widespread globalization of business, it has become important to be competitive at international level. This, in turn, requires good company governance that includes strict following of regulations and norms, and ensuring that the staff and the shareholders are happy. The Company Secretary plays an important role to ensure that the company fulfils these ideals.

Desirable Personal Qualities

To be successful in this field, a person must:

- have a good personality and a cheerful disposition. It helps create a good impression in general.
- have good analytical skills. This will be important to appreciate business trends.
- have respect for laws and lawmakers. A good knowledge of Company and other related laws is important.
- be fond of reading and studying new developments. Rapid changes are taking place every day. It is important to know about them.
- possess self-confidence. This comes from a thorough knowledge of one's work and situations.
- generally be well aware of the business scenario. Delayed decisions can prove expensive.

- be computer literate. Computers are overtaking many office activities.
- know how to manage time well. Pressures of time will need to be coped with almost every day.

Role of a Company Secretary

A Company Secretary has a wide range of responsibilities. One would do well to understand them before considering taking up this career. Let us consider the more important ones:

- **Advising the Board of Directors:** With a wide range of responsibilities within the Company Act and other laws, the Company Secretary needs to advise the Board of Directors on the legal aspects of their decisions. Therefore, it is necessary that the Company Secretary must be well acquainted with the latest developments and changes.
- **An Important Link:** The Company Secretary is an important link between the Board of Directors and the staff, shareholders and government agencies.
- **Establishing Good Systems:** Since the Company Secretary serves as an important link between various agencies that keep the company in operation, s/he plays an important role in formulating and executing good systems of operation.
- **Planning Future Development:** By the very nature of the work, a Company Secretary is in the best position to identify opportunities for development of the company. S/he must be on the lookout for opportunities for company acquisitions, mergers, take-overs, collaborations and future growth. One can also suggest setting up of subsidiaries and new ventures. The Company Secretary plays an important role as a planner for the company.

Educational Facilities

To qualify for a Company Secretary's position, a person must be a member of The Institute of Company Secretaries of India, Delhi. The Institute has regional offices for the north in

Delhi, for the east in Calcutta, for the west in Mumbai and for the south in Chennai.

To become a member of The Institute of Company Secretaries of India, a person must pass the Foundation, Intermediate and Final examinations conducted by the Institute, followed by 16 months of training on the job. The coaching for the exams is primarily through correspondence. One can pursue the Foundation course after 10+2 or equivalent. Graduation in any field other than Fine Arts is necessary for the Intermediate course and examination. The Final examination and on-the-job training complete the preparation for the position.

Important Address

Institute of Company Secretaries of India,
A-1/111, Safdarjang Enclave,
New Delhi-110016.

Opportunities for a Company Secretary

The Companies Act makes it mandatory that every company with a paid-up capital of over Rs. 50 lakhs must have a full-time Company Secretary. Those companies that do not have a full-time Company Secretary, but have a paid-up capital of Rs. 10 lakhs or above need to file a certificate issued by a full-time practising Company Secretary that the company has fulfilled the requirements prescribed in the Companies Act.

With globalization of business and many new companies being established, the need for good Company Secretaries will always be there. Presently there are 15,000 members attached to the Institute. The Institute registers about two lakh students for various exams. About 25,000 fresh applications are received for registration as students every year.

Making a Beginning

Since one can register for the Foundation course after 10+2, one can continue to do one's graduation in a regular college and simultaneously study for the course through correspondence. One will need to apply for the Intermediate course only after graduation. After the Final exam, 16 months of on-the-job training is important. At this stage people get involved with a company job, gradually rising to the position of a Company Secretary. Some people may prefer to join an independent practising Company Secretary and work as an assistant for sometime before getting into independent practice.

Income as a Company Secretary

The position of a Company Secretary is an important managerial position in the company. Therefore, the remuneration is good. Depending upon the size of the company and the ability of the person, there are good prospects for growth.

Opportunities for Self-employment

It may not be possible for a person to set out as an independent Company Secretary immediately after qualifying for the position. However, after a period of work as an assistant to an established Company Secretary, one can set out on one's own as an advisor to several smaller companies.

Cooking

27

Food is a basic necessity of all people. With more women moving out of their homes to pursue regular careers along with men, they are gradually devoting lesser time to cooking. Eating out at a variety of eating places to suit all kinds of income is on the increase. A variety of fast-food establishments, restaurants and hotels with several speciality restaurants are coming up steadily not only in the larger towns and cities, but also in small towns.

Catering as a vocation is now widely recognised. The increasing number of residential schools, colleges and other institutions need boarding facilities. All these places require good cooks and supporting staff. Cooking has come of age. Good cooks are recognised and appreciated all over the world. Opportunities in the field of cooking are waiting to be filled by young people.

Desirable Personal Qualities

To succeed in this field, a person must:

- have a taste for good food. Those who love food learn to cook it well.
- be willing to experiment with food. Progress depends upon regular experimentation.
- be creative and innovative. Many cooks have made it big with new ideas.
- understand aesthetic food presentation and colours. The first impression of food comes from its appearance. Taste follows later.
- be willing to work hard for long periods. Customers can come at odd hours.
- not mind working without a break or during holidays.

When others are on holiday, the cooks need to work harder.

- know the use of kitchen equipment. Life is becoming easier with new gadgets. Most gadgets aim at making kitchen work easier.
- be ever willing to learn new dishes. Learning leads to progress.

Opportunities in Cooking

Opportunities in careers in cooking are steadily increasing. Never before was there as much need for good cooks as we have today. Earlier, this field was not recognised with as much dignity as it is today. Good cooks receive immediate attention and appreciation. They are important people in the hotel trade. More people are eating out than ever before. There is a great need for good cooks in wayside restaurants, fast-food chains, and speciality restaurants and in institutions that provide boarding facilities.

Catering is an important activity. There is such a great variety in Indian food that many restaurants hire cooks to provide a wide range of dishes. Indian food is appreciated around the world. Many enterprising young people have moved out to service this need. Whereas competition at lower levels is high, there is an ever-increasing need for good cooks.

Speciality Cooking

With a very large variety of foods from within the country and abroad being appreciated by people, cooking has become specialised. People are devoting their efforts to particular types of food and dishes rather than cooking every kind of food. Some of the popular specialitics are:

- Fast foods—both Indian and foreign.
- Baking—food items and confectionery.
- Mughlai food.
- Tandoori dishes and *rotis.*
- South Indian food.

- Continental food.
- Chinese and Thai food.
- Indian sweets.

Educational Facilities

In India, besides the private cooking classes conducted by some people, there are few institutions dedicated exclusively to teaching cooking. This art is taught as a part of courses in hotel management and catering. There are several Food Craft Institutes spread out in various parts of the country. Please see the chapter on Catering and Hotel Management. Most people graduate in a hotel management institute after 10+2, and then opt for kitchen work in a large hotel. One begins at the lowest level. The competition is tough, and promotions slow. But one can gain valuable experience, and move into better positions in a restaurant or elsewhere. One can even set out in a business.

Making a Beginning

Depending upon one's education and level of specialisation, one starts in this field at the lowest level as a trainee, or Commie Chef, in a kitchen. One will need to work hard to prove one's abilities. At this level one needs to do all kinds of work that include chopping vegetables and meat, cleaning deep freezers, and doing a variety of odd jobs.

The promotions that are slow and far in between are in this order. Commie Chef—Demi Chef de Partie—Chef de Partie—Assistant Sous Chef—Sous Chef—Executive Chef. If one is working in a hotel chain, one may ultimately rise to become the Corporate Chef responsible for several locations. Those who have their foundation in hotel management may rise to important managerial positions.

Many young people with cooking abilities coupled with self-confidence set out on their own and started small eating joints, fast-food counters, canteens, restaurants, catering service and similar work to rise to develop the business in a big way. Examples exist in almost every town.

Income from Cooking

The income at the lower levels in careers in this field range between Rs. 3,000-5,000, rising slowly with time. With much competition promotions are slow. At medium levels the income grows to a five-figure salary. At higher levels, the salaries can be very good. Self-employed young people need to struggle hard but can earn very well.

Opportunities for Self-employment

With everybody needing to eat, there are many opportunities for self-employment in this field. Depending upon their area of interest young people in this field can work almost anywhere around the world. There are young people who have a *tandoor* mounted on a pushcart and serve hot *rotis* and vegetable, making a thriving business of it. Similarly, there are a variety of items ranging from fresh sandwiches to *chaat*, cutlets, and even *idli/sambar* being served from mobile units. One's imagination is the limit to what can be served.

At higher levels, young people have opened canteens, catering service, bakery shops, fast-food joints, restaurants and even cooking training institutes. Many young people opt to become self-employed after gaining valuable experience in some of the leading restaurants in big hotels. Indian food is liked around the world. Taking advantage of this fact many Indians have opened restaurants in other countries, making a grand living out of it.

Cottage Crafts

28

There are several cottage crafts peculiar to particular areas in the country. There is a total lack of formal education or training on the subject. However, individuals have passed their skills from one generation to another. This has provided useful employment to a large number of young people. Most of the crafts are restricted to certain areas only. This is due to restricted availability of raw material and availability of skilled individuals in these areas only.

With development of marketing techniques, and export marketing, the demand for several items has gone up. This has created opportunities for many more young people to specialize in these crafts. There is a great need for the development of these cottage crafts, at both production and marketing levels. This would mean additional opportunities for young people. As these crafts develop, the results can be shared worldwide. Young people can build profitable careers in this field of work.

Desirable Personal Qualities

To be successful in this field, a person must:

- possess skills required for the craft. Each craft requires different kinds of skills.
- have artistic ability. Most crafts aim at providing a personalised item of art.
- be quality conscious. Consumers are more quality conscious than ever before. Consistency in work is important.
- be willing to work hard. Personalised items always require greater attention and effort.
- know how to pack and dispatch products. Poor

packaging has resulted in the failure of best products. Packaging must be attractive and protective.

- have some marketing knowledge and skills. Without these skills most craftsmen are at the mercy of the middlemen who eat away the profit.
- be willing to upgrade personal skills. There is no end to learning even for the best craftsman.

Opportunities in Cottage Crafts

Opportunities in cottage crafts exist in definite lines of specialization. Amongst the most popular are making of ornamental metalwork. Making bangles of different kinds and shapes, those made of glass, lac or plastic, is another specialized craft. Ceramics offers a big field of specialization. Handloom fabrics, ladies stoles and shawls, scarves and gents ties too have a large field of cottage crafts to offer. Cane items, toy making, bone and horn items, novelties of soapstone, marble and other kinds of stones, things made of sea shells offer career opportunities where the necessary raw material is available.

Lacquerware, incense and perfumery items, handmade paper, papier-mâché work, sandalwood items, ornamental wall carpets and decorative pieces, wooden screens, tables, bookstands and similar items, baskets, and a variety of other items are in good demand not only within the country, but also abroad.

In the recent past, there has been a significant development of these cottage crafts, particularly as the craftsmen are beginning to appreciate the importance of a good finish to the product, and the need for attractive packaging and presentation. Many of the crafts are restricted only to particular areas as skilled craftsmen are available only there. Even when they move out to other areas, the non-availability of raw materials, lack of knowledge of changing trends, and a restricted market do not allow the craft to be developed.

However, since many of these items have a great potential for export marketing, these need to be developed more seriously through organized education of new craftsmen, and use of newer manufacturing techniques. Many of the crafts can be developed even in the rural areas, providing useful employment to the workers there. Furthermore, rather than be restricted to particular areas only, the development of the crafts in new areas will also provide useful opportunities for careers to many young people interested in this field of work.

Educational Facilities

Educational facilities are available for only a few restricted items like ceramics. For most of the other items, there are no organised educational facilities available. Several state governments have taken steps to gradually organize the activities for several crafts. Craft fairs are being organized. Better marketing techniques are being taught. However, scope exists for further developing many of the crafts through rural educational outlets where young men and women can develop these crafts and find useful employment.

Making a Beginning

Most of the people engaged in cottage crafts begin their careers very early as children helping their parents at work. With time, they develop their skills until they become master craftsmen themselves. However, it would be worthwhile to develop organized education through institutions and polytechnics for imparting theoretical and practical knowledge of these skills to young people interested in these careers. This would enable large-scale development of these skills. In turn, the production of various items would increase, and provide greater employment to interested people. Many of the items have a great demand in the overseas markets. Young people with initiative can explore the potentialities through better presentation and packaging, and selling abroad.

Income from Cottage Crafts

Until the recent past, most of the able craftsmen were an exploited lot. The greater part of the income went to the middlemen who arranged for the sale of the craft items. With greater awareness amongst these workers, and with greater demand for the craft items, the craftsmen are assured of a reasonable income. People who can unite to form co-operative sales counters can earn more. Many of the enterprising workers are now selling directly to overseas customers to get good returns for their work.

Opportunities for Self-employment

Some craftsmen are working for employers who work on a larger scale, or when large sums of money need to be invested. Many of the craftsmen are self-employed. They sell their own items, or produce them for purchasing agents on a piecework basis. Organized co-operative selling will help get many more craftsmen to work on their own, and earn much more than what they can through a job.

Courier Service

29

One field of service that did not exist a few years ago, but one cannot do without it presently is courier service. Earlier, all mail and parcel packets were sent through post. Even the magazines were posted in the mail. Since everyone was using the mail services, very often there were big bulks of mail that had to be moved swiftly not only to every town and village in the country, but also overseas. At the destination the mail had to be sorted and delivered from home to home. It was a fairly efficient service, but sometimes when there was more mail as would happen during festival periods when hundreds of thousands of greeting cards would be posted delays in delivery could not be avoided.

To overcome the problem of delayed and uncertain delivery of mail courier service was established. Whereas postal services are offered as a government service, the courier services are efforts of private operators who guarantee an assured delivery of mail and parcel packets within a fixed time for a nominal charge. This has greatly promoted business activities and most businessmen have switched to these services. Many courier companies have come up. They have built individual networks and offer services within the country and abroad. These services have provided employment to many people.

Desirable Personal Qualities

To be successful in this field a person must:

- be very clear about the kind of service that is being offered to the clientele.
- appreciate the importance of the package to the person who has sent it and to the person who will receive it.
- understand that time is an important factor for delivery of the packet.

- understand that security of the package is an important factor.
- be well acquainted with the locality where one is working. Without this knowledge the deliveries will suffer.
- be outgoing and should build as many contacts as possible. Volumes are important to business.
- be able to work as a team. Good teamwork promotes efficiency.

Opportunities in Courier Service

The purpose of courier services is to carry mail and packets swiftly and efficiently. One of the major users of postal services is the government. They have offices spread in every part of the country. However, the government offices do not use courier service, as the government owns the postal service and issue special stamps for official use. The biggest users of courier service are the private businessmen and institutions.

Banks need to send a large number of communications every day. Since they desire both speed and definite delivery, courier services have found great favour with them. Courier companies compete with each other to pick up their business. Many business houses too need to send mail everyday and avail of the mail pickup service until evening. Postal services close for the day earlier. The delivery of the mail is faster, reaching the next day in most cases. The larger courier companies have air-links to send mail to distant towns. Where the mail is not enough to justify daily pickup, courier companies have established collection centres that collect mail packets against cash payment.

Magazines that are published in a particular town or city offer the greatest opportunity for courier service. The local distribution and that in nearby towns is swift and gives the courier companies regular business. The distant mailings work out cheaper by post. Book publishers also use courier services. Companies and organisations that need to send bills, circulars, newsletters and other literature locally also offer opportunities for local courier service. It costs the same as postal charges, and the delivery is recorded.

Many companies need to send out samples and goods everyday. Rather than send these by parcel post most people are now sending these through couriers. Special rates are offered to those who avail of this service every day.

Courier service is labour intensive. At every step people are required to fulfil the many responsibilities involved in the work. Courier services have provided a very large workforce at all levels. With greater development of business, the opportunities in this field will also increase.

Educational Facilities

The major workforce in this field has passed the 10th class or done 10+2. They serve as delivery and collection personnel. To do their job they need to know the area where they serve well. To move swiftly they need a bicycle or a motorized two-wheel vehicle. Their responsibility includes making of run-sheets where lists of documents to be delivered are recorded, and to get the recipient's signature on these at the time of delivery. A neat handwriting is an asset.

The work in the office requires more responsible people. They do not only supervise the field staff, but also maintain office records, details of cash and credit sales, and details of packets received from outstations and those handed over to the vehicles that carry the packages. Graduates who understand accounts and office routine can fulfil these responsibilities. An office manager oversees the entire work. There are no educational institutions that impart specialised education in this field. The work has evolved over a period of time.

Making a Beginning

Efficient courier work is based upon a network of people and services spread over a well-defined area. A team of personnel who need to know the area where they are posted does the collection and delivery of documents/packages. They must be well acquainted with the sectors, roads and house numbers. They must have a knack of identifying an address quickly. A personal vehicle is necessary. These positions are filled through personal negotiation.

One begins in a courier office as an assistant and gradually learns the routine. One grows with the ability of handling more responsibility. Those who handle accounts must understand accounting procedures. One can grow to be the manager of a centre.

Since it is not practical to cover large cities from a single office, most companies appoint franchisees to serve a particular area. The franchisee hires and supervises the staff that does the collection and delivery of documents. The franchisee is really a manager working on contract basis for a particular area. To facilitate the collection of documents, many companies appoint collection centres in markets or shopping complexes. This provides the collection centres part-time additional income besides the work they may already be doing.

Income from Courier Services

The delivery personnel may be working on a salary that is at par with that of most delivery boys, or may even work piece-work with the income dependent upon the number of documents collected or distributed. The income of the office staff is at par with those doing similar work. Many services like carriage of documents to different stations are on contract basis.

Opportunities for Self-employment

Since efficient courier services are dependent upon good teamwork, the scope for working individually is limited to being a franchisee for a courier company, and handling a local centre. To make it especially remunerative one can strive to develop more of local business.

Dairy Science

30

Milk is a primary necessity in everyone's life. From the time one is born until the end one consumes milk and milk products as vital food provided by nature. With a very large population there has been a great pressure on milk supplies. There have been times when milk was imported in different forms to cope with the demand. However, with the 'white revolution' the scene has changed. Modern technology was able to bring about a great transformation. Milk is now available in abundance.

Many milk products are being manufactured to utilise the excess supplies. The principal target before the dairy technologist is to ensure that fresh milk and milk products reach the consumer. There should be the least loss from the point of supply to the point of consumption. There is a continued effort to extend the shelf life of milk and milk products.

Desirable Personal Qualities

To be successful in this field, a person must:

- be highly quality conscious about products. Dairy products are liable to rapid deterioration.
- be health conscious. A stale product can be harmful for health.
- have a love for animals. Unless one is fond of the animals one cannot operate a dairy.
- be a stickler for cleanliness. Cleanliness at every level is related to contamination and deterioration of food items.
- be technically competent. New techniques are promoting products with longer shelf life.

- be disciplined and self-motivated. Looking after a dairy can be monotonous and hard at times.
- possess business acumen. One cannot progress without keeping an eye both on expenditure and income.
- have the ability to work as a team. It is necessary to seek the cooperation of the staff at all times.
- be willing to work hard at odd hours. One needs to rise early, and work till late many times.

Opportunities in Dairy Science

There was a time when individuals reared cows and buffaloes and personally sold milk from home to home. Those who were unable to do so sold the milk to intermediaries who reached the milk to the consumers. Although this system continues in some places, but by far it has given way to organized milk collection, treatment and distribution at controlled prices. The milk producers get a fair price and the consumers too are assured of a uniform product at a reasonable price.

Opportunities for careers exist at different phases of the work. It begins at the dairy farm stage where a person can rear cows and buffaloes and produce milk. The size of the operation is immaterial. There are people who rear just one or two animals, looking after them personally. At the same time others keep larger numbers and hire help.

The milk from this stage passes on to the second stage where a large group of people collect the milk at purchase centres, and reach it to the central dairy plant. At this stage the milk is treated for uniform fat content and also pasteurised to ensure a healthy product. The milk is packed in flexible packaging and is ready for the last stage. The final stage is sale at distribution points from where the consumers pick up their requirements.

Like most food products milk has a short life. To cope with excessive purchases the surplus milk is converted to dairy products like cream, butter, cheese, *ghee, khoa,* skimmed milk and milk powder. Large quantities of milk are consumed in making sweets.

At every stage of milk production, treatment, conversion to milk products and sale of the final product there are opportunities for employment. One can select avenues that are in harmony with one's personality. With the entire process more organized and with Indian companies coming up with products that compare well with products in developed countries, the opportunities for further development are bound to increase.

Educational Facilities

Most of the people employed at the primary stage of milk production are not formally educated in the line. They learn on the job, following instructions of the local veterinarian or the local personnel in the animal husbandry department.

Those who aim for positions in the dairy plants go on to obtain the B.Tech or B.Sc. (Dairy Technology) after 10+2 with Physics, Chemistry and Maths. There are colleges spread all over the country that offer these courses. Admission is through competitive exams. The Indian Council for Agricultural Research also conducts an All India examination for admission to these institutions where 15 per cent of the seats are reserved for those who qualify in this exam. The training includes an all round study followed by 6 to 12 months of practical training in purchasing, quality control, plant operation, packaging, storage and sale.

At higher levels one can go on to qualify for the M.Tech in Dairy Technology or a Ph.D. There are several related options like fruit preservation, food technology, biotechnology and brewery science. In larger plants the work of marketing and overall management could be in the hands of specially qualified individuals who may have done a MBA in marketing or administration.

Making a Beginning

At the milk production stage one can make a beginning at any time, and on a scale that the individual can handle. Most people grow gradually, increasing the strength of the cattle and the necessary infrastructure. Cleanliness and personal supervision is most essential.

Those interested in working in milk plants join as management trainees or trainee executives. Private companies participate in campus recruitment. Jobs are also advertised in newspapers and on the web. After gaining the initial experience one is promoted as a junior executive, a shift in-charge, superintendent and manager. At the plant level, one could serve as a Deputy Dairy Manager or Deputy Plant Manager, rising to become as Assistant Manager and then Manager. At the top level there is the General Manager and the Managing Director.

Besides the management positions one could also join in specific lines like product development, quality maintenance, planning or systems development. Those who have specialised as Dairy Engineers oversee plant maintenance. For looking after the financial aspects, those who have specialised in that field are employed.

Income in Dairy Science

The income from milk production was erratic until the entire sector got organized. It is now a source of regular income to millions of rural families, both big and small. Those who do it on a larger scale are doing well. There are taxation benefits for those involved in this field.

Those involved in the plants begin with salaries that are in harmony with those in similar fields. Private companies pay higher salaries, but entrust greater responsibility. As in other fields there is steady growth and promotion.

Opportunities for Self-employment

The opportunities for self-employment that exist are at the level of milk production. If one is willing to invest in this field there is scope for installing smaller plants in small towns and cities that are presently not served by the larger milk plants. There is also scope for developing new dairy products and marketing them even in the larger cities. Manufacturing of ice cream, sweets, butter and *ghee* is popular all over the country.

31 Dancing and Dramatics

Careers in dancing and dramatics have never received the attention that they rightly deserved. In the past many people attached a stigma to careers in this field. Very often, the capabilities of very talented young people were just wasted. However, the situation is different now. There is a very big field of careers in this field. People spend large sums of money on these all over the country.

The area covered by these careers is still limited to larger cities. There is a great scope for expansion not only in the smaller towns, but also to the vast rural areas. We have a very large variety of folk dances in different parts of the country. These can provide useful careers to many. Many new ideas need to be tried out. These can be adapted for use in this field of careers.

Many young people are attracted to these careers because of the glamour attached to such vocations. Many are attracted by prospects of becoming rich quickly. Such hopes are ill founded, as like all other careers, there is only one place to begin from. That is right at the lowest rung of the ladder. The success one achieves is directly proportional to one's capabilities and the hard work one is willing to put in. There are indeed many opportunities to be availed. It is for the talented young people to gain by them.

Desirable Personal Qualities

To be successful in this field, a person must:

- be endowed with talent for the field of choice. Without basic talent one cannot go far.
- have a deep interest to excel in the field. Personal interest is a great motivating force to move ahead.

- possess musical ability. Part of it is inborn. Partly it is developed.
- have an understanding of grace and rhythm. Dance depends entirely upon these qualities.
- have an aesthetic sense. Crudity can be repelling.
- have the ability to express emotions convincingly. Without it one cannot influence the audience.
- have a sense of showmanship. The best of artists fail without showmanship.
- understand the mood of the audience. Audiences behave differently at different times. Making adjustments is important.
- be willing to train and improve continuously. There is no end to learning. Be prepared to learn every day.
- have the ability to work in a team. One cannot succeed without cooperation from others.
- be ready to work continuously for long hours. Continuous practice is important.
- be willing to travel and stay away from home. One will need to travel to perform in other towns and cities.

Opportunities in Dancing and Dramatics

India has a rich heritage of arts like music, dancing and dramatics. It is the largest producer of films in the world. Indian music and dancing have won wide acclaim in the affluent Western world. There is still a great demand for good performances. There is always a gap between the supply and demand. Talented young people are always in need. Even within the country, there is a great need for good entertainment. It will be long before the need can be satisfactorily fulfilled.

Music forms a part of the curriculum in many schools and colleges in the country. Those who are talented proceed to specialize in particular fields. On attaining proficiency, they join groups which stage shows, or even perform independently at special shows, or on the radio or television. Singing and music in restaurants, hotels and clubs are becoming popular.

Besides, musicians are always in good demand on occasions like weddings, parties, fetes, *melas*, etc.

Dancing is an art that is especially appealing in both the urban and rural areas. Classical Indian dances have received great appreciation all over the world. India being a vast country has a variety of folk dances that offer a great opportunity for being developed into refined and acceptable performances. This talent can be used to fulfil the entertainment needs in smaller towns and rural areas, and in the larger cities. These dances offer newer patterns of grace and rhythm. In the same way, the talent in the larger cities can be shared in smaller towns.

Theatrical groups have achieved good success in the larger cities. The young people in smaller towns can start such groups to present plays that can be both entertaining and educative. The demand for such entertainment is obvious from the success these groups have achieved in new and small towns.

Educational Facilities

Music as a subject of study is offered in many schools and colleges. One can pursue the studies according to one's personal interest. Dancing is also taught as an extra-curricular activity in some institutions. To qualify for higher levels one can study the art under the guidance of an established expert in a school, or even independently. One begins in dramatics too at school or college level by taking part in institutional performances. Those interested in it as a career can pursue a three-year course in Acting, Direction, Stagecraft and Dramatics after graduation. An aptitude for acting is necessary. The details of the courses offered can be had directly from:

The National School of Drama,
Bahawalpur House,
Bhagwan Dass Road,
New Delhi-110001.

There are several smaller institutes managed by individuals or groups who provide training in this field of careers. They advertise in popular newspapers and magazines from time to time. Some of these institutions are good. A few are not.

Check the record of an institution before signing for a course with them.

Making a Beginning

Most senior people engaged in this field of careers have come up through sheer hard work. However, the younger generations interested in such careers confirm that proper training has been a great asset in their rise in the career. Interest in music and dancing begins early at the school stage. Success at that stage encourages young people to pursue further studies under a capable guide who may be working independently, or may be connected with one of the many schools spread all over the country. There are no established channels for employment and growth in the career. One needs some initiative to form a group, or join an established group of artists, and work one's way up by displaying personal capabilities. It is a slow process, but those with interest and zeal have made it to the top.

Income from Dancing and Dramatics

The income from careers in this field of careers varies greatly. The artists who are in good demand can ask for any amount they can justify. At the lower levels, the salaries are negotiable according to supply and demand. Those working as groups share whatever they earn. Established artists can earn a steady income, and can rise to great heights of fame and prosperity. The lot of the artists working at the lower levels is not very encouraging. They cannot be certain of continued work unless they are attached to a group, and receive a salary each month.

Opportunities for Self-employment

Young people beginning a career in this field of work may prefer to accept a job as it ensures regular income through a salary. Most artists prefer to work as groups, and divide income as negotiated mutually. There is ample scope for self-employment if one has the requisite qualifications and the connections to find work regularly to ensure a steady income. There are enough openings for freelance artists. Those with initiative and imagination find success a constant companion.

Defence Services

32

The Defence Services offer excellent opportunities for careers for young people interested in working in the army, the air force and the navy. We have vast frontiers that need to be guarded. Even the great Himalayas that stood as a wall impenetrable by possible invaders until the recent past now need to be protected as the increasing routes of communication have made it easier to cross them. The coastline of almost 6,000 kilometres also needs to be guarded by the navy against the enemies of the country.

One can serve in the Defence services in many ways through one of the three services. There is great honour and prestige in these careers. The remuneration and benefits offered are good. Young people have continued to find careers in the Defence services very satisfying. Each day greater numbers are getting interested in serving their country through them.

Desirable Personal Qualities

To be successful in this field, a person must:

- believe in discipline in various aspects of life. All defence services insist upon discipline in everything.
- be physically healthy and strong. The work can be difficult and arduous.
- possess stamina for physical work. One may need to work continuously for long periods.
- have a love for nature and the outdoors. Much of the time will be spent outdoors.
- love a variety of games and sports. These help maintain good health and stamina for physical exertion.
- be a willing learner. New situations need new techniques. Learning never ends.

- be ready to work as a team. One cannot succeed without the cooperation of others.
- have the ability to gain confidence quickly. Self-confidence is important in many situations.
- possess leadership qualities for higher positions. When one works as a team, someone has to lead. Those who have the ability will do it.
- be willing to work at odd times for long hours. Many situations will require it.
- be ready to stay away from home for long periods. Families are not permitted in the front areas.

Opportunities in the Defence Services

Opportunities exist at all levels for young people interested in careers in the army, the air force and the navy. Whereas at the lower levels there are opportunities for working as Sepoys, aircraftsmen and sailors, opportunities also exist for joining the services directly in the officer cadre. There are opportunities for promotion at both levels of service according to time-scale, and according to the selection grade. Everyone is provided enough opportunity to rise to the highest levels provided he is capable and exhibits qualities of service, dependability and leadership.

At the lower levels one joins the army as a Sepoy, and rises gradually to serve as Lance Naik, Naik, Havildar, Naik Subedar, Subedar and Subedar Major. In the air force one joins as an aircraftsman, and is promoted to Leading Aircraftsman, Corporal, Sergeant, Jr. Warrant Officer, Warrant Officer and Master Warrant Officer. In the navy one joins as a sailor/artificer/apprentice, and rises to become an Able Seaman, Leading Seaman, Petty Officer, Chief Petty Officer, and Master Petty Officer.

In the officer cadre one begins the career in the army as a Second Lieutenant, and rises to become Lieutenant, Captain, Major, Lt. Colonel, Colonel, Brigadier, Major General, Lt. General, General and Field Marshal. In the same way, one joins the air force as a Pilot Officer, and is promoted to positions of Flying Officer, Flight Lieutenant, Squadron Leader, Wing Commander, Group Captain, Air Commodore, Air Vice Marshal, Air Marshal, Air Chief Marshal and Marshal of the Air Force. In the navy, beginning as Acting Sub-Lieutenant, one goes up the ladder as Sub-Lieutenant, Lieutenant, Lt. Commander, Commander, Captain, Commodore, Rear Admiral, Vice Admiral, Admiral, and Admiral of the Fleet.

Substantive promotions to the ranks of Lieutenant, Captain and Major in the army, and their equivalent positions in the air force and navy, are admissible by time-scale on completion of 2, 6 and 13 years of service respectively. Acting promotion to the rank of Captain is admissible after three years, to the rank of Major after six years, and that of Lt. Colonel after 16 years. A Major, who is not granted the substantive rank of Lt. Colonel by selection, is granted the rank on completion of 24 years of service.

Besides the opportunities for careers at different levels of the three services, positions also exist for civilian workers in the engineering and construction sections for repair and maintenance work.

In each of the three services, there are various kinds of work assigned to each person. For example, in the army one may belong to the Infantry, Artillery, Armoured Corps, Engineers, Army Supply Corps, Army Medical Corps, etc. In the same way, the officer cadre in the navy is divided into the categories of Executives, Engineering, Electrical, Supply and Secretariat, Instructors and the Medical branch. The air force is not restricted to the flying branch of pilots and navigators. It has a large ground support staff with people engaged in the technical branch pertaining to Aeronautical engineering, further sub-divided into Electronics and Mechanical sections. The non-technical branch consists of the Administrative, Logistics, Education, Accounts and Meteorological sections. There are many opportunities for making a selection of a particular line of choice in any of the three services. Those who are capable do well in careers in the defence services.

Educational Facilities

To qualify for careers in the Defence Services one needs to qualify the high school or the 10+2 examinations, appear for the competitive exams and the interview. On selection training is imparted at the defence establishments. For the technical branches it is essential that one should specialise in a particular field, and join whenever the need is advertised. Whatever additional training is required shall be imparted at a defence establishment.

Making a Beginning

The entry into the career at the lower levels is through recruiting centres spread all over the country. For entry into the air force and the navy, the minimum educational qualification is high school, higher secondary, or a pass in an equivalent examination. Those with lower qualifications can join the army, and certain sections of the other services. Those who are better educated enjoy greater chances of rising in the career. Sound health and good physique are essential in all cases. After one year's training, each one is assigned to a particular unit, in different trades and categories. Those in technical lines have better opportunities for promotion as Non-Commissioned Officers and Junior Commissioned Officers.

For higher cadres of services in the Defence Service, there are competitive examinations conducted by the Union Public Service Commission, Dholpur House, P.O. Box 186, New Delhi. Those who have passed the higher secondary, 10+2, or an equivalent examination can appear for the examination conducted twice a year by the U.P.S.C. for admission to the National Defence Academy at Khadakvasla near Pune. Candidates who do well in the written test are invited for interview by the Services Selection Board, and for the medical check-up. A merit list is prepared on the basis of marks obtained in the written test and interview. Selected candidates receive three years' training at the National Defence Academy. A one-year specialized training for the three services is conducted separately before one is commissioned as an officer.

Young people who have passed the 10+2 or an equivalent examination can appear for the competitive examination conducted by the U.P.S.C. for entry into the Air Force College for the Pilot's Course. The Air Force Selection Board invites successful candidates for an interview. For final selection, each candidate must secure the minimum qualifying marks in the written examination, the pilot aptitude test, the officer potentiality test, and the physical endurance test. Selected candidates are sent for training as pilots at the Air Force College.

Similar to the direct recruitment in the air force, young people who are 19 to 22 years old, and have graduated from a university approved by the Government of India, or possess an equivalent qualification, can appear for the Combined Defence Services examination for direct entry to the Indian Military Academy at Dehradun, or the Naval Academy at Kochi. One is commissioned as an army officer after a two-year training at the I.M.A. at Dehradun. The Naval Academy at Kochi prepares candidates for regular commissions in the navy. The selection is based upon the merit list compiled on the basis of the written test and the interview by the Services Selection Board.

N.C.C. cadets who are graduates, 19 to 22 years old, have passed the "C" Certificate examination of the N.C.C., and were discharged from the N.C.C. 12 months earlier can also apply for a regular commission in the army without having to appear for the U.P.S.C. examination. A permanent regular commission is granted after training at the Indian Military Academy at Dehradun.

N.C.C. cadets who have passed the 10+2 examination or its equivalent, and have served for three years in the Senior Division of the N.C.C. Air Wing, and possess an Air Wing "C" Certificate, and also a certificate of good conduct from the principal of the college, can within 12 months of leaving the N.C.C., apply to join the Flying Branch of the Indian Air Force. For complete details, the cadets can write to:

The Director General, N.C.C.,
Ministry of Defence,
Government of India,
West Block No. 4, R.K. Puram,
New Delhi-110022.

Young men who have done the two years' training course on T.S. Rajendra (See Chapter on Merchant Navy) are also eligible for direct entry into the Indian Navy.

Young men who have a degree, or a diploma equivalent to a degree, in civil, electrical or mechanical engineering, in mining, architecture, telecommunications, electrical communications, or in automobile or radio engineering, recognized by the Institution of Engineers (India), in exemption of passing Section A of their Associate Membership examination, or a degree or diploma in various engineering fields recognized by the Ministry of Education for recruitment to superior posts in the Government of India, or the M.Sc.(Tech.) in Radio Engineering and Electronics of the College of Science & Technology, Kolkata, or Diploma in Electronics & Technology (DMIT), Chennai, or M.A./M.Sc. (Physics) with Wireless, Electronics, Radio Commission as a special subject, are eligible for permanent regular commissions in the Corps of Engineers, Signals and Electrical and Mechanical Engineers. There is no written test. However, the Services Selection Board calls the candidates for a test and interview. Selected candidates receive one year's training before being commissioned as officers.

Those who have passed the M.A./M.Sc., hold a degree or diploma in teaching, and possess 2 to 3 years' teaching experience in high school, college or university, can join the Army Education Corps. Those with a degree in Dairy Science or in Agriculture (with Dairy Science as a subject) can join the Military Farms Service. Those who hold the M.Sc. (Organic Chemistry/Biochemistry/Microbiology), or M.Pharm. or M.Sc. (Food & Drugs), with two years' research experience, can join the Army Service Corps (Food Inspection Organization). The Services Selection Board calls candidates for these services. On selection, they are sent to the Indian Military Academy for one year's training, and then commissioned as officers. The details for joining these services can be had from:

Army Headquarters,
AG Branch, Recruiting Directorate,
Rectg. 6 (SP), R.K. Puram,
New Delhi-110022.

In the navy, one can join the Executive branch if one possesses the Ministry of Transport & Communication's Certificate of Competency either as Second Mate, Mate or Master (See Chapter on Merchant Navy). If one has a degree in marine or mechanical engineering recognized by the Government of India, or by the Institution of Engineers (India), or in electrical, electronic or telecommunication engineering, one can join the Engineering and Electrical branches of the navy. Openings also exist for those qualified in naval architecture, aeronautical engineering, civil engineering and metallurgical engineering. Graduates are also eligible for services in the Supply and Secretariat branch, and the educational branch. Posts are advertised according to need. On selection the candidates are sent for training to various naval ships/ establishments for varying periods, and commissioned as officers. For further details, please write to:

The Director of Personnel Services,
Naval Headquarters,
R&R Section, DHQ P.O.,
New Delhi-110011.

Young people, who have a degree in engineering or technology in electronic communications, or electrical engineering, or have passed sections A and B of the Associateship examination of the Institution of Engineers (India), or possess a degree in mechanical or aeronautical engineering, can join the technical branches of the air force. Openings also exist for graduates and post-graduates in the Administrative and Logistics branches. Graduates with a teaching degree can join the Education branch. Qualified accountants with B.Com. are eligible for the Accounts branch. For the Meteorological branch, one must be a M.Sc. with Meteorology as a special subject.

Qualified doctors, both men and women, who possess a recognized degree of an Indian or foreign university, and are below 30 years of age, are eligible to join the Army Medical Corps. The age-limit can be relaxed for those with higher post-graduate qualifications. Young people, who are selected for the Armed Forces Medical College, Pune, on qualifying, are also absorbed in the Army Medical Corps.

Besides regular permanent commissions in the army, air force and the navy, there are also short service commissions in various categories for 2 to 5 years, and commissions in the Territorial Army. The vacancies are advertised as and when they occur. Those in the short service commissions can be absorbed in the regular commissions subject to their capabilities and availability of vacancies.

Income from Defence Services

Income from careers in the Defence Services is good. Besides the salary, the personnel are entitled to many other benefits like outfit allowance, free rations, residence, healthcare for the family, canteen services, two months annual leave, 30 days' casual leave (20 days for officers), free railway warrant for self and family, and a whole lot of other amenities. On retirement, they are entitled to a pension.

Opportunities for Self-employment

As is obvious, there are no opportunities for self-employment at any level of the Defence Services. However, at lower levels there are schemes for training services personnel to become self-employed after retirement. Many ex-servicemen find employment in security services in the industry after retirement. The officers are also able to find useful employment in management cadres after retirement.

Dentistry

33

Another field closely related to medicine is that of Dentistry. Despite the importance of oral hygiene in maintaining good health this aspect is often neglected. This is so not only in the vast rural areas where only the basic health services are available, but even in the urban areas where people are educated. This aspect of health has not received the importance it deserves.

In sharp contrast to the general scenario of dental care, those who appreciate the need for it have encouraged the development of several lines of specialization within the field of oral hygiene and care. The field is very vast. With growing education and awareness for oral hygiene the opportunities in this field are bound to grow.

Fields of Specialisation

Although the field of Dentistry is restricted to a small part of the human body—the mouth, the jaw, gums and teeth, yet within the field there are several lines of specialization. Some of the popular ones include:

- **Periodontics:** pertains to the treatment of diseases and disorders of the periodontium, that is, the gum and tissues surrounding and supporting the teeth.
- **Prosthetics:** pertains to replacement of teeth artificially.
- **Pedodontics:** pertains to tooth related diseases in children.
- **Prosthodontics:** pertains to restoration and replacement of missing teeth and other oral structures by artificial devices.
- **Orthodontics:** pertains to the correcting of irregularities in the teeth.

- **Oral Pathology and Microbiology:** pertains to the pathological aspects of the mouth.
- **Cosmetic Dentistry:** pertains to cosmetic improvement of the teeth.
- **Oral Medicine and Surgery:** pertains to general medical and surgical needs.
- **Conservative Dentistry:** pertains to a cautious approach to preserving existing conditions.

Desirable Personal Qualities

To be successful in this field, a person must:

- have a pleasing personality. This helps win the confidence of the patient immediately.
- observe good etiquette and manners. This enhances the effect of a pleasing personality.
- have the ability to gain confidence quickly. Most patients are afraid of pain often associated with dental treatment.
- be able to comfort people. Some pain is imminent. The ability to comfort people helps reduce it.
- possess a gentle touch. This helps win patient's confidence.
- be sensitive to others' pain. This too helps comfort the patient.
- have an aesthetic sense. This is important when performing cosmetic surgery.
- be artistic in approach. Artificial teeth are the handiwork of an artist.
- have good communication skills. This helps keep the patient's mind away from pain.

Opportunities in Dentistry

There are good opportunities for careers in Dentistry in general and specialised practice. A small percentage of parents are conscious of the need for timely dental care for children. However, this awareness is growing. Even amongst grown-ups the need for good teeth and oral hygiene is being appreciated. More people are visiting a dentist as a part of regular oral healthcare.

Most residential schools have dentists who look after the children's dental care. However, the day schools have yet to make a beginning. With the parents not fully conscious of the importance of dental care for children, a start by the schools can be an important beginning. The doctors may need to take an initiative in this field. It will open up a vast need for providing timely dental care.

The vast rural areas too hold unlimited opportunities for extending dental services to new areas. With low rural incomes, cheaper treatment will need to be devised. But the need for such services exists, and appropriate initiatives will need to be taken.

Educational Facilities

There are dental colleges offering the Bachelor's degree (BDS) and the Master's (MDS) in several fields of specialization spread all over the country. Selection to these colleges is on the basis of the all-India competitive examination. For a Bachelor's degree one needs to have passed 10+2 before taking the competitive exam. For the Master's degree one must have the BDS degree.

All medical practitioners need to update knowledge periodically. Besides personal study this requires regular participation in medical workshops conducted by respective medical associations.

Making a Beginning

One can begin dental practice soon after obtaining the BDS degree. However, it is advisable to specialise in one of the many fields that are available. There are two work options available. One can take up employment in a hospital or clinic. In the alternative, one can start a practice. To do this, it will be necessary to have a clinic and dental equipment required for such practice. If a person can partially pay for the equipment, banks are willing to finance the balance.

As with other fields, a practice builds up slowly when people get to know of one's capabilities. Many begin their careers in a hospital or clinic. After gaining experience, and building contacts with patients, they separate to establish personal clinics.

Income from Dentistry

Dentistry is a popular field of medical practice. The income in this field is good. However, with increasing number of young people entering this field and with growing competition, many of the established dentists have been complaining about it. It is not that the income is not attractive, but that the patients are becoming aware of better facilities at more competitive rates.

Opportunities for Self-employment

This is one field of medicine where a person can practice all on one's own with the help of an assistant, who can be trained to assist in routine jobs like sterilizing the equipments, ushering in the patients and doing simple jobs.

Dressmaking

34

Dressmaking pertains to getting ready clothes that we need to wear for different occasions in everyday life. Just as we need food to appease our hunger, we need to dress up not only to protect, but also to project ourselves. Steps involved in dressmaking include selecting an appropriate fabric, picking out the best design for the purpose, and having it ready. Both appearance and comfort are important. The dress must enhance the personality of the individual.

Desirable Personal Qualities

To be successful in this field, a person must:

- know the technology involved. Some learn it through experience. Others learn it through education.
- be original and creative. People want to look exclusive. A good dress can make them so.
- be a stickler for detail. Details sometimes appear unimportant. But they are not. Little details enhance the appearance and utility of a dress.
- have a good imagination and artistic abilities. A good dress is piece of art.
- have an eye for colour balance. Colours create harmony. They can also be jarring sometimes.
- have good communication skills. Unless one knows what a customer desires it is difficult to provide it.
- be hardworking. Like all other fields one needs to work hard to progress in life.

Opportunities in Dressmaking

With Indian trade opening up to the world, there is a great demand for readymade dresses particularly in the developed countries. Business houses that fabricate, buy or export garments regularly need personnel for dressmaking. Since people at every level of the society need to wear clothes, there is scope for smaller units in the smaller towns to cater to the needs of the local people. Making of school dresses, uniforms for service personnel and other organizations also require a steady supply of dresses for a variety of needs. Clothes wear out with time. They will need replacement periodically. Therefore, there is a steady need for dresses and dressmaking.

Educational Facilities

There are several institutions that are offering courses in this field. However, the National Institute of Fashion Technology (NIFT) is a premier institution in this field. It has several centres serving in different parts of the country. Admission is through a written test followed by an interview.

Other important institutions offering courses include South Delhi Polytechnic, International Polytechnic, The Pearl Academy, The Academy of Fashion Studies, The Apeejay Institute of Design, Senorita College of Fashion and Young Women's Christian Association, all in Delhi. Similar institutions exist in many cities around the country.

Admissions are after passing 10+2. One will necessarily need to file applications for admission when in the 12th class to be able to join the course soon after the 12th class results are announced.

Making a Beginning

Training in many of the institutions includes practical training in established fabrication units and export houses. If one is capable, there is a chance that one may be absorbed there. If one wants to set out on one's own, one can start a boutique or a small fabrication unit to supply the needs of schools. Those who do not have the resources to establish a boutique can join an established boutique as an assistant, and gain valuable experience. Many people have started by fabricating dresses for a small school, and gradually grown with the needs of the school. With experience people add on other institutions. Young people can even set out on their own specialising in particular kinds of clothes like shirts, trousers, *kurta/pajamas*, nightwear, etc.

Income from Dressmaking

At the lower levels incomes from this field are similar to those from other careers. However, those who have the ability to set out on their own and work hard, rise quickly to earn substantially. Many people start in a small way, but gradually expand in a very big way. People have amassed fortunes in this field.

Opportunities for Self-employment

Dressmaking is a skill. One can use this skill anywhere. There are enough opportunities for young people in this field to be self-employed. It is immaterial whether one is living in a small town, or in a big city. One needs to wear clothes. You can put your skills to use wherever you are.

Engineering and Technology

35

Careers in engineering and technology continue to fascinate young people. However, few understand that the field of engineering and technology is very vast. It leads to many lines of specialization.

As is obvious, the word "engineering" is derived from the word "engine", but engineering includes many lines as varied as mechanical engines and equipment, electronics, computers and even building roads and bridges.

Technology refers to the application of sciences for developing and controlling techniques of treatment or manufacture of industrial or consumer products. The scope of technology is as diverse as products like soaps, plastics, foodstuffs, ceramics, textiles, paper, leather, etc.

With development of greater skills and knowledge, specialization in engineering and technology continues to grow. New horizons are opening. Opportunities for further development are waiting to be exploited for the welfare of mankind. This, in turn, will mean more careers in engineering and technology for young people.

Desirable Personal Qualities

To be successful in this field, a person must:

- make precision a matter of habit. There is no place for approximation in this field.
- understand design and execution of plans. That is a part of careers in this field.
- be proficient in Physics, Chemistry and Maths with the ability to make neat drawings.
- understand shapes, figures and numbers. They are the backbone of this work.

- be able to visualise objects as three-dimensional units.
- have an understanding of mechanical contraptions. One will need to work with them every day.
- be willing to work with one's hands. Those who are shy of work never make progress.
- be willing to work in faraway places. Very often the work sites are at distant places.
- have the ability to cope with sudden emergencies. If things can go wrong, they will.
- be creative and have a good imagination. Great progress has come about because of these abilities.
- possess the ability to work as a team. Cooperation of other workers is as important as personally extending cooperation to them.

Prospects for Employment

In any developing economy, there is bound to be an increased demand for engineers and technologists to fill the positions in new industries. With the establishment of new polytechnics and technical colleges particularly in the private sector, the number of qualified personnel has also increased considerably. Unfortunately, the need has not grown at the same pace. The industrial growth has been slow because of lack of initiative amongst young people. Unsettled market conditions have also contributed to slow growth of industry. This has resulted in unemployment of qualified personnel. Many are tempted to migrate abroad in search of better openings.

With the demand for qualified personnel in several countries less developed than our own, many possibilities of technical collaboration have been successfully exploited. Many more can materialize. Rather than wait indefinitely for the right kind of jobs the unemployed young people have the option of becoming self-employed. They can take advantage of financial assistance available from several government and private agencies. Besides finding personal employment, this will also create opportunities for many more young people to be employed profitably.

Engineering Specialities

The word "engineer" refers to a person engaged in any one of the specialities in engineering. With growing knowledge and experience, specialization in various fields of engineering is growing. However, most of this specialization is at the post-graduation stage. At the undergraduate level, there are specific fields of study. While the syllabus is common for all students in the first half of the course, the students study subjects of their choice in the second half of their study in a college. Some of the more important engineering specialities are discussed in the following paragraphs.

Civil Engineering

Civil engineering refers to a wide field of engineering activities. It includes making of buildings, roads and bridges, the railways, irrigation barrages, dams and canals, water drainage and sewerage schemes, building docks and harbours, development of power projects and other similar works.

This is a growing field of engineering. Its basic purpose is to use the natural resources for the welfare of mankind. With growing pressure on natural resources because of the population explosion, there is always the scope for making improvements. As a civil engineer, one can specialize in public health engineering, docks and harbours engineering, railway engineering, and other similar lines through postgraduate diploma or degree courses.

Of all the fields of engineering, the greatest demand is that for civil engineers. They can find employment with the State and Central Public Works Departments, the Railways, in the Defence establishment, Municipal Boards, Irrigation Department, and other such employers. There is scope for employment of specialists in different fields of specialization.

Mechanical Engineering

Mechanical engineering pertains to designing, fabrication and maintenance of machines of all kinds. With mankind depending upon machines of varied descriptions to do a million different jobs, the mechanical engineer has a big role to play in everyday life. Their expertise is important in the home, the field, or the factory.

After a degree in mechanical engineering, one can pursue postgraduate studies in specialized fields like automobile engineering, aeronautical engineering, marine engineering, production management, air-conditioning, machine tools engineering, etc. For qualified engineers, there are good openings in public and private undertakings. One can also find profitable self-employment. Designing of simpler and better machinery will always hold innumerable opportunities for work. Those with some imagination and an inventive outlook can always try their skills in this lucrative field of employment.

Electrical Engineering

This branch of engineering refers to the study of the science and technology of electricity. It includes generation, transmission and utilization of electrical energy. It also pertains to various aspects of designing, manufacture, installation and maintenance of electronic equipment and devices.

Specialization can lead to the specific study of electronics, telecommunications, radar engineering, microwave engineering, power station instrumentation engineering, high voltage line transmission engineering, television and similar lines after graduation. Electrical engineers are in demand by the State Electricity Boards, Municipal Boards, Railways, the defence establishment, industrial undertakings, All India Radio and Doordarshan, Post and Telegraphs, overseas communications, etc. Self-employment opportunities are also open to creative young people who would like to go into business themselves.

Chemical Engineering

Chemical engineering is comparatively a new field in engineering. It aims at designing, construction and maintenance of plant and works where substances undergo a change of state and composition. A chemical engineer needs to understand chemistry and the basic sciences. He must also possess knowledge of mechanical, electrical and structural engineering to be able to design and construct new plants.

Specialization can lead to reaction engineering, chemical plant designing, process engineering and design, etc. Opportunities for employment exist in industries dealing in paints and dyes, varnishes, drugs, chemicals, plastics, soaps, petroleum, rubber, fertilizers, glass, etc. A capable chemical engineer can work as a consultant to several small units.

Metallurgical Engineering

This branch of engineering deals with various problems of smelting, refining and testing metals. There is a search for newer methods of extraction of metals. Young people who are qualified in this field of engineering can find employment in metal extraction industries and plants, in foundries and rolling mills, in fabrication workshops, in industries working with metals, in research laboratories, etc. One can specialize in the study of particular metals, and their extraction from the ores.

Mining Engineering

As the name implies, mining engineering refers to the exploration, extraction and processing of all kinds of ores and deposits for transmission to actual consumers or refining industries.

This field of engineering can lead to the specialization in mine safety engineering, coal mining, natural gas and petroleum production, drilling engineering, limestone and non-ferrous metal extraction, metal extraction, etc.

Mining engineers can find employment with the mining departments of the government. Many engineers are also self-employed, and extract minerals from leased mines. They also work as consultants to mine owners, and commercial firms working as contractors to extract minerals from mines.

Industrial Engineering

Industrial engineering is another new field of engineering. It aims at better utilization of men, material and machinery. An industrial engineer studies manufacturing techniques. He is responsible to plan work and time schedules to obtain maximum production. One can specialize in areas such as motion study, methods engineering, planning engineering, factory designing, etc. Industrial engineers are in demand by the larger concerns that wish to eliminate wastage, and increase production. A capable industrial engineer can find useful self-employment as a consultant to several small industries in the area.

Agricultural Engineering

With emphasis on better utilization of agricultural land and resources, agricultural engineering has emerged as a special field of engineering. It aims at applying engineering techniques to solving problems like water supply, rural electrification, irrigation and drainage, soil conservation, farm buildings, dairy science, implements and machinery, and other activities connected with agriculture.

Specialized courses are available at selected centres in India in subjects like farm machinery, soil and water conservation, crop process engineering, etc. Government departments that specialize employ agricultural engineers in related subjects. Private business concerns, which deal in agricultural inputs, also offer opportunities for employment.

Making a Beginning

Young people interested in a career in engineering can make a beginning in various positions depending upon their educational qualifications and personal capabilities. Whereas there are young people with poor academic achievements who have taken to engineering fields as apprentices and assistants to mechanics, and learned things the hard way, there are others who have first taken the necessary training, both theoretical and practical, and begun the career on a stronger foundation.

Those who aspire for the lower levels of employment in engineering fields can begin after obtaining a Certificate of Proficiency through training at an Industrial Training Institute, a Vocational Training Centre, or through a Secondary Technical course, after completing high school, higher secondary or 10+2 examination. Six months' work as an apprentice is essential after training. After this one can join one of the many trades like welders, fitters, carpenters, draughtsmen, lathe operators, mechanics, etc., depending upon the line of training received. Many engineering firms insist upon some in-plant training before giving independent responsibility. Those who do well can rise to become supervisors and junior engineers.

Those who aspire for higher positions must undergo advanced training in polytechnics and engineering colleges. After obtaining a degree in engineering, they can specialize in the line of their choice before seeking employment in a suitable position in a government or private undertaking.

There are a large number of Industrial Training Institutes, Vocational Training Centres, Polytechnics and Engineering colleges run by the State governments, and private or charitable organizations. These institutions offer a variety of courses at all levels for preparing young people for a career in engineering. Admission to these institutions is on merit. For admission to engineering colleges, and the Indian Institutes of Technology, competitive examinations are held at State and national level. This is followed by an interview. At lower levels, one can join after high school. However, the basic requirement to qualify for the competitive examination is 10+2.

Many polytechnics offering courses specifically for women have come up in the recent past. They offer diploma and degree courses of particular interest to women. Most of these courses require 2 to 3 years of study, followed by apprenticeship that may extend from 6 months to a year.

Engineering colleges, engineering departments of universities, and the Indian Institutes of Technology offer degree courses. For a complete list of institutions, please refer to the directories being published by publishers who specialise in books and magazines on careers. Admission to these colleges is through a common entrance examination. Please verify the dates for filing applications and dates for examinations. The details are published in national and regional newspapers.

Postgraduate courses are available in specific fields of study after graduation. Research degrees like the Ph.D., the D.Sc., etc., are awarded based on original research and work. Facilities for research are available at the Indian Institutes of Technology, the Council of Scientific and Industrial Research, and at several research laboratories and centres spread all over the country.

There are several institutions that conduct professional examinations, which make it possible for those who have obtained only the basic knowledge through a Certificate or Diploma, but having work experience, to qualify for higher positions in the career. The Union Public Service Commission and various State governments recognize these examinations as being equivalent to a university degree. One could qualify through part-time study in an institution, or even through a correspondence course offered by some schools. The details of the professional examinations can be obtained directly from the institutions concerned, or through those institutions that offer courses of study for appearing in these examinations. Some of the institutions that offer these examinations are:

The Institution of Engineers (India),
8, Gokhale Road, P.O. Box 669,
Kolkata-700020.

The Indian Institute of Chemical Engineers,
Raja Subodh Mullick Road,
Post Box No. 170001,
Kolkata-700 032.

The Institution of Mechanical Engineers (India),
Janmabhoomi Chambers,
29, Walchand Hirachand Marg,
Mumbai-400001.

The Aeronautical Society of India,
13/B, Indraprastha Estate,
New Delhi-110001.

The Institution of Surveyors,
Kashmir House, King George Avenue,
New Delhi.

The Institution of Automobile Engineers (India),
85, Mount Road, Teynampet,
Chennai-18.

The Institution of Tele-communication Engineers,
C-95, South Extension,
Part II, Ring Road,
New Delhi-110016.

The Institution of Electronics and Telecommunications,
P.O. Box 3040,
New Delhi-110003.

The Institute of Town Planners (India),
Institution of Engineers Building,
Mathura Road, New Delhi.

The Society of Engineers,
21/23, Messop Street,
London SW3 2LW,
England.

Skills For Progress (SKIP), 72, Brigade Road, Bangalore-25, is a service association of private Technical Training Centres in India, and publishes a directory giving the details of all centres which are affiliated to it. The details include the courses offered and the basic qualifications required for pursuing them. There are several unrecognized private institutions that provide practical training in some fields like radio and television. Many young people have benefited from the knowledge so gained. Those interested in rising to higher positions in their career can also enrich their knowledge through a variety of correspondence courses available in various fields. The details of such courses are advertised in the national press from time to time.

Careers in Technology

Several polytechnics and colleges in the country offer courses in technology. The admission to these institutions may be based on the marks obtained in the higher secondary examination, the intermediate or 10+2 examination, or through a competitive examination followed by an interview. Courses may vary from two to three years, depending upon the subject of study. Degree courses take three to five years, depending upon entrance requirements and the need for practical training. Some courses like Chemical Technology, Sugar Technology, etc., are for graduates with science subjects. Postgraduate studies in technology can be pursued for diploma or degree courses. While a diploma may be for just one year, the degree course will require two years.

After qualifying as a technologist, one is known by the subject of specialization, such as paper technologist, food technologist, jute technologist, glass technologist, leather technologist, etc. One can find employment in a suitable industry in the private or public sector. There are several industries where technologists are required. Depending upon individual capabilities there are many kinds of jobs available for various lines of specialization. Job opportunities are growing. There is good scope for self-employment also if the person has the necessary initiative, finance, and drive to operate an independent business.

Looking for a Job

Although careers in engineering and technology have become very competitive, job openings continue to be advertised in the national press. This has been possible because of growth in industry, and opening up of the world market. Great opportunities exist in the developing countries. For positions at the lower levels, one should register at an employment exchange, and a call will be sent as soon as there is an inquiry. Many young people have profitably contacted private employers directly, and found the kind of work they were in search of.

For senior positions in the government, engineers are recruited based on special selections or competitive examinations held by the Union and State Public Service Commissions from time to time. These openings are advertised in the national press. Through these tests one can enter services like the Indian Railway Service of Engineers, the Central Engineering Service (Buildings and Roads), the Central Engineering Service (Mechanical/Electrical), etc.

The defence services also recruit qualified engineers for regular and short-term commissions under technical graduate courses. After training, they are placed with Corps of Engineers, Corps of Signals, Corps of Electrical and Mechanical Engineers and Corps of Artillery in the army, and for the Mechanical, Marine and Electrical branches in the navy. There are openings in the navy for engineers who have degrees in naval architecture, civil, aeronautical, metallurgical and mechanical engineering. The Indian Air Force has need for graduates in electronics, telecommunications and electrical engineering.

Industrial undertakings in both the private and public sectors need a large number of engineers qualified in various fields of specialization. Many countries advertise for their requirements of engineering personnel. This has provided employment to many engineers. Foreign-trained engineers who have not found suitable positions can join the Scientists' Pool of the Council of Scientific and Industrial Research where they are assured of a nominal income until they find suitable employment.

Income from Engineering and Technology

Competition for jobs is very keen, but salaries are reasonable. Different States have adopted varying pay scales, but most of these are similar to those for other technical services. Provided a person is competent in his work, opportunities for gradual promotion are good.

The salaries offered by employers in the private sector are slightly higher at the lower levels of employment. At higher levels, the difference is very significant as senior engineers and technologists in the private sector are highly paid as compared to those in the public sector. Self-employed engineers have to be content with small incomes when they begin on their own. When one is capable and hardworking, the growth is fast. The income becomes attractive. Many engineers have established very profitable business concerns for themselves.

Opportunities for Self-employment

When the public and private sector is unable to absorb the large number of engineers and technologists produced each year, the only course open to many is to become self-employed. The number of such self-employed young people is on the increase. There are many opportunities for qualified young people in every field. If one were to take the initiative and be willing to put in hard work, self-employment offers better income as compared to working for an employer. Besides finding work for themselves, self-employed engineers and technologists create opportunities of employment for others also. Many government and financial institutions are offering liberal terms for industrial sheds, machinery, raw material and other needs. Interested young people can avail of them.

Many commercial concerns are also offering dealerships to unemployed engineers and technologists. This way, sales outlets for tractors, two wheelers, agricultural implements, pumps, etc. can be opened. There is scope for opening service points for different items. It is for young people to survey the requirements in their particular area, and use their skills accordingly to build a career for themselves in engineering and technology.

Entertainment

36

Once the basic needs of human beings—food, clothing and shelter are met, they turn their attention to other things. Suddenly they become aware of getting bored. There is nothing new about it. Even our predecessors felt bored. To rid one of boredom there is the need for entertainment.

Entertainment is a big industry. Over a period it has expanded to many fields. It has provided vocational opportunities to millions of people around the world. We are nowhere near the saturation point. Opportunities continue to grow. Mankind will continue to experience boredom. There will be individuals who will come out with newer ideas of entertainment, and find useful vocations in the process.

There is a lot of glamour attached to careers in this field. Wide scale publicity is a part of this industry to attract volumes. Besides, those who reach the top gain tremendous popularity and money. Many times what people see is not what an individual is in real life. The projected image is deceptive. Yet most people find it attractive. There is, therefore, a special attraction for careers in this industry.

Changing Trends of Entertainment

A very significant feature about careers in entertainment is that trends change periodically. Sometimes, they change fast affecting long-term investments in the industry. Those investing in this field need to be particularly careful about this fact.

At one time entertainment came by way of snake charmers, those that had trained animals like monkeys and bears, or were street performers doing magic shows, hypnotism or rope walking. Music and dancing has always been entertaining in its many forms.

Radio ushered entertainment to the homes. The broadcast services were limited and came at fixed times. People looked forward to special programmes. The gramophone was another addition in some homes. However, it depended upon records and had to be wound before each playing. At that time it appeared to be the ultimate, but better things were yet to come. The single playing record was replaced by long playing records, and then by a variety of tape recorders using cheap audiotapes. Today we have CDs and DVDs.

The development of cinema brought in tremendous changes in the last century. From black and white silent movies we moved to sound and then to colour. This was further developed into three-dimensional movies, cinemascope and the wide screen with special sound effects. For a long time cinema remained supreme, and people earned vast sums of money catering to one or the other need of the industry. Large sums of money were invested in infrastructure and films.

Television changed the scene. It brought entertainment to people's homes. It started with black and white sets, which were replaced by colour and supplemented with video-cassette recorders and players. The widespread use of tapes depended upon piracy of film rights, and the film industry suffered. The manufacturing, recording and renting of videotapes was good business for some years until the video-cassette recorder was replaced by the CD player and now the DVD player.

With personal computers becoming high tech and affordable, music and movies can now easily be played on them. With a wide range of computer games, the personal computer is now becoming the entertainment centre within the home. Internet has opened the world to everyone. The possibilities are endless.

With growth in television channels across the country, the source of programmes is no longer restricted. There are many channels broadcasting programmes not only of regional interest, but also those of national and international interest. To keep these channels running there is a widespread need for all kinds of programmes that are fit to be televised. Besides news and business programmes there is a great need for entertaining programmes that may include serials of different varieties, musical programmes, programmes for children, reporting on games, live programmes, etc.

Whereas TV programmes are prepared on large scale and people in smaller towns are involved more as spectators than as a part of the production process, there are other aspects of entertainment that affect people even in the smaller towns also. These include theatre groups, music groups and bands and musicians that cater to local functions like weddings and special parties. The larger restaurants and hotels too have need for singers and musicians. These have opened up opportunities for employment at the local level even in the smaller communities.

Desirable Personal Qualities

There are a variety of activities in the field of entertainment. It would be wrong to generalize one set of qualities that may be desirable for success in this field. Depending upon the kind of activity one is interested in, one needs to possess several qualities to succeed in a particular activity.

In general, those in the field of entertainment need to:

- have the quality of showmanship. A person in this field stands out in a crowd.
- be an extrovert. It is necessary to be friendly with people.
- understand what the audience wants. That ensures success.
- be able to create a rapport with the audience. That is the purpose of a show.
- be innovative and creative. People are attracted to novel ideas.
- be able to communicate well.
- have an ear for music. It helps to play a musical instrument.
- be able to work as a team. Without it success is not possible.

- be willing to work for long periods at odd hours.
- have skills to handle mike and music systems.

Opportunities in Careers in Entertainment

The field of entertainment is so vast that there are innumerable opportunities. Singing, music and performing arts are the basis of this vast area of activities. There are opportunities at the local, regional and national level. Some outstanding performers make it to the international level. In each field, opportunities exist for a variety of needs requiring different skills.

The making of a film is not the work of a single person. It begins with the producer who makes the film. There is the need for a variety of professionals who make the film possible. One sees the actors on the screen. There are many people who are not visible on the screen. Script writers, dialogue writers, musicians, lyricists and music directors, photographers, film processors, editors, directors and a whole lot of supporting staff and other people are not seen on the screen, but the work is not possible without them.

TV serials and programmes require a different treatment in that they have to be mass-produced as compared to a film. However, they too have their requirements of producers, writers, actors, musicians, singers, photographers, directors and technicians and supporting staff.

The field of music alone has requirements for a variety of professionals other than singers and musicians. It is a high tech field and each day there are marked developments. With video photography of musical presentations, there is the need for models, singers, locations and support staff other than photographers.

The need for recreation and entertainment has also increased the demand for stereo systems, tape recorders, cassette players, video players, compact disc systems, and televisions. The need for recorded music and films has created a huge demand for audio and videotapes and compact discs. These also need to be marketed through a network of retailers all over the country. All these present opportunities for careers in this field.

With the field of entertainment growing rapidly, opportunities too have grown in every sphere. Besides the requirement for people in films, serials and other productions, there is the need for singers and musicians in restaurants, hotels and at special functions like birthday parties, weddings and special meetings. There is also a need for puppeteers, magicians and those who have special skills to entertain people. As people get recognition at lower levels, they move to larger cities and metros, and into bigger avenues like TV and films.

Another line within the field of entertainment that is growing fast is that of parlours where a variety of video games are installed. Other lines of entertainment include private centres where billiard and snooker tables are installed, or there may be a bowling alley. A variety of games and rides too provide opportunities in the field of entertainment.

A circus is attractive to both the young and the old. There are now restrictions on keeping wild animals in captivity, but there are still many lines that make a visit to a circus worthwhile.

Educational Facilities

Earlier, most young people started as amateurs singing and entertaining at school and college level, and gradually moved to professional assignments where they searched both recognition and some financial gain. However, the present trend is professional in that young people like to learn the basic skills at recognised schools and institutions. There are short-term and full-fledged courses available in a variety of areas in this field of activity. A good educational foundation helps in finding work, and ensures growth with experience.

Those interested in technical fields like recording music, editing and processing films, reproducing audio and video tapes, CDs or VCDs and DVDs need specialised knowledge in using high tech equipment. They will need to be trained at institutional level, or be trained on-the-job.

Making a Beginning

Most young people begin in a small way in this field of activity. Initially they are attracted to this field because of the recognition they might have received at school and college level, and gradually at local social functions. Many young people get together to form theatre groups, music groups and even work independently in cooperation with one or two persons. Those who can afford the cost of the equipment hire assistants and become disc jockeys. The field is glamorous in that many young people find it attractive. However, success requires personal ability. Those who are efficient rise steadily. Sudden rise is more imaginary than real. Success can always be traced back to persistent hard work.

Income from Careers in Entertainment

This is a very competitive field. With a lot of glamour attached, there is a great rush of young people who wish to enter this field. Unless one is talented and specifically qualified for specialised positions, the income at entry levels is low and erratic. A lot of hard work is involved. Only after an individual is able to prove one's ability does one rise in this field. Those who reach the top earn very well.

Opportunities for Self-employment

Self-employment in this field is limited to those who give individual performances of their field of specialization. Most people work in a group and then find self-employment. Many people in this field are free lancers in that they have a full-time work, and are also involved in the entertainment business part-time whenever a need arises.

Event Management

37

Although the history of event management can be traced back to more than hundred years, as a full-fledged career in India it is comparatively new. Earlier the ad agencies were providing the service to a limited degree. It has now emerged as a line of specialization. Many young people have found good careers in this field. Many more are regularly attracted because of the excitement of organizing big events and meeting important people from all walks of life.

Desirable Personal Qualities

To be successful in this field, a person must:

- understand the requirements of the client. Every client is bound to have very specific needs.
- have the vision and creativity to translate the expectations of the client into reality. That is what event management aims at.
- have a pleasing personality and enjoy good public relations. This helps build good clientele.
- be resourceful. Many needs of the client will require a person to be resourceful to cope with them.
- be committed to the work at hand. One cannot succeed without commitment.
- be able to work in a team. One needs the cooperation of everyone in the team.
- know how to deal with difficult situations. When things can go wrong, they will. The ability to cope with them is very important.
- have the stamina to work untiringly for long periods. The execution phase of the work can require a lot of stamina and hard work.

- be willing to travel and stay away from home for long periods. Most of the events may be far away from one's hometown.

Opportunities in Event Management

Event management involves planning and executing an event with a specific purpose for a client. When companies have a message to convey to its dealers or clients, and the stakes are high, they cannot take chances to have the message lost somewhere on its way. To ensure that the message reaches where it needs to go, the solution lies in passing on the responsibility to a firm of event managers who look to every aspect in detail. This may include creative planning, invitations and printing, arrangements for hotels, catering, entertainment, gifts and other such details.

Weddings in rich families, or those who come from abroad, have also come within the scope of event management. Every aspect of the wedding like fixing a venue, issuing invitations, decoration, seating, catering, arranging for special music, photography and even arranging for the religious ceremonies has become a part of event management. It is a growing field and with time newer activities will come within its fold. It is up to enterprising young people to seek avenues where they can help organize functions better. People who can afford it prefer to pass their responsibilities to a professional for a fee.

Educational Facilities

This field of careers is new. Most of the people who have entered this field have come from advertising. The knowledge required is varied. Specialized institutions imparting training in this field have yet to emerge. A bachelor's degree from a good college is useful as a foundation. For newcomers the training is necessarily on the job. Those who are creative and have a sharp mind learn the work quickly. Commitment and hard work are essential for success. A good all-round knowledge of people and things is a great asset. One must know how to maintain one's cool during a crisis.

Making a Beginning

One will necessarily need to begin in this field as a trainee. The work begins with a client conveying what he wants. It is then conceptualised and execution planned in detail. The work can require a variety of skills. If one has the ability to learn quickly and convince the superiors of one's commitment and reliability one can grow quickly.

One needs to be a stickler for good manners and etiquette as one meets a lot of important people as a part of work in this field. At time of need one must be willing and ready to do any kind of work. At the final stage of execution one may need to work very long hours without rest.

Income from Event Management

Income from careers in event management at the lower level is similar to those for trainees in any field. Those who are talented and hardworking rise quickly to a five-figure salary. At the top level the going is very good for the people who manage the company.

Opportunities for Self-employment

The concept of event management depends upon good teamwork. Therefore, the opportunities for self-employment are limited only to those who want to start a company with hired help. It would be worthwhile to experiment on smaller scales in the smaller cities of the country.

Fashion and Design

38

One field of careers that has grown significantly in the immediate past is that of Fashion and Design. The words conjure an image of immaculately dressed men and women. Earlier, it was the outstanding tailoring establishments that took the credit for creating fine clothes. Presently, we need to differentiate between those who fashion and design clothes, or do the tailoring job. Mass production of clothes is yet another line of specialization.

This field of service had been serving the rich and the fashionable in the developed Western world for a long time. Now we have it in India with people designing exclusive clothes for a variety of occasions. These are sold at exclusive boutiques. Some of the people who entered the field earlier have etched a name for them in this field. They have a clientele of the rich and discerning people, who want the best. Some names are as good as brands.

The successful fashion designers have not only succeeded in developing a good clientele within the country, but have also ventured to developed countries to woo the rich Indians and the locals alike with the latest fashions from India. The desire to look smart and immaculate has no end. It will continue to provide opportunities for vocations in this exclusive field.

Desirable Personal Qualities

To be successful in this field a person must:

- have a good imagination and be creative. Creativity is the basis of the careers in this field.
- be aware of the world scenario in this field. We are literally living in a global village.

- be able to look ahead at the changing trends and foresee what is to come.
- have an aesthetic sense of matching clothes to personalities. The design must enhance the individual's personality.
- have a good sense of mixing colours and designs.
- be able to work as a team. Many times several people together create a special dress.
- appreciate the need to work to strict time schedules. There is no scope for delays.

Opportunities in Fashion and Design

The need for clothes is a basic human need. Over a period this need has transformed to the need to look smart, beautiful and attractive. To fulfil this need people dress in keeping with their personal spending ability.

India has a vast population with a variety of traditional dresses. Whereas a *sari* is a typical Indian dress, so is *salwar-kameez*. However, with the use of a variety of fabrics and regional variations in the way they are worn, together they present many forms. The traditional *ghagra-choli* also has its variations. The clothes and designs that emerge from the rural and tribal sections of the population present an equally interesting range of clothes and jewellery.

With greater Western influence in thought and work, the everyday dress too has seen Western influences and changes. A combination of traditional Indian designs and Western way of dress has also presented a variety of possibilities to the fashion designer.

India has a vast leather industry spread all over the country. Footwear designs vary from one region to another. So do other accessories like belts and bags. As a combination with clothes, these too offer infinite challenges to creative designers looking forward to create exclusive designs.

Those who can afford to pay talk of wearing particular 'brands' of clothes. Ladies talk of buying their clothes from particular boutiques. Some boast of getting their dresses designed by top names in the field.

The field of fashion and design is not restricted to clothes alone. There is a vast field of accessories that includes a variety of bags, belts and footwear. The field of jewellery is equally important. It is a specialised field and discussed separately in the chapter on Gemology.

Looking at the vast variety of designs and clothes existing in various parts of the country, the field of fashion and design offers great opportunities to young people who have a flair for good clothes and elegant designs.

Educational Facilities

This field of vocations is so large that it offers a great potential. To utilize this potential a large number of institutions that offer courses in Fashion and Design have emerged in almost all cities. However, National Institute of Fashion Technology with its six branches in Kolkata, Mumbai, Chennai, Bangalore, Hyderabad and one in Gujarat is the premier institute. Several other institutions of repute sponsored by leading export houses have also come up.

These institutions offer courses both at the Bachelor and Master's levels. Short-term diploma courses on a variety of areas are also offered. One can join after 10+2. Admission is on the basis of a written test, followed by a test for creative ability, group discussion and an interview. The basis of these tests is to select the most talented candidates.

Making a Beginning

Those who are inclined towards careers in this field can begin training after 10+2. Since admission is on the basis of competitive tests, not everyone can get into the leading institutions. In that event it would still be preferable to join a lesser important institute and receive professional training than to join another field where one does not hold interest. Graduation courses are better than diploma courses. Personal effort and creativity will eventually distinguish those who achieve success in this field of work.

After qualifying from a training institute one can join as an assistant in an established boutique or manufacturing unit, or set out on one's own by opening a personal boutique. Through experience one learns about what the public in a particular town demands. Many times two young people join to set out together. Whereas both could be involved with the creative work, one can follow up production, and the other can look after the sales. Many young people have made it big in a small time.

Income from Fashion and Design

Those who take up a job as an assistant will necessarily need to start at the lowest level. However, if one is creative one can grow quickly. In one's own business one may have to work with lower margins initially, but gradually people earn very well. Many of the leading names today started in a very small way, but grew really big. Good clothes are a regular need. One can expect steady work over the years.

Opportunities for Self-employment

Careers in this field offer ample opportunities for self-employment. One can set out on one's own soon after completing the necessary training, or work for some time with an established party for some time, gain useful experience, and then set out independently.

Films and Serials Making

39

Films are way ahead of other forms of entertainment because they combine and present the best of arts. They provide quality entertainment at a price that most people can afford. Making a film is a complicated procedure requiring the efforts of hundreds of people who are not seen on the screen. It also involves large sums of money for both making and exhibiting it.

India has the largest film industry in the world. It provides a variety of jobs to a very large number of people. Besides the size and the impact of the industry, a lot of glamour is attached to this field of vocations. It is because of this glamour that many young people are attracted towards careers in this field. However, they must understand that this glamour is superficial. The limelight falls only on a limited few. The rest struggle just like those in other vocations.

The expansion in television has opened new opportunities for employment of more people in the ever-growing field of entertainment. There are dozens of channels making presentations on the television. All these channels need serials, films and a variety of other programmes. All kinds of activities, educative and entertaining, have been brought into the average home through television programmes. All these mean additional opportunities for work for young people.

Making of a Film or TV Serial

Making of a film or a TV serial is not a simple thing that can be done by an individual. It requires a combined effort of a large number of people. Each of them possesses special abilities, and is trained for these activities.

The work starts with a producer who conceptualizes the

film or serial. He is responsible for financing and carrying through the project. The film or serial is based upon a story written by a writer. The story is converted to a script and the dialogues are written. Writing professionals do this work.

The director is responsible for converting the script into a film or serial. For this there will be the need for actors, musicians, photographers supported by lighting staff, choreographers, stunt-men who double for actors, film processors and editors who give the final shape. All these people need to be supported by many more that prepare the sets, help the actors with make up and provide a variety of facilities to look after the whole unit. When the film is ready it is sold for exhibition to distributors who deal with cinema hall owners.

The serials for television require different treatment in that they are bulk produced. Their production is not as expensive as films. But the following of a tight time schedule is very important.

Desirable Personal Qualities

Since making of films and TV serials is a team effort rather than an individual effort, the different members of the team will require a variety of abilities. The abilities of one may not match with the other. The director coordinates the working of the team, and together they produce the finished product.

To be a successful actor a person must:

- have a love for films, TV and theatre. It provides good motivation.
- possess self-confidence, a good memory and personal charm.
- have the ability to express emotions convincingly. Without it one cannot influence the audience.
- have a good command over the language. Without it one cannot deliver the dialogues convincingly.
- possess some musical ability. Part of it is inborn. Partly it is developed.
- have an aesthetic sense. Crudity can be repelling.

- have a sense of showmanship. The best of artists fail without showmanship.
- understand the role well. This will require one to be adaptable and versatile. Making adjustments is important.
- be willing to train and improve continuously. There is no end to learning. Be prepared to learn everyday.
- have the ability to work in a team. One cannot succeed without cooperation from others.
- be ready to work continuously for long hours. Continuous practice is important.
- be willing to travel and stay away from home. One will need to travel to different sites for filming.

Opportunities in Films and TV Serials

With India boasting of having the world's largest film industry opportunities for work will continue to emerge in this field. There are two aspects of this industry. The first is the people you see on the screen as actors, anchors, newsreaders and sometimes the news reporters. The second is the people who work to make the films and TV serials possible through a variety of production activities. While we see the first group on the screen, and a lot of glamour is attached to their role, the second group does all of the production work, but no glamour is attached to their work. Whereas most young people are attracted to the glamorous opportunities to be visible on the screen, the real opportunities exist in roles off the screen.

There has always been a need for good writers, lyricists, choreographers, photographers, editors and a whole lot of support staff both in films and in the field of TV serials and programmes. With the great variety of channels, there is a need for programmes on almost all subjects that you can think of. The work is not restricted to field of entertainment only. There is need for programmes on business, religion, better living, general knowledge, sports, nature and whatever you can think of.

The need to keep updated about everyday happenings has

helped promote several news channels that operate around the clock. This has required the channels to build a network of news reporters around the country, offering many opportunities in this field.

The films and TV serials in India are not restricted only to the Hindi-speaking public. There are several channels that serve different areas through the regional languages. Even the film industry is not restricted to Hindi films. Films are being produced in almost all the regional languages spoken in the country. This has broadened the opportunities for vocations in this field.

Educational Facilities

With the variety of abilities required to make films or TV serials, people specialise in different fields acquiring knowledge from an appropriate institution. Writers go to schools that teach journalism, musicians go to music schools and photographers to schools where they teach photography. The technical aspects are taught in specialized schools too.

Courses in film acting, photography, direction, editing, etc. are available for those interested in such careers. The details of the courses can be had directly from:

The Film & Television Institute of India,
Pune. (Maharashtra)

Several private institutions are also providing instruction in different fields of this work. They advertise in the national press. One can get in touch with them to obtain details of courses offered.

Making a Beginning

As in all other careers one needs to begin at the lowest level. If one is selected to play a lead role, one must consider it good fortune. However, this is only an opening. The ultimate success will depend upon repeated offers for good roles. Real success comes from knowing one's work and putting in one's best efforts. One cannot overlook that people who enjoy the limelight today had their days of struggle and hard work. Very few saw them at that.

The field of acting is uncertain in that it depends upon various factors. Besides personal ability, the role, the audience and the time of release of the film are important. Very often the careers depend upon the unpredictable audiences who may accept or reject one for reasons that are difficult to understand. Many actors get stereotyped for particular roles. A few are acclaimed and get repeated offers. Most continue as mediocre actors. A lot let go after some frustration.

In the technical field one begins as an assistant to a person already working in that sphere of work. One has to prove one's competence before being accepted as efficient. Progress comes slowly. However, once a person is accepted as reliable for a particular assignment one can look forward to a gradual permanence in that sphere of work.

Income from Films and TV Serials

Careers in films can be very uncertain. Some young people suddenly skyrocket to fame and prosperity because of their personal capabilities and the right opening. However, a large number have worked all their lives earning just enough to make ends meet. They have grown only with time, effort and experience.

Just as with other careers people have realized the importance of appropriate training. This has added more certainty to this field of careers. Courses on various aspects of film-making are available. Training has provided a certain amount of professionalism and permanence. As a trained person one can look forward to a reasonable income.

Opportunities for Self-employment

Since making of films and TV serials is basically a team effort, the best opportunity of self-employment can be as an entrepreneur where one sets out on one's own to make them. However, the investment is so high that newcomers cannot think about it. Those who provide services as contract workers like actors, lyricists, singers, musicians, photographers and others can be said to be self-employed in that they can provide their services to several producers at the same time.

Fitness and Beauty Business 40

Everyone wants to be fit and look beautiful and charming. These needs have opened up a variety of opportunities for useful vocations for young people. It is not that these needs did not exist earlier. Perhaps they are as old as mankind itself However, the far-reaching electronic media has made people more conscious of these needs than ever before. The advertising world has further brought them to the forefront.

This field of vocations is steadily growing. Fitness and beauty is good business. Many gymnasiums are being established. One hears of people joining health clubs. Many are visiting slimming clinics. People are getting conscious of what they eat. Yoga is getting popular not only on the TV, but also in the homes. Nature cure clinics are being widely advertised. Many are visiting them. It has become fashionable to visit spas and saunas. Beauty clinics for both men and women are popular. Massage parlours are advertised in the national dailies. The important thing is that all these activities are providing careers to a lot of people.

Desirable Personal Qualities

To be successful in this field a person must:

- be well acquainted with the particular line of specialization.
- exemplify what one is trying to achieve. Those who operate a gymnasium must have physiques that justify the work.
- not exceed the call of responsibility. These fields are related to but should not replace medical treatment.
- have good manners and etiquette. These will be appreciated.

- be ethical in dealings with individuals. No false claims must be made.
- be willing to work as a team. Many responsibilities require it.

Opportunities in Fitness and Beauty Business

The opportunities in this field are gradually growing, as people are becoming more conscious of the need of remaining fit and looking beautiful. The desire to be strong and healthy through regular exercise has encouraged many young people to establish gymnasiums. People have hired premises, purchased the necessary equipment that is now freely available within the country and established gymnasiums. Both men and women are using these facilities.

Health clubs have additional facilities besides the exercising equipment. These are bigger premises with facilities like saunas. There may be sections for those interested in slimming. Aerobic exercises may be a regular feature. Health foods may be also available.

Nature cure clinics are a speciality in that many provide both outdoor and residential services. The persons operating these clinics must appreciate the limits of each system of treatment. It will also be necessary to be aware of the past medical history of the individual.

Yoga is receiving attention of a very large number of people not only because of the camps being organized by specialists in different towns, but also because of the wide publicity given to it on the TV. Yoga as a system has its strengths, but like other systems has its limitations too. It is best when used to learn good breathing and exercise techniques that can be followed daily at home as a means of being fit.

Too many people are over-weight and becoming conscious of the fact. Many decide to slim down because they realize that obesity takes away one's charm. Some do it at the recommendation of a doctor. Many of these people who want to slim down find their way to slimming clinics that are becoming big business. The control of diet is important, but exercise is equally important. Since many people are too lazy to exercise, these clinics use special equipment that helps do away with fat in certain parts of the body. The investment on equipment is high. So are the charges for the treatment. Some dieticians are also attached to these clinics, particularly in the larger cities.

Many star hotels and resorts have health clubs with a spa or Jacuzzi and sauna baths. Besides the fitness equipment they also have massage parlours.

One comes across beauty parlours of all descriptions for both men and women. Most of them offer the facilities for hairdressing, dyeing, manicure, pedicure, waxing, etc. In the larger cities some of these have gone hi-tech where they offer facilities for hair removal by electrolysis treatment, acne treatment, hair weaving treatment, hair straightening treatment and a whole lot of other things for which the charges are high.

Full-time make-up artists are employed by the film and TV industry. Many are offering services for advertising agencies or for bridal make-up at marriages. The application of *mehndi* is a specialized line. It is now a big thing at weddings and during some traditional festivals.

With a trend towards herbal cosmetics, India being the home of Ayurveda, many people have taken to manufacturing herbal cosmetics of all kinds. One can appreciate that even in the field of fitness and beauty business there is enough opportunity for selecting a line from amongst the many that are available.

Educational Facilities

Educational facilities are available for specialized training in physical training and for beauticians. People learn yoga from teachers at school or elsewhere. The use of hi-tech equipment requires special skills. One may need to take special training to use this equipment. In some cases specialized medical care of dermatologists may be necessary. For slimming clinics it may be necessary to avail of the services of trained dieticians. To be able to manufacture cosmetics one will need to obtain a degree in Pharmacy.

Making a Beginning

Most people make a beginning in a small way. They may serve as an assistant to provide some service in this field of careers. Those who have received specialized training can take up an appropriate position right away. Only after a person has gained some experience on the job should become an entrepreneur and open a fitness club or beauty clinic.

Income from Fitness and Beauty Business

The beginning in this work may be rather small. One may earn just like an average craftsman. But once established one can expect a good steady income gradually increasing with time. The larger beauty clinics are offering franchise arrangements and working like a company. Some people have made great progress with herbal cosmetics that are exported abroad. Yoga is another field that has attracted people from all over the world.

Opportunities for Self-employment

At every level there are many opportunities for self-employment in this field of vocations. At higher levels when big centres or clinics are established, people take up jobs as assistants. With some experience they set out to become self-employed.

Forensic Science

41

Forensic science refers to the use of scientific methods in the investigation of crime. When medical knowledge is used for such a purpose it is referred to as Forensic Medicine. An allied subject, Criminology, refers to the scientific study of crime and criminals.

Forensic Science involves the study of several subjects like chemistry, physics, botany, zoology and medicine. It also involves the study of the human body. The use of fingerprints is an old use, but it has now been greatly refined with the use of computers. Blood analysis, dentistry, fingerprinting and analysis of the voice and speech are also a part of this field of careers.

A variety of chemicals are used for criminal purposes. Therefore, the study of drugs and poisons through chromatography is important. Similarly, the study of ballistics, or the use of bullets, also forms a part of Forensic study. Since valuable documents are important in criminal cases the detailed study of documents is yet another aspect of this work. The latest addition has been the use of the DNA test to identify genetic factors or the electroencephalogram (EEG) to study brain reactions.

As can be understood from the kind of work involved, careers in Forensic Science mean working in a sophisticated forensic laboratory to trace out valuable clues to ensure that a criminal is tracked and punished.

Desirable Personal Qualities

To be successful in this field a person must:

- be well acquainted with the field of specialization.
- have an analytical outlook. It is necessary to analyse every aspect of the problem.

- have a good imagination. The person must be able to visualize the situation as it might have existed.
- have a good all-round general knowledge.
- be willing to work at odd times. It may be necessary to work beyond working hours.
- be computer literate. Computers have changed the way things work.

Opportunities in Forensic Science

Forensic Science is a growing field of opportunities for careers. With increased population and crime, there is greater pressure on the police and the investigation agencies. At the same time there is greater pressure on the existing forensic laboratories.

The Directorate of Forensic Science, Union Ministry of Home Affairs, oversees the work in this field. Presently there are three Central Forensic Laboratories, three Government Examiners of Questioned Document Laboratories and nine State Forensic Science Laboratories.

To ease this situation, the government has planned to invest more money to modernize the police services. This would include the availability of forensic facilities throughout the country. There are approximately 700 districts in the country. It is proposed that there will be about 3000 mobile forensic labs, one in each sub-division of every district. Each lab would have a forensic scientist, a criminologist and assistants. This way the forensic facilities will be available close by.

It is also proposed that the existing forensic labs will also expand their services, creating opportunities to induct more people into the work.

Private investigation agencies also require forensic scientists to help them in their investigative work. There is a great variety of investigative work being conducted by these agencies. Many handwriting experts are self-employed. Banks too have a need for experts to study documents, signatures, forgeries, etc. Experts also verify counterfeit currency.

Private laboratories that conduct analysis work also need experts from this field. With analysis becoming hi-tech with

DNA tests and EEGs of suspected people there is greater involvement of medical specialists. If criminals are becoming careful, so are the investigating agencies. With better analytical work new opportunities are emerging for vocations in this field.

Educational Facilities

Forensic Science and Criminology require proficiency in several fields. Although a few colleges offer subjects at the graduation level, most of the colleges offer a Master's degree in Forensic Science and Criminology. Some institutions offer short-term diploma courses. In Forensic Science one may specialize in fields like Examination of Documents, Ballistics or Toxicology. In Criminology there may be further specialization in fields like Human Rights, Rehabilitation of criminals, Crime Investigation, or Environmental Crime. Medical analysis will require specialization in that field.

Making a Beginning

Those who have the necessary proficiency through specialization can join as scientific assistants. The Union Public Service Commission advertises jobs. One can also join through the State Public Service Commissions.

Private employers hire employees directly from the campus or through advertisements. Private investigation work has become a big business with many employers desirous of checking on their employees, or individuals verifying the fidelity or activities of others. For more details please refer to the chapter on Investigation Services.

Those who desire to work on their own as handwriting or document specialists may first join an established individual for some time. After gaining some experience one can set out as a self-employed professional. Banks require personnel to study documents, signatures and forgeries. The study of counterfeit currency too offers opportunities in this field.

Many science graduates join a laboratory as assistants. Later they study further and progress to higher positions. Analytical skills are very important in this field of work.

Income from Forensic Science

At lower levels the salaries are at par with those joining similar vocations. When one joins as a gazetted officer the salaries are according to government scales. Capable individuals with good analytical skills rise well in private labs.

Opportunities for Self-employment

By the very nature of the work it is necessary to work as a team. Under such circumstances it becomes difficult to become self-employed. However, there are many that are self-employed in the field of examination of documents or verifying signatures and forgeries. Many enterprising people have started their own firms in these fields of investigation.

Forestry

42

India has a vast forest wealth spread in different parts of the country. An intelligent exploitation of this wealth offers many useful vocations. In the past, there was emphasis only on the exploitation of this wealth. Presently, there is an equal amount of stress on the simultaneous development of this wealth. This is very important because if we do not do it, we would soon deplete the country of this very important wealth. Considering the importance of trees and forests in controlling weather and the environment, the planting of trees is attracting special attention.

Forests are being replanted. Simultaneously, special belts of trees on roadsides and in barren areas are being developed. To provide greater employment opportunities, new industries dependent upon the forest wealth are also being developed. There is a good future for those interested in this field of work. A variety of careers in forestry are available. A person can choose one that suits best.

Desirable Personal Qualities

To be successful in this field, a person must:

- have a special love for nature and the great outdoors. One will need to spend a lot of time outdoors.
- enjoy a good health and physique. These are important for outdoor physical work and movement.
- have a good knowledge of the subject of specialization. Within the field there are several branches of work.
- appreciate the need to work as a team. It is important to seek the cooperation of others.
- not be sensitive about living alone in the wilderness. It can be very lonely sometimes.

- be willing to stay away from the family. It may not be possible to have the family if one were living in the forest.
- be adaptable to varying conditions. Life can be uncertain in the wilderness.

Opportunities in Forestry

There are opportunities in forestry at all levels of the career. At the lower levels, there are nursery planters, forest guards, supervisors, timber markers and estimators. The overall in-charge at the forest range level is the Forest Ranger, or Range Officer. At the divisional level, there is the Divisional Forest Officer, or the Assistant Conservator of Forests. Much of the work like felling of trees, sawing them into timber, and transporting them from the site to the timber sale depot is done by contractors through labour working on piece-work basis. In some States, the governments have eliminated the contractors. They are doing some of the work departmentally.

Forestry holds many opportunities for allied businesses like obtaining crude turpentine and resins, operating saw mills, making plywood and paper, etc. In the hill areas, floating it in streams and rivers moves much of the timber. In the plains, its movement provides a lot of work to truck operators. With greater development of the forest resources, and better utilization of all portions of trees, newer opportunities are opening for careers in this field.

Educational Facilities

Specialized training in forestry and allied subjects is provided by the following institutions in India:

1. Forest Research Institute, Dehradun.
2. Indian Forest College, Dehradun.
3. Northern Forest Rangers' College, Dehradun.
4. Southern Forest Rangers' College, Coimbatore.

Making a Beginning

The lower positions in the forest departments are filled through selection at the divisional level. The recruits learn their work through some preliminary training and working with those already in the line.

The State Public Service Commissions, the Subordinate Services' Selection Board, or the Chief Conservator of Forests of the state selects the candidates for the post of Forest Rangers. To qualify for selection one must be 18 to 24 years old, be physically fit, and must have graduated with subjects like Botany, Zoology, etc. After selection, the candidates receive training for two years at the Northern Forest Rangers' College, Dehradun, or the Southern Forest Rangers' College, Coimbatore.

Foresters are selected from amongst young men, who have passed high school, and are 18 to 24 years old. The Chief Conservator of Forests makes the selection based on a written test and an interview. The selected candidates receive one year's training at the Forest Training School. They help a Range Officer in his duties.

For senior positions, the Union Public Service Commission conducts the Indian Forest Service examination once a year. To qualify, one must be 20 to 26 years old, and should have graduated with subjects like Botany, Zoology, Chemistry, Geology, etc., or should have graduated in Agriculture, or hold any equivalent qualification. Those who qualify in the written test are called for the personality test.

The State Public Service Commissions also conduct examinations for senior positions in forestry. Successful candidates receive two years training at the Indian Forest College, Forest Research Institute, Dehradun. On completing their training, they are attached to the office of a Divisional Forest Officer. Gradually they rise to high positions in the Department of Forestry.

Those interested in taking up careers as forest contractors, timber merchants, timber brokers, etc., learn the trade by joining those who are already established in the line. There are several industries connected with forestry. Those who live near forest belts can establish an industry for which sufficient raw material is available nearby.

Income from Forestry

The salaries for jobs in the Departments of Forestry are at par with those in other government departments. In the Indian Forestry Service, one begins the career as a Class I gazetted officer. Income from self-employed business ventures as forest contractors vary greatly from year to year, but are good. Many a person has earned a fortune from these careers.

Opportunities for Self-employment

The only opportunities that exist for self-employment in this field of work are connected with extraction of forest produce. Interested young men can become forest contractors depending upon local requirements. Many young people have successfully established industries dependent upon timber and other produce near the forest belts.

Franchising

43

As a measure to add value to their product or service, businessmen go to great lengths to develop a 'brand' name. Earlier, a customer wanted to know who had manufactured a particular product, or was offering a service. A reputed manufacturer would have an edge over others. Now people look for the 'brand'. It does not matter whether it is soap, a shampoo or a particular 'brand' of shirt or trousers. It may even be a service like a coaching centre, the 'brand' name is important. It is the name that sells.

Just as it is important to have a 'brand' name that inspires confidence to buy, it is equally important to have volumes to offer competitive prices and get good profits. Besides, the larger the coverage of a product or service, the better its visibility. This adds to the value of the brand. Since it is not practical for any business to have operations to provide products and services over a large area, a convenient way to achieve this aim is to establish franchise centres.

A franchise is a licence or permission granted by a company to a person or group allowing them to use the company name to sell the company's products or services under a definite agreement. The terms and conditions of different companies vary in that some may charge a premium. Others may not. They may want to keep a certain amount as security with or without interest. However, all companies require that the franchisee will provide the infrastructure by way of premises furnished to a common design and colour as approved by the company, and exclusively sell their products and services. The franchisee gets a definite commission on the sales.

Desirable Personal Qualities

To be successful in this field a person must:

- choose the correct products and services to offer in a community. Getting enough business is important.
- be very clear about the company's requirements. Most companies have lengthy agreements that tilt towards the company's interests.
- preferably have one's own premises for the franchise centre.
- be clear on the support services offered by the company. If these are not available, one can lose on one's profit.
- personally establish and operate the centre to ensure the quality of service.

Opportunities in Franchising

A variety of opportunities to open franchise centres exist in almost every town and city. Through these one can offer products and services that would be most suitable in the place where one desires to establish a centre.

It is interesting to note the variety of products and services that are being offered. Amongst eatables, beverages and ice cream are leaders. The franchisees ensure that local hoardings, boards, bottle coolers and ice cream freezers conform to a common pattern. In the larger towns there is opportunity to open franchise centres for fast foods like burgers, pizzas, etc. Ice cream parlours too offer opportunities for new franchise centres.

There are a variety of branded T-shirts, shirts, jeans, trousers and other kinds of apparel for which companies desire that exclusive stores be opened. However, since many of these are priced high and interest only a limited number, an exclusive store may not be able to generate enough business. In such cases the companies have agreed upon exclusive counters in large stores where their products are displayed and sold.

Every town and city has its educational requirements. This has attracted the attention of many coaching centres and those providing vocational training. Young people who have the necessary infrastructure by way of premises can open franchise centres for a variety of courses. Information Technology spread at a very fast rate because of these centres.

Many young people who could repair motor cycles, scooters and cars have after some training opened exclusive repair centres for particular brands of bikes, scooters and cars. The repair and maintenance of particular brands of electronic equipment too offer opportunities for opening centres where specialized services can be provided.

Fitness centres, slimming clinics and pathological labs have also opened franchise centres where complete or limited facilities are available. Gift shops, courier services and a variety of marketing services are offered for particular towns or localities. An individual needs to study the possibilities in one's area and then work out a franchise agreement with a company.

Educational Facilities

There is no specialized formal training that would suit all those interested in opening a franchise centre. Depending upon the kind of work a person is interested in one must be proficient in the particular field of one's choice. When technical services are provided in a franchise centre, the company provides the necessary technical training at its own centre. The franchisee may have to pay the necessary charges. It may also be necessary to take refresher courses periodically.

Making a Beginning

Opening a franchise centre is a business preposition. If one is interested in a particular field or the work of a company it would be advisable to visit the stores or centres already in operation at different places. One should observe how the centre is being operated. Without expressing one's interest one can talk to the employees and the customers. One should then evaluate the products or services on the basis discussed earlier. When one sees an opportunity for that work in one's own locality or town one can write to the company expressing the desire to open such a centre. The details must be thrashed out. If there are certain clauses in the franchise agreement that need clarification, these must be discussed in detail. If necessary, clarifications can be sought in writing. Once the arrangement is finalised, one can go ahead and establish the centre.

Income from Franchising

Most franchise arrangements are on commission basis. It is not possible to assess how the arrangement will work out. However, one must evaluate the products and services meticulously. One can also meet the prospective customers without giving the details. A franchise centre is a business preposition. The initial period of establishment is bound to go through the usual teething problems that all business activities face. Only with time one settles down to smooth working and a steady income from a business arrangement.

Opportunities for Self-employment

Establishing a franchise centre is a step towards self-employment where one finds a useful vocation and an avenue to invest one's money. It helps generate work for a lot of other people that work in the centre.

Games and Sports

44

Games and Sports are activities that attract a lot of young people initially. Their interest is short-lived. Because of frustration they move to other fields. Unfortunately, this has been one of the most ignored fields in our country despite the great potential it promises.

India has a vast population. There should be an equally large number of sportsmen. People assert that being a poor country the scope for growth of this field is very limited. However, this is not true. The 'middle class' that does all the spending and has attracted industrial giants from all over the world to woo this group of people is equivalent to the population of the whole of Europe. In Europe when each of the countries can produce great sportsmen, why can India not do the same with better potential that exists?

The major problem for the lack of growth in this field has been the wrong attitude of the people who are responsible for imparting education to the youth of the country. To compound the problem parents have been supporting this attitude. Finally, the leadership that guides the games and sports activities at all levels—district, state and national, is guilty of not supporting talented young people sufficiently. The training facilities too are in short supply as compared to the demand for them.

Desirable Personal Qualities

To be successful in this field a person must:

- be proficient in a particular game or sporting activity.
- be physically very fit. Physical fitness is the primary requirement in this field.
- have a winning attitude. Physical success follows mental success.

- believe in personal discipline at the field and off it.
- be willing to undergo constant training and practice. Without it one cannot rise in this field.
- be willing to work as a team. Most games require a joint effort for success.

Opportunities in Games and Sports

Everyone may not be able to take advantage of the opportunities in the field of games and sports. If one were to look back since the time the country attained independence, an ever-increasing number of young people have made significant achievements in this field. They have become icons in their areas of specialization achieving not only national applause, but have been acclaimed at the international level.

Just take a look at the achievements in the areas of cricket, tennis, chess, golf and shooting. For years the country excelled in hockey. When the games are shown live on the television everyone is tuned on to the channel. All good schools have playgrounds and other facilities. Professionally trained physical trainers impart training at the school level. Almost in every district there are games and sports where school and college students participate. From amongst these winners there are participants at the State level. Finally, there are events organized at the national level.

To achieve success at higher levels it is necessary to select talented young people at school level. Talented sportsmen are not just born. They need to be trained. This training must start early. Unfortunately, few schools realise this truth. There is greater emphasis on academics than upon this field of activity. The few talented sportsmen are often attracted to careers in Defence Services or Police Services. They find positions there. Only a few take the risk of joining the field of games and sports. They eventually become physical training instructors and coaches in schools and colleges.

Economic reasons have held back talented young people from rising in this field. There is lack of training and support. At one time it was difficult to find this support altogether. In the present times when millions of rupees are being spent on sponsoring games and sporting events by national and international business giants, it should not be difficult for schools to identify young people and also seek support for their training.

In the recent past there has been an unprecedented growth in a variety of educational institutions sponsored by leading industrial houses. Large amounts are also spent on sponsoring games and sporting events. A part of these funds can definitely be diverted to utilise the opportunities for training centres for games and sports. The government is aware of this need and could provide the necessary land and support.

Few countries are as fortunate as India to be blessed with natural resources like mountains, rivers, lakes and wide fields. India is also blessed in having a large section of people knowledgeable in martial arts like wrestling, fencing and archery. Many tribal people are expert gymnasts. River sports are common in some parts of the country. The basic need to utilise the opportunities in this field is to select talented persons and to train them to international standards just as we have been able to do so in academic and technical fields.

Educational Facilities

Facilities are available to train physical instructors, who eventually find employment in schools and colleges. From amongst these some specialize as coaches in some games and sports. The government has established some sporting institutions to provide training to young people. There is need for many more of these training institutions.

Making a Beginning

Most young people make a beginning through good performance in particular games and sports at school level. At this stage they may be encouraged to compete at district level. A few outstanding sportsmen move on to play at the state level. The local coaches train them. They deserve greater support by specialist coaches from training institutions. Much of the effort of the talented sportsmen is directed towards winning the favourable approval of the selectors at different levels. This stage needs greater transparency. More people should be accorded the opportunity to show their talent. Once a person has achieved national attention various organizations that oversee the various areas of games and sports begin to look into the potentialities of the sportsmen.

As a measure of encouragement, earlier, some of the talented sportsmen were employed by government departments and banks to fulfil their need for a livelihood. Presently, some of the corporate bodies have undertaken this responsibility. However, the support that is coming forth is very small. Many more corporate bodies need to cut on the advertising and spend it in the support of sportsmen and training facilities.

Income from Games and Sports

It is very difficult to foretell what a person can earn through a career in this field. The physical training instructors in schools and colleges receive a salary at par with that of other staff. However, most sportsmen need to have another source of livelihood to maintain a family until such time as they gain national importance. Those who reach the top earn very large incomes through endorsements of products. There are exceptional instances where some sportsmen have earned fortunes to last them a lifetime.

Opportunities for Self-employment

In many games team effort is necessary. It is not possible to work single. However, in some areas one can be self-employed by becoming a coach holding training sessions or by running a training institute. Many field judges and radio and TV commentators work as freelancers offering services as required.

Gemology

45

A gem is a precious or semi-precious stone, or a piece of mineral substance. Diamonds, rubies and emeralds are precious stones. Jade, amethyst and garnet are semi-precious stones. Gems are also known as jewels. However, this word is used more in reference to precious stones than to semi-precious stones.

Indians have a great love of gems and jewellery. They also believe that the stones have a profound effect on the personality. Different stones are suggested for all the twelve signs of the Zodiac. Besides, it is believed that several stones protect individuals from the malefic influence of the planets. That explains why many people wear a variety of rings or adorn a charm, or children wear a stone around the neck.

Gems and jewellery are big business. It has always been that way. However, in the recent past our attitude has changed. Previously this trade passed on from one generation to another. Even the craftsmen who made the jewellery taught the craft to their children, and life moved on. Presently, it has been accepted as a need of the people and has acquired the status of a vocation that can be pursued by newcomers.

Desirable Personal Qualities

To be successful in this field a person must:

- have a good knowledge of gems and jewellery.
- have a good imagination and be creative. Everyone is looking for new designs.
- have an artistic bent of mind. After all jewellery is a piece of art.
- have a good sense of balancing colours and designs.

- be careful and honest. The work requires handling of high value gems and jewellery.
- have a steady hand and be precise with the fine work.
- be computer-literate. Computer-aided designing and manufacturing is being done.
- have a bit of showmanship. That is necessary to sell high value items.
- be fashion conscious and keep a track of current trends.

Opportunities in Gemology

India is a vast country with a huge population. Although 70 per cent of the people live in the rural areas and are in general termed poor, but gems and jewellery play a significant role in the lives of all Indians. The urban population may think in terms of precious stones, platinum and gold, but even the poorer sections think in terms of semi-precious stones set in silver. The vast population presents many opportunities of fulfilling their desire with well designed modestly priced jewellery. The vast international market too has its eyes on India. The exports are likely to rise manifold.

The work is not restricted to one stereotyped routine of making jewellery. Opportunities exist at various levels where people do different kinds of work. For instance, designing jewellery is a creative art. New designs are always welcome. Designers provide this service. Gemologists help test and identify various kinds of stones. Professional grinders grind the gems to definite specifications. They are finally given a smooth finish by gem polishers. The gem setters set the gems in the jewellery. Another specialized line is that of engravers who engrave designs and patterns on the jewellery. Besides these professionals there are researchers and scientists that create gems from other substances.

With the entry of foreign operators in the jewellery market one can expect steady growth with increased jewellery exports. Even at the national level, the jewellery manufacturers are trying to streamline the manufacture and marketing of jewellery to give the purchaser value for money. Investments in gold have been popular, but with confidence building measures manufacturers are encouraging people to invest in precious stones like diamonds.

Local jewellers do much of the semi-precious jewellery and silver jewellery work, but with newer techniques and designs there is ample scope for growth.

The marketing of all kinds of jewellery is a sophisticated business that will also develop in the near future. That will open up many opportunities for smart young men and women interested in this field of work.

Educational Facilities

In the past people learnt about the work through those who were already working in the field. The things have changed in that organized training facilities are now available. National Institute of Fashion Technology, New Delhi, offers a three-year course in Accessory/Jewellery Designing. South Delhi Polytechnic also offers a two-year course. There are several other institutions that offer short-term and long-term courses in this field in different parts of the country. Many of them advertise in the national press. One can get in touch with them directly to verify admission requirements, fees, etc.

Making a Beginning

Jewellers who have their own showrooms and also fulfil export orders conduct the jewellery trade. To keep their operations within control they do the manufacturing personally. Therefore, one will necessarily need to get in touch with an established jeweller who may have an opening in the particular area of specialization. Those who are capable are picked up for more responsibilities. By the nature of the work promotions are bound to be slow unless a person adds on to one's abilities.

Income from Gemology

Since one needs to handle high-value items, these careers are for responsible people. Trained designers are always required. The remuneration is reasonable keeping in view the nature of work. Many of the operations are on the basis of work done. However, the possibilities of growth are limited.

Opportunities for Self-employment

Many of the people who are paid on the basis of work done are self-employed. To ensure regular work they may be connected with one or more jewellers. Many young enterprising people have gone into the field of selling semi-precious jewellery and made a big success of it.

Government Service

46

The government continues to be the largest single employer, offering jobs at different levels of service in its many departments. The jobs are particularly attractive to young people who come from middle-class families in urban areas. They offer the maximum security of service. The variety of jobs that are offered makes it possible for young people with different educational backgrounds to find appropriate openings to suit their needs.

All government departments follow a definite system for enlisting employees at a particular age, and retire them at a fixed age. This ensures a steady turnover of employees, making it necessary to recruit a certain number each year. With growing development in all spheres of life, there has been a gradual expansion of many government departments. This has created many opportunities for service by young people interested in this field of work. Newer avenues will continue to open. However, with greater demand for efficiency recruitment in some offices is at a standstill.

Desirable Personal Qualities

The qualities desired for different positions in government service depend upon the kind of service one is interested in. Several kinds of services have been discussed in chapters on Accountancy, Engineering and Technology, the I.A.S. and Allied Services, Law, etc. For general responsibilities in government services, a person must:

- possess clerical ability. Most responsibilities require a lot of written work.
- have a good command over Hindi, English and the regional language.

- possess good communication skills. This is important when one wants to understand others' point of view, and express one's own.
- have good knowledge in general. Many situations will require it.
- be willing and able to work with different kinds of people. This can sometimes be very demanding.
- be able to work as a team. Seeking the cooperation of colleagues is important to make progress.
- be prepared to work in different locations. Most jobs are transferable. One will need to comply with them.
- work within a definite discipline. This is important to succeed at work.

Opportunities in Government Service

The vacancies in the Indian Administrative Service and Allied Services are filled by the Union Public Service Commission through competitive examinations just as it does for the Defence Services, Engineering Services, etc. These are discussed in separate chapters. There are several vacancies at all levels in the government administration that need to be filled by new candidates each year. Since the country is divided into states, and the government within each state administers within its territory, vacancies are declared according to need. The set-up in each state varies slightly according to need and custom.

In general, each state has vacancies in the Civil Service, Judicial Service, Subordinate Civil Service to enlist Naib Tehsildars and Tehsildars, Forest Service, Police Service, Jails Service, Educational Service, State Finance and Accounts Service, Clerical Service, Excise Department, Sales Tax Department, Industries Department, Employment Department, Agriculture Department, Civil Supplies Department, Social Welfare Department, and for filling positions of Sub-registrars, Assistant Registrars, etc.

Besides these positions, vacancies also occur in the State Public Boards, and such other government organizations providing civic services. The variety of jobs offered is very big.

Since many young people are interested in this field of careers, there is a lot of competition. Only the most capable young people find their way into these services, particularly in those lines that lead to top positions in the government.

Educational Facilities

Candidates who are selected for the various services are sent to duty right away if they are so qualified. If they need special training, this is provided to them at special centres run by the government for this purpose. In certain cases, they are also sent to special educational institutions to receive further technical training required by them to be able to perform their duties efficiently. During the training, the government may pay small amounts to meet the personal expenses of the candidates. Full salaries are only paid when they join service to fill a particular vacancy.

Making a Beginning

It is only fair that everyone should have a reasonable chance to join the various government services. Therefore, the State Public Service Commission in each state fills positions through competitive examinations followed by an interview/ personality test. The basic requirement for almost all responsible positions is a minimum of graduation in Arts, Science, Commerce, Agriculture, Law, Engineering, etc., as required for the particular line of one's choice. A good academic background and a good general knowledge of men and matters are helpful. Since the details of the services and the competitive examinations vary from one state to another, it is not possible to give the details of the same here. They can be obtained directly from the State Public Service Commission in your own state. You can also look out for advertisements issued periodically.

Income from Jobs in Government Service

All personnel in government service are paid according to the scales declared for particular positions from time to time. The scales of pay offered by the State governments are slightly less than those paid by the Central Government. All government employees derive benefits like dearness allowance, provident fund, medical facilities, pension, etc., as allowed by rules of particular service. There is great prestige attached to senior positions in government service.

Opportunities for Self-employment

There are no special opportunities for self-employment for those who are in government service. The opportunities that are available to doctors, engineers, accountants, and others can always be availed of whether one joins government service or private employment. The top positions in the government are mostly administrative positions. One can take advantage of the experience gained after retirement.

Homoeopathy

47

Homoeopathy is a field that has for long been associated with being a hobby rather than a profession. Many did not hesitate to equate it with quackery because of lack of scientific reasoning. However, for several years now it has been accepted as a system of treatment of diseases. The government recognises it as such. The millions of people who have been cured confirm its efficacy not only in India, but also in developed countries like U.S.A., U.K. and Germany.

India is a vast country with 70 per cent of the population living in the rural areas many of which do not have the facilities of medical care. With low incomes and inability to pay for the conventional medical treatment, Homoeopathy offers a reasonable alternative. Young people trained in this field can conveniently take the benefits to the vast rural areas making a reasonable career out of it.

Desirable Personal Qualities

To be successful in this field, a person must:

- be a motivated person. Those who practice conventional medicine often look down upon this field of medicine.
- be observant and analytical in his approach. The system of treatment depends upon observing and understanding the symptoms of the patient.
- be very painstaking to understand what the patient is trying to convey. Many patients that cannot communicate well cannot explain their symptoms. One may need to question them in a variety of ways.
- possess good communication skills. This helps understand the patient easily.

- have a good understanding of human behaviour. This is an important aspect of this system of medicine.
- be forever ready to refer to books to understand a patient. Matching symptoms and drugs is important. Several drugs produce similar symptoms.
- be computer literate. It has made following up symptoms and drugs easier.

Opportunities in Careers in Homoeopathy

With the government having recognized Homoeopathy as a system of treatment of diseases, the opportunities in this field are growing. Conventional medical treatment is expensive and not available in the rural areas and smaller communities. Besides, with many side effects of the conventional system of medical treatment more people are moving to systems like Homoeopathy. This form of treatment has no side effects and is safer.

Many government hospitals now have a Homoeopathy department. The medicines are comparatively much cheaper and easily available. They are easily dispensed. The practitioners in this field have drawn vastly from the field of Ayurveda where many Indian herbs and drugs have been successfully tried and used in treatment of diseases.

Educational Facilities

All earlier practitioners learnt Homoeopathy through self-study or by studying for a diploma in many of the institutions run by private organizations. To practice Homoeopathy it is necessary that a person must possess a degree in Homoeopathy and be registered with the government as a practitioner.

There are more than 100 universities in India that offer courses in Homoeopathy. Both government and private colleges offer the Bachelor's degree in Homoeopathic Medicine and Surgery (BHMS). The course is for four-and-a-half years followed by one year's internship. Admissions to the course are on merit after 10+2 with Physics, Chemistry and Biology.

Some universities also offer diploma courses. Before seeking admission into any course, one must ensure that the particular course is recognized by the government and registration for practice would be granted after the completion of the course.

Making a Beginning

The job opportunities in this field are not very good. Most young people join an established practitioner after their internship. Depending upon availability of jobs, some join private or government hospitals. Very few set out on their own. Many join private charitable hospitals where they get an opportunity for gaining valuable experience, and then move out on their own. One builds a practice only with time. The medicines used initially by Dr. Samuel Hahnmann, the founder of Homoeopathy, are still used today. Hundreds of new ones have been added. The secret of success lies in understanding the medicines and the patients well.

Income in Homoeopathy

One necessarily begins at the lowest level. The income at this stage is at par with those in similar fields. However, with increasing self-confidence and valuable experience, the income rises gradually. Most practitioners dispense their own medicines. This augments their income. Many young people earn well when they are well-known in the community. Exceptionally intelligent practitioners have risen to great heights and received both recognition and financial gains.

Opportunities for Self-employment

As a professional a Homoeopath can practice anywhere. Most practitioners run a retail store selling branded Homoeopathic medicines that are in good demand.

Horticulture and Floriculture 48

A good garden is a place of great admiration for all people. Everyone enjoys the pleasure of being close to nature in a garden. It is this pleasure that motivates people to have small gardens within their homes. If space does not permit it, people have plants in pots placed in verandahs or even have some indoor plants. The greenery is a source of oxygen for all people. This need has given rise to several careers in this field.

Horticulture is the art or practice of cultivating and managing gardens. It includes the growing of a variety of plants that are decorative, or bear fruits and flowers. Floriculture refers to the specialization of cultivation of flowers and flowering plants, very often in adverse weather conditions under artificial shelters. The place where young trees and plants are raised is known as a nursery, and the person who owns or looks after a nursery is known as a nurseryman. The need for cut flowers has created opportunities for florists, who sell and arrange cut flowers into bouquets or vases.

Desirable Personal Qualities

To be successful in this field, a person must:

- have a great love for nature. One will need to work outdoors amongst trees and plants.
- enjoy time amongst plants and flowers. This is important to succeed in this field.
- enjoy good health. Outdoor work can be strenuous. Good health is an asset.
- be willing to work with one's hands. One cannot wait for assistance.
- have a sense of commitment towards nature's bounty.

- be aesthetic and artistic in outlook. A beautiful garden is a piece of art.
- have some business acumen. Without it the middlemen take away the profits.

Opportunities in Horticulture and Floriculture

The need for fruits and flowers always existed in our country. With greater development in agricultural practices, import of newer varieties and greater awareness amongst the people for greenery around the home, the opportunities are growing. With demand for cut flowers from metro cities and foreign countries and with the development of swift transport services the opportunities for specialized floriculture has also grown. There is a growing need for both fruits and flowers.

With the need for potted plants for homes, nurseries have come up around every town and city. The modern offices have not ignored the benefits of plants and hire personnel to supply and maintain these for them. There is also the need for the maintenance of parks, roundabouts and other public places. There are also the opportunities to supply plants of different kinds, garden supplies like insecticides, fungicides and equipment, and the supply of seeds, bulbs and cuttings.

Many people also look forward to hire professional landscape specialists to plan the area around the home. At functions there is the need for potted plants to decorate entries and the area around the stage. Those who have the necessary skills are also experimenting and researching for newer varieties of flowers, fruits and vegetables. The growing of medical plants is also drawing great attention of people around the world. This field holds greater promise of treatment without bad side effects. Flower and fruit shows draw a lot of public attention. Skilled people are also writing regularly for magazines guiding people towards greater love of nature.

Educational Facilities

Although many people join this field because of their interest in the subject and learn on the job, to be successful it is advisable that one should do at least a bachelor's degree in agriculture after 10+2. There are several colleges spread all over the country offering this facility. It would be preferable if one follows the B.Sc. (Agri.) with a Master's degree in Horticulture, that prepares one better for success in the specialized lines in the career, and puts one ahead of the others that are not that qualified. Short-term diploma courses are also available. The best training comes from doing things with one's hands.

Making a Beginning

To make a beginning in this field one can join an established nursery, and gradually learn the basics of the business on the job. There are many that may be involved in agriculture, and devote a part of their land and time to growing fruits and flowers, or even running a nursery. Many people who have some land attached to their homes are using it to grow potted plants and operate a nursery. For growing flowers on a larger scale more land would be required. It would also be necessary to have a firm contract for their supply because they cannot be stored. Fruit growers normally sell the fruit on the trees to contractors in advance. However, some people are gradually beginning to market it on their own directly in the market or to bulk purchasers like the fruit preservation industry.

Income from Horticulture and Floriculture

Interestingly most people who specialize in this field through special courses prefer to join government departments or business houses where they get a steady income that is at par with income from other lines. Only those who have a great urge to do the work personally enter the practical field.

This work is greatly dependent upon nature, and there are bound to be variations periodically. More people get into this field because of their love for nature rather than their desire to earn large sums. For many people it is not a full-time work unless they take it up on a larger scale. Initially, the returns are likely to be moderate, but with experience the incomes improve. With use of modern methods returns can be stabilized.

Opportunities for Self-employment

There are ample opportunities for self-employment in this field. Most people take on one or more assistants and do the work themselves. Many people have successfully become florists. Many are operating small or large nurseries depending upon the need. Those with experience and goodwill are handling work for several business houses, hotels and other organizations simultaneously.

I.A.S. and Allied Services

49

Among the most prestigious vocations in the country is working for the I.A.S. and Allied Services. The Indian Administrative Service, or I.A.S. as it is popularly called, is the successor to the Indian Civil Service (I.C.S.) started by the British. The members of the I.A.S. are the backbone of the civil service in India. They hold all the important executive positions in the government. Their responsibilities include district administration, development work, coordination of various government services, improvement and management of the secretarial services at the government level, and such other duties. In brief, it would be correct to say that I.A.S. is responsible for the executive responsibilities of the administration in the states and at the centre. In the same way, the Allied Services provide personnel for other responsible positions in the government. They include the Indian Foreign Service, the Indian Police Service, the Indian Revenue Service, etc.

Desirable Personal Qualities

To be successful in this field, a person must:

- possess high intellectual ability. The jobs in this field are top of the line.
- enjoy a wide range of interests. This helps one face a variety of situations.
- have a pleasing personality. One looks up to people in this field.
- have a good observation. This prepares one to gauge situations quickly.
- have an interest in understanding of people and situations.

- have a sense of determination and purpose. These help develop leadership qualities.
- enjoy the strength of character. Ethical superiority is important for good leadership.
- be able to take decisions swiftly. Many situations require urgent decisions.
- have qualities of good leadership.
- be willing to learn continuously through experience. There is no end to learning in high positions.
- be able to face difficult situations with a smile. Solutions to most difficult problems have to be found by the top leadership. One cannot afford to buckle with problems.

Opportunities for Employment

Since the basic purpose of the I.A.S. and Allied Services is to provide the administrative and management skills for government administration, there are few openings to be filled up each year. The competition in this field of service is very stiff. Only those who have achieved a high grade in academics, have many interests, and possess a good personality with qualities of leadership have an opportunity of entering this field of work.

Young people who have average capabilities would do better to look for opportunities in fields other than those like the I.A.S. and Allied Services. It would be of interest to note that almost half of the direct recruits to the I.A.S. are the children of people working for the government. Four out of every five come from middle class families in urban areas.

Joining the I.A.S. and Allied Services

Recruitment to the I.A.S. and Allied services is through a competitive examination conducted by the Union Public Service Commission, Shahjahan Road, New Delhi, in September/October each year. The announcement is made in the national press about six months earlier. There is a combined examination for the I.A.S. and Allied Services. The minimum educational requirement is a university degree, and the age limit is from 20 to 26 years. The Government of India fixes the basic requirements in consultation with the Public Service (Qualification for Recruitment) Committee, U.P.S.C., and the State governments. The examination is for the following categories of services/posts for which recruitment is made:

CATEGORY I

1. The Indian Administrative Service.
2. The Indian Foreign Service.

CATEGORY II

1. The Indian Police Service.
2. The Delhi, and Andaman and Nicobar Islands Police Service, Class II.
3. Posts of Assistant Security Officer/Assistant Commandant/Adjutant, Class II, in the Railway Protection Force.

CATEGORY III

A. Class I Services:
   1. The Indian P & T Accounts and Finance Service.
   2. The Indian Audit and Accounts Service.
   3. The Indian Customs and Central Excise Service.
   4. The Indian Defence Accounts Service.
   5. The Indian Income Tax Service (Class I).
   6. The Indian Ordinance Factories Service (Class I) (Assistant Managers—Non-technical).
   7. The Indian Postal Service.
   8. The Indian Railway Accounts Service.
   9. The Indian Railway Traffic Service.
   10. The Military Lands and Cantonments Service (Class I).

B. Class II Services:
   1. The Central Secretariat Service, Section Officers Grade (Class II).
   2. The Indian Foreign Service, Branch 'B' Integrated Grades II and III of the General Cadre (Section Officers Grade).

3. The Armed Forces Headquarters Civil Service, Assistant Civilian Staff Officers Grade (Class II).
4. The Customs Appraisers (Class II).
5. The Delhi and Andaman and Nicobar Islands Civil Service (Class II).
6. The Pondicherry Civil Service (Class II).

The candidates are free to compete for any one or more of the categories of services/posts mentioned above. However, the preference must be clearly indicated. It cannot be changed later. The competitive examination is divided into two portions —a written test and an interview. The standard of the written test is equivalent to that of an Honours degree of an Indian university. It consists of three compulsory papers: General English, Essay and General Knowledge, and a wide choice of optional papers on subjects commonly studied at university level. The number and choice of the optional subjects vary with the category of services/posts preferred.

The result of the examination is generally announced by April. The candidates who have achieved the requisite number of marks are invited for an interview for the personality test. The marks for the interview are added to those of the written test, and a merit list based on total marks is prepared. This list depends upon the number of vacancies that need to be filled.

The successful candidates, subject to their fulfilling the health requirements, are sent for training as I.A.S. probationers at the National Academy of Administration at Mussoorie. The training comprises a fundamental course of five months to make them aware of the aims and obligations of the civil services, the ethics of the profession, its objectivity, integrity, impartiality, thoroughness, etc. This is followed by another course of seven months.

The training is thorough, and includes practical assignments. The basic idea behind the training schedule is to help the probationers develop an all-round personality, to understand and develop their strong points, and to learn to get over personal weaknesses. During training, special emphasis is given to subjects like Economics, Criminal Law and Procedure,

Administrative History of India, General Administration, District Administration, etc., along with knowledge of the state to which the candidate is posted.

Service Prospects

I.A.S. is recognized as an All India service by the constitution. The power to regulate recruitment and conditions of service is vested in the Parliament. The Parliament has empowered the Central Government, in consultation with the State governments, to make rules under The All India Services Act to regulate recruitment, probation, pay, travelling allowance, medical and other benefits, conduct, cadre, regularity of seniority, etc. These are, therefore, subject to revision through rules made by the Government.

Since a good administrator is required to keep up-to-date in his knowledge and managerial skill, officers are given opportunities for higher training after they have gained some experience. Among the institutions where officers receive higher training are the Administrative Staff College, Hyderabad, the Indian School of Public Administration, New Delhi, the Central Institute of Community Development, Mussoorie, and the National Council of Applied Economic Research, New Delhi. Some officers have received training in foreign universities also.

Beginning at the lowest administrative post as in-charge of a sub-division in a district, or of a government department at the district level, there is gradual promotion to the position of a Collector, or District Magistrate, or Deputy Commissioner in-charge of the whole district. Depending upon personal capabilities and seniority, there are important positions in the government departments at the divisional level, and again at the State level in various departments and ministries. Senior I.A.S. personnel also man the administrative positions in the Central government.

Income from I.A.S. and Allied Services

The prestige, authority and status that go with this field of service attract and motivate young people to join the I.A.S. and Allied Services. The salaries are at par with all first class jobs. However, although the I.A.S. personnel hold key executive positions all over the country, their salaries are not at par with those of the senior executives who hold key positions in private business and industrial undertakings.

The I.A.S. personnel enjoy great respect in their communities. They are in themselves a privileged class. The positions that they enjoy, and the power they wield as administrative heads in the districts, and the government departments, open the gates for all kinds of temptations that come their way. Young people need to specially guard themselves against these.

Opportunities for Self-employment

Young people who join the I.A.S. and Allied Services do not do so as a temporary measure. They build a full-time satisfying career from their capabilities and efforts. One learns gradually from the training and the experience that the career offers. Therefore, there is no scope for giving it up in favour of self-employment at any stage of the career. A few have done it to become entrepreneurs. Such instances are exceptional. They cannot be accepted as normal. Therefore, it is clear that there are no opportunities for self-employment. Even after retirement, rather than be self-employed, one prefers to use the skills and experience by working for large private undertakings.

Information Technology

50

One field of vocations that witnessed an unprecedented growth after the mid-nineties is computer-related vocations. Just as pocket calculators hit the scene ten years earlier, computers were doing it now. There was no planned growth. Computers were introduced. They spread just like a wild fire. People did not know enough about them. Anyone who could barely operate a computer was running a private training institute. People were lapping it up.

The larger training institutions were financially stronger and more organized. They opened franchise centres. Firstly, in the larger cities where the students had better capacity to pay, and then in the middle level cities and towns. Soon they were everywhere.

The children told their parents that if they were to remain competitive, they needed computers. The parents obliged. With the world of trade opening up, the government too saw the need for computerization. Special import concessions were announced, tax rebates were given and the prices came down to be at par with the international prices.

The use of computers spread to almost all businesses and professions. With dedication and hard work, the youth gave India a special international status in the field of Information Technology. The fears of the Y2K repercussions created demand for Indian IT professionals all over the world. There was an international demand for computer literate professionals.

Understanding Computers

One needs to understand that a computer is an electronic device that is capable of processing information and storing data according to a set of instructions. It is like a huge calculator that is capable of doing a variety of functions. Just by possessing a computer one cannot avail of all the benefits a computer can offer. To be useful, the computer depends upon the software for what it can do. When the software is installed in the computer, the next important thing is the capability of the person using the software. When the individual understands the software, one is able to achieve wonders with it.

The simplest kind of information a computer can handle is words and figures. It can handle figures and pictures also. Since the kind of information that a computer can handle can be used in many vocations, it is necessary to have software for different kinds of work. Therefore, the opportunities for vocations in this field can be divided into various categories like:

- Hardware engineering that aims at producing better and faster computers and peripheral equipment like storage devices, printers, etc.
- Software development for a variety of activities related to different vocations.
- Computer applications. More people are training for this than any other field.
- Multi-media use. Computers are useful tools both for education and entertainment.

Desirable Personal Qualities

To be successful in this field a person must:

- be computer literate. The person must know the basics of using the machine.
- be well acquainted with the field of specialization. Technical competence is important.
- be creative and have a good imagination. The ability to visualize situations is necessary many times.
- be adaptable to situations and circumstances that may change suddenly.
- have a logical bent of mind.

- be responsible to work on one's own. This is possible through good self-motivation.
- be willing to work as a team. This is necessary to get good results.
- be willing to work for long hours to achieve targets and meet deadlines.

Opportunities in Information Technology

No vocation has seen the kind of growth that the field of Information Technology witnessed in the last few years of the twentieth century. It not only emerged as the fastest growing vocation, but also revolutionized the way people think. This is one field that touches every other vocation. Just as it is necessary to be able to write to communicate well, it has become necessary to be computer literate to progress in one's vocation.

Many vocations cannot now exist without the use of computers. Accountancy, Banking, Designing, Insurance and even fields like Management when managers carry their laptops wherever they go. Speed and accuracy are the key words. In fact many new vocations have come up because of computers—Call Centres, Medical Transcription and Business Process Outsourcing.

The world of journalism or mass communication cannot think of a life without the use of computers. Electronic media, newspapers, magazines and even the book publishing trades are totally dependent upon the use of computers.

Internet and websites have brought easy communication and the world of knowledge to the home of every person who has a computer. The computer has become the education and entertainment centre of the family. Those who do not own computers use them at Cyber Cafes.

Just take a look at the index and the list of all the careers that are discussed in this book. Can you identify even a single field of careers where computers can be avoided? This just goes to show how different vocations have utilized what Information Technology could offer them. The field has gained such importance that most schools and colleges now have training centres to teach the use of computers. Many young people now own computers in their homes.

Educational Facilities

Just as there was phenomenal growth in the field of Information Technology, there has been an equally rapid growth in the field of educational facilities to train the personnel. Every town, small and big, has institutions providing education in this field. Before taking admission in one of the institutions one must ensure that the training provided is related and beneficial for the exact area of work one desires to do. The larger institutions provide the Bachelor's and the Master's degrees in Computer Engineering and applications.

Since a lot of young people take to the field of software development, it becomes necessary for them to obtain the certification of the company that has made the software. Different companies have their own requirements for this certification.

An important aspect of the careers in this field is that developments in this field are growing so fast that one is not taught about them. It is, therefore, necessary that a person must search for and acquire such knowledge to be updated on the subject. Without it one can easily fall back. Continuous study is important. Many prefer to take up short courses periodically.

Making a Beginning

A computer is like any other office equipment. It is a combination of a typewriter, an advanced calculator, a storage machine and a printing device. Depending upon the field one wishes to pursue, one can join soon after qualifying for a particular position. Knowledge of the particular software that can do the necessary work is essential.

To be able to get into the field of software development one needs to be well-versed with the different languages used. Companies that specialize in software development hire software developers. It is necessary that one must obtain certification from the parent company about one's knowledge and ability to use it. Trends in this field change quickly. The selection of the software is important. When there are further developments, additional certifications will be necessary.

Young people who desire to join the work as data entry operators or desktop publishers need to learn particular software and handle particular responsibilities. Many business houses have developed software to suit their personal requirements. One will need to get acquainted with this software if one takes up a job to use the software.

Multi-media and entertainment companies too require personnel that are specialized in this field.

Income from Information Technology

The entry-level salaries of personnel who can just do the normal office work are at par with the salaries of most office staff. However, those who are capable of software development, web designing, multi-media applications and specialized activities earn well. Many young people who got to start software firms have earned fortunes from their efforts. Capable people rise swiftly in the field.

Opportunities for Self-employment

If one has a personal computer there are enough opportunities for self-employment. Many young people are busy maintaining accounts for businessmen, doing desktop publishing work, or even doing a variety of things in one of the many Business Process Outsourcing operations. One can earn a steady income through self-employment activities.

Insurance

51

Till recently the insurance business was restricted to the Life Insurance Corporation of India and to the General Insurance Corporation and the companies attached to it. The four subsidiary companies are the New India Assurance Co., Oriental Insurance Co., United India Insurance Co. and the National Insurance Co. Whereas the former promoted the life insurance business, the latter companies are involved with all forms of general insurance.

With the opening of the insurance sector to private and foreign operators the whole business is rapidly undergoing a significant change. Many companies, some of them jointly with leading operators around the world are offering top rate services. The customers can now expect better services at more competitive prices. There is now a wider choice of policies to choose from. The business is bound to grow slowly but steadily.

Desirable Personal Qualities

To be successful in this field, a person must:

- be an extrovert fond of meeting people. The greater the number of people one knows the better the business.
- have the ability to network in the society. That helps one make great progress.
- have good mathematical ability. Insurance aims at dividing risks amongst many people.
- have an analytical outlook. One must know what would suit a customer best. One must also know how this need can be fulfilled.
- have good communication skills. That helps explain benefits to potential customers.
- be trustworthy, sincere and service-minded. People buy

insurance from people they can trust. Good follow-up service is important.

- be an aggressive seller. This is a very competitive field of selling.
- have an optimistic outlook. Those who are optimistic help enthuse others. This is a great asset to progress in this field.
- be available at odd hours to the customers. Customers buy insurance to avoid bad times. These come at odd times.

Opportunities in Insurance

The large population in our country is still not fully aware of the benefits of insurance. This is not so only in the rural area, it is equally true for the urban areas. With the entry of several new operators in this field, better services and pricing, advertising and aggressive selling the general awareness about benefits of insurance is growing. New opportunities are emerging in the field.

The insurance companies require actuaries, marketing and sales personnel, agents or consultants who secure business and surveyors who assess losses. In addition, there is need for administrative and office staff. Selling insurance requires a positive outlook. The training of sales staff and agents is very important. The Insurance Regulatory and Development Authority oversees the insurance business in the country.

An actuary is a person who compiles and analyses statistics in order to calculate insurance risks and premiums. Marketing and sales personnel include Development Officers who promote and sell business directly, or through agents or consultants. Agents work on commission basis. Assessors and surveyors are independent operators connected to insurance companies to assess losses and claims when clients seek compensation for losses, damages, thefts, etc.

New Companies

Some of the new companies who have entered the field of insurance include Tata-AIG, ICICI-Lombard Insurance, Metlife,

Reliance Life Insurance, Prudential ICICI, Birla-Sun Life, HDFC Standard Life, Allianz Bajaj Life Insurance, Aviva Life Insurance Co., Max New York Life and AMP Sanmar Assurance Co.

Educational Facilities

To work as an actuary it is necessary to have passed the examination conducted by the Actuarial Society of India, Mumbai. It takes several years to qualify in all the 10 subjects for which one is tested. Those who qualify in six subjects ecome associates of the Society. Several universities offer courses that train people to appear in the examinations conducted by the Society.

Assistant Development Officers are appointed on the basis of a written test and interview after graduation in any discipline. The General Insurance Corporation and CBSE are jointly offering general insurance subjects at +2 level in some schools.

Agents and consultants are appointed on the basis of a written test and interview. One need not be strong academically to become an agent. Even 10+2 will suffice. However, one must possess first rate communication and selling skills.

Surveyors and assessors are technical people, who must have a bachelor's degree in a particular field in engineering, or are a chartered accountant, or have the fellowship or associateship of the Institute of Insurance Surveyors and Adjusters.

The senior administrative staff in the public sector is selected on the basis of an all India examination followed by an interview. Six months training is imparted after selection. The staff at lower levels is selected according to need.

Some Important Addresses

Insurance Institute of India,
Universal Insurance Building,
Sir P.S. Mehta Road,
Mumbai-400001.

Actuarial Society of India,
9, Jeewan Udyog Building,
278, D.N. Road, Fort,
Mumbai-400001.

Delhi Insurance Institute,
78, Janpath, 1st Floor,
New Delhi-110001.

Making a Beginning

Depending upon one's choice of the work involved in the field of insurance, one needs to begin work in different ways. At the office level, the lower staff is selected and trained on the job as required. The Assistant Development Officers join after training and begin by developing the insurance business. At still higher level, the officers may be attached to the administration, development, accounts or insurance departments.

Agents or consultants are self-employed people who set out on their own after some preliminary training. They work under the guidance and supervision of the Development Officers.

Like agents, the surveyors and assessors are also self-employed people who start their work in their own field of specialization. Later, they may get attached to one or more companies. They need to be available as and when called by the insurance company.

Income from Insurance

Income from careers in insurance is in harmony with that of income from selling business. The perks are good. Since the business comes through agents or consultants who work on commission basis, the income in this area is dependent directly upon the individual's selling skills and application to the work. The harder an agent works, the better the income. It grows with time as new clients are attracted to give business. The surveyors too get a commission on a claim. Their income depends upon how well they can balance the claim of a client and the liability of the company.

Opportunities for Self-employment

The entire field force that sells insurance is self-employed. They work under the guidance of the Development Officer. Those who learn the business well take their work directly to the office. Surveyors and assessors are also self-employed, working in cooperation with the administration staff of the company. Since the incomes of the agents rises gradually as new business is added every year, some of the senior agents in the insurance field receive very large sums as commissions every year.

International Trade

52

With efficient international travel and cargo services and the countries opening up to procure products and services around the world the opportunities in international trade have witnessed a rapid growth. The world has suddenly shrunk to make several countries dependent upon each other for a variety of products and services. This has promoted international trade.

International trade has existed for a long time. Nature has been more benevolent to some areas than to others. The population is also more concentrated in some countries as compared to others. This has created vast disparities in the level of labour values. Wherever possible people have sought advantage of cheaper labour to promote trade and business.

Our country is truly blessed with some of the finest 'brain power', with a variety of ores and minerals and with some of the finest crafts that have no comparison anywhere in the world. This has encouraged many young people to avail of the opportunity to export products and services around the world. Since the country is fast developing and rather than wait to develop technology and manufacture many of the necessities, importing these items has made the export and import of products into a truly growing international trade. With constant growth, the opportunities in this field are on a steady rise.

Desirable Personal Qualities

To be successful in this field a person must:

- look at the whole world as a potential market. It is necessary to perceive the world that way.
- have knowledge of the country and its people with whom one wants to do business. People around the world look at the same thing differently.

- understand the needs of the people of the country where one wants to do business.
- understand international procedures of business. Without it one can get into trouble.
- appreciate that at the international level, there is no compromise on quality. One must supply the best.
- appreciate that at the international level, there is no compromise on time. The supply must be made on time.
- be personally a disciplined person with great respect for business ethics, behaviour and time.
- be ahead of competition. At the international level the competition is tougher.

Opportunities in International Trade

As a nation we are fortunate in that we are well blessed by nature. There is a great variety of ores and minerals. Almost every kind of fruit and vegetable that grows around the world is grown in the country. We have a rich tradition of excellent handicrafts. Above all, we have a large population that includes some of the finest craftsmen around the world. We have a great variety of products to offer. We also have the capacity to innovate new products that would be attractive to the people around the world.

Already we are exporting a variety of fabrics, ready-made clothes, household linen and items, handicrafts made of leather, wood, marble and a variety of metals, gems and jewellery, many kinds of food grains and processed foods, indigenous medicines and cosmetics and a whole lot of industrial items. Many of these are being exported to developed countries, but considering the big variety we have to offer, there are innumerable untapped opportunities waiting to be utilized. There is a growing need for young people in this field of selling as more and more companies are looking forward to expand their sales by selling in overseas markets. The underdeveloped countries look up to India for many of their requirements.

We are a developing country. To accelerate the growth

there are many industrial inputs available that could be useful. There is a need to bring these into the country to hasten development. All these are opportunities waiting to be developed into useful careers in international trade.

Educational Facilities

Due to lack of educational facilities many people entered the field of international trade through a hands on experience. People already working in the marketing departments of the companies were entrusted with the responsibility of export marketing. Connections were built in another country and the business was gradually promoted.

However, the approach is very methodical now in that young people are training to qualify with degrees in marketing supplemented with short-term courses in Export Marketing and Procedures. Several institutions offer courses in marketing. After completing the course one can specialize in the field of international trade. Learning about export procedures is important. The courses are advertised in the national press.

Making a Beginning

In the past people working in the marketing departments built connections in other countries, and depending upon the need and circumstances gradually developed international trade. There are many organizations and facilities to help build up connections now. One needs to have a good product range that interests the customer. With improved telecommunications one can keep in constant touch with business partners. With time one can understand the needs better and increase the range of products.

Income from International Trade

International trade is very competitive in that people from all over the world strive to promote their own products and services. It aims at a high level of efficiency. When one supplies large volumes even low margins are profitable and worthwhile. Besides, there are incentives for export marketing. If the products are unique as many handicrafts are, one can get a fair margin.

Opportunities for Self-employment

The bulk of the international trade is done between larger companies, but there are many individuals who work at their own level to represent foreign suppliers making sales to Indian companies. At the same time there are smaller proprietorship concerns that export specialized handicrafts and special items to foreign customers through personal connections.

This field of selling opens the whole world as a potential market for selling goods and services. Many young people have achieved significant success in this area of selling even without much personal capital to invest. However, knowledge of export marketing is essential along with the ability to understand the needs in other countries. It is undoubtedly a competitive field. It offers interesting possibilities of building vital contacts and a very satisfying career.

Investigation Services

53

Everyone loves reading murder mysteries. Everyone loves to see films and serials that portray detectives in hot pursuit of crooks and criminals. The principal reason for the great love and interest in these activities is the human nature to identify oneself with the detective to solve the case. Every scene holds one's attention and excitement to look for the right clue. That explains the great popularity of mystery books, films and serials.

In real life the situation may not at all be exciting. However, a need exists to carry out investigations to verify facts in many cases. Besides the investigation work done by the police to maintain law and order, new opportunities have emerged for investigators or detectives, as some prefer to call them. There are opportunities in both the government and private sectors.

Desirable Personal Qualities

To be successful in this field of activity a person must:

- have above-average observation qualities. Many times the truth is verified from a very fine point.
- have an analytical outlook. All facts must be analysed to arrive at definite conclusions.
- have a smooth tongue telling lies as easily as the truth. One sometimes needs to pretend to be what one is not.
- have an inquisitive disposition. Fine investigation requires it.
- be hardworking willing to put in continuous effort. Being in pursuit is necessary.
- have the ability to look at things differently. That is what makes it revealing.

- be willing to work in a team. Support from others is necessary.
- maintain a low profile, talking only when necessary. Nobody should guess what you are looking for.
- be prepared for difficult situations. Crooks and cheats could do anything.
- know how to cover tracks on an assignment. Someone may be following you.

Opportunities in Investigation Services

Besides the Indian Police Service (IPS), there is the Criminal Investigation Department (CID), Central Bureau of Investigation (CBI), Intelligence Bureau (IB), Research & Analysis Wing (RAW) and a few others and the private investigators.

The role of police is well-known to all in maintaining law and order by booking the guilty. The CID, CBI and the Crime Branch are involved with investigating fraudulent activities and scams at different levels. They conduct research, search records, analyse them, interrogate individuals and conduct open investigations before drawing any inferences. The IB personnel basically collect important information. RAW officers are involved with building connections and collecting information to help formulate policies.

Private detectives carry out investigations pertaining to industries, trademark and copyright infringements, manufacturing spurious goods, collecting information about employees, verifying authenticity of insurance claims, and even collecting information about activities of individuals. Maintaining a low profile is important in that carrying out snooping activities is a legal offence.

Educational Facilities

Those working in government agencies are trained in schools run by the government. Private investigators can be trained in special schools, or even at the agency level where special on-the-job training is imparted. The training is through a short-term course of 2 to 6 months. Retired personnel from police can join agencies directly, or can even start one.

Making a Beginning

Government agencies like IB and CBI conduct competitive examinations through UPSC to select Assistant Intelligence Officers. Examinations are also conducted to recruit Sub-Inspectors. Announcements about the examinations are made in both the national and state level newspapers.

RAW may appoint Deputy Field Officers directly or through the Civil Services. Technical and scientific staff may be recruited from universities and the Department of Science and Technology.

Those joining private investigation agencies are selected directly at the agency level and trained for the particular kind of work assigned to them. Those who join private training centres can apply directly to agencies for work. One gains experience on the job.

Income from Investigation Services

The income from government positions is at par with those for similar jobs. The salaries are reviewed periodically. In the private sector, the beginning salaries are good. Increments come fast when one is capable and understands what needs to be done. The perks in the job are attractive. Many capable young people are drawing very handsome salaries.

Opportunities for Self-employment

The work involved in this field is such that one needs to work in a team, and not as an individual. Therefore, individual working has its constraints. After some experience, a group can get together to start their own agency.

Journalism

54

Perhaps few thrills in life equal that of seeing one's name in print. Young people interested in becoming writers enviably look up to the power that journalism enjoys in influencing people. With growing interest in education and in reading for better knowledge and awareness of the world around us, there is a growing need and market for newspapers, magazines and books of all types. Besides, an ever-increasing network of radio and television centres has its own requirements of good writing.

In the field of education, there is a great demand for new and better textbooks, and for presenting technical work in a simpler form so that the average person can benefit from it. We cannot overlook the huge market for entertaining fiction or the need for good literature for children. When we add up all these needs, we can well visualize the vast storehouse of opportunities that exist and can be profitably used by young people interested in writing for a career.

Desirable Personal Qualities

To be successful in this field, a person must:

- enjoy expressing oneself in writing. To be a writer, one must be fond of writing.
- be capable of writing interesting letters. This means that a person knows what interests people.
- have an urge to put thoughts on paper. Many people blank out when asked to put their thoughts on paper.
- be willing to learn the knack of good writing. Few writers are born. Most of them learn the necessary techniques.
- have a good knowledge of the language. Writing is

playing with words. You cannot do it without the knowledge of the language.

- have a good general knowledge. Writers must be well informed.
- have an insight into human thinking and behaviour. One writes about people for people.
- be intelligent and observant to note details. Good writers are good observers. They write what they observe.
- have a good imagination and interest in people, places and everyday affairs.
- know how to talk their way around. They need to collect as much information accurately as possible.
- learn how to keep cool in awkward situations. It is not easy to deal with a variety of people, both good and bad.
- have a sense of the dramatic to put interest into their work. A good writer sees a story even when others do not.
- appreciate the need to be disciplined. A good writer must produce a certain amount of work everyday.
- learn to maintain time schedules. Publishers do not tolerate delays. Many stories become stale the next day.

Opportunities in Journalism

To get an idea of the many opportunities that exist for young people interested in a career as writers, one need only see the variety of newspapers, magazines and books at newsstands at bus terminals, railway stations, on the pavements, and in the thousands of bookshops spread all over the country. There are several hundred newspapers and thousands of magazines in all the principal languages published regularly in our country. These are very few considering the population of our country. One can understand that there is ample scope for starting many more periodicals, particularly to cover news and events at the local level.

There are magazines for men, women and children. There

are magazines pertaining to housekeeping, entertainment and various trades and businesses. Many companies and organizations have their own house journals. The book trade too is by no means small. India is one of the largest publishing countries in the world. Publishers are always on the lookout for books on all kinds of subjects, be they textbooks for schools and colleges, or books for entertainment and reading during leisure time.

Radio and TV also require a regular supply of written work. With increasing number of channels and programmes, this requirement is on the increase. We have the world's largest film industry. This too has its need for good stories and scripts for films. To these markets, if we can add the very large publishing market abroad that is always on the lookout for new and better written work for publishing, there seem to be endless number of opportunities that can be used by young people who would like to set out in a career in journalism.

Educational Facilities

Many colleges and universities offer courses in journalism. The details can be obtained directly from the institutions concerned. The details of colleges offering courses in journalism are given in directories published by publishers who specialize in publishing career-oriented publications. Many private institutions also offer different kinds of courses in journalism. The details are advertised in the national press. Correspondence courses offered by important correspondence schools can be useful if a person is capable of persevering independently, and turning out some written work regularly.

Making a Beginning

Most writers have made a very humble beginning in their younger years. It may have been when their contributions were published in school or college magazines. It could also be when letters or comments were published in a newspaper or a magazine that had nothing to offer except for the satisfaction of having broken into print.

There are many fields of work in a career in writing. Before one can make a sound beginning one must consider whether one would like to work full-time with a newspaper or magazine, or would like to pursue writing only as a freelance. Even then one needs to decide whether to specialize in reporting, article writing, short story writing, writing for children, or may be for the stage, the radio or TV.

Besides the ability to write well many possess technical knowledge about a particular subject. Therefore, they specialize in writing on specific subjects like aviation, finance, medicine, commerce, the environment, etc. Even in the field of fiction writing, writers specialize in writing for children, light romances, murder mysteries, etc. There is a big field of self-improvement subjects also. There is a wide range of subjects that would interest beginners in writing. However, gradually one is able to understand personal preferences, and specialize in that field.

The real beginning for a writer comes when he can produce good work regularly for a newspaper or magazine as a regular reporter/contributor. He can then send his work for consideration of the editors of various newspapers and magazines that find it of interest. Although freelancing has its advantages, most successful writers agree that the finest lessons they learnt in the trade were when they were reporters for newspapers and magazines. There they learnt how the trade operates. It also afforded them the opportunity to come into close touch with people and events. They learnt those realities of life on which they could base their future work.

Those interested in writing books have to hunt around for a publisher who would be interested in the kind of work they produce and can offer. Rejection slips from editors and publishers should not frighten enthusiastic writers. No writer worthy of a name has achieved success without getting his due share. There have been many instances when books turned down by important publishers went on to create publishing history when they were published by some other publisher.

Responsibilities Involved

The basic responsibility of a writer is to produce the kind of work that editors and publishers want. To be able to do this one must understand the needs of the market well.

In any newspaper, it is the reporter who regularly covers events, and 'turns in a story' about the happenings at the end of the day. The work of a reporter can be tedious. It may vary from reporting the arrival of a dignitary at the airport to visiting the police station and other places to report on a bank robbery, or even murder! Of course, outstation reporters (or correspondents) send in news from outstations. Many of these do not work full-time. They are paid according to work involved in a particular assignment.

The reporters work directly under the Chief Reporter who assigns responsibilities to each one. When reports are received, he sorts out those that are worthy of publishing. The sub-editors cut down, or re-write the subject matter highlighting the important facts, and adding headlines as required. Depending upon the scope of the newspaper, different persons are assigned duties as feature writers, sub-editors, etc., with chief editor having the overall responsibility. Supporting executives look after advertisements, circulation, business development, etc., with the overall charge being the responsibility of the Managing Director.

The staff maintained by house journals is invariably small. The news is collected from different branches by post. It is edited and published by the editor on behalf of the company or organization.

Book publishers employ editors and sub-editors to go through various manuscripts they receive for publishing. Some publishers hire freelance readers to assess manuscripts for their scope in the book market. Editors also prepare the manuscripts for the printer by making necessary corrections, improvements, additions, etc.

Income from Writing

The small local newspapers and magazines do not employ many members of the staff. Those on roll are hired on mutually negotiated salaries. However, the staff writers and sub-editors with good newspapers are assured of regulated wages revised from time to time by the Government Wage Boards. They receive steady increments with increasing experience. Many staffers have written books on topical subjects using the experience gained through their work. Many of these have fetched handsome royalties for the authors.

The income of freelancers depend very much upon their output, and the market they cater for. The payment depends upon the length of the contribution. Good newspapers and magazines with good circulation pay well. Contributions of a sensational and topical nature fetch high and exclusive prices. If the author can get his work published abroad, the returns are much higher when he is paid in foreign currency.

Book publishers may offer to buy the copyright of a book by a new author at a mutually negotiated price. However, authors prefer to get their work published on royalty basis. The usual royalty offered by publishers is 10 to 15 per cent for books published in hardback, and 5 to 7½ per cent for the paperback editions. The usual first print order for hardback editions may be about 1000 copies, and 3000 to 5000 copies for paperback editions.

One cannot predict when the work or a book by an author will become a best-seller. Once this happens, a writer can look forward to a comfortable and easy time. He can work to his own personal convenience, hoping that each new work will bring in still greater returns. Some authors have earned six-figure royalty incomes from a book in a single year.

Opportunities for Self-employment

Few careers offer as free a choice for self-employment as does a career in writing. In fact, most people writing for magazines and publishers are freelancers who regularly submit their work for the consideration of editors. Since written work can be marketed all over the world, provided the work meets the standard of publication, a steady writer can look forward to a reasonable income from writing if he has found the right markets for his work. To ensure greater security, many writers have combined a career in writing with another career such as teaching, running a bookshop, a printing press, publishing a weekly magazine, or even running a small publishing house.

Languages

55

Proficiency in more than two languages open opportunities for a variety of careers. More than ever before young people are learning foreign languages to take up specialized careers based upon the knowledge of a particular language. With this in mind people are learning Spanish, German, French, Arabic, Persian, Chinese, Russian, Japanese, Korean, Portuguese, Italian and other languages.

With trade opening up with countries around the world there is need for professionals who know the language of the country one is dealing with along with the knowledge of English. Many foreign companies are establishing businesses including manufacturing units. With the senior staff speaking a language that is different from what the local staff speaks there is need for interpreters. They can help establish a two-way communication soon.

The knowledge of different languages also opens opportunities for translating documents and books. Foreign missions in India and abroad also require multi-lingual staff. The foreign inward tourist traffic into India is steadily increasing. Tourist guides who can speak languages other than Hindi or English are required as interpreters. The opportunities for careers will continue to grow.

Desirable Personal Qualities

To be successful in this field a person must:

- be proficient in the language of choice besides knowing English and Hindi.
- possess good communication skills, both verbal and written.

- have a good personality. One will need to interact with a variety of people.
- have good manners and etiquette. This helps in making cordial relationships.
- continue to improve language skills. Learning is a continuous process.
- have additional knowledge of business procedures, or of one's country depending upon the place where languages are used. This is helpful at work.
- be willing to work long hours at odd times. Most of the time it is not a 9 to 5 desk job.
- possess computer skills. This is helpful in many situations.

Opportunities in Languages

Opportunities in languages exist in a wide spectrum of activities. With international trade growing, both inward and outward, opportunities exist in business and manufacturing houses that are dealing with non-English speaking countries around the world. This includes countries like China, Japan and Korea. The countries in Europe predominantly use French and German. Knowledge of Spanish is essential to deal with countries in South America.

The tourism industry too has need for multi-lingual young people who can converse with tourists in their native language. This helps promote the business, gives the tourist a better in-depth knowledge of what they see and promotes greater goodwill.

The need for translating documents and books of interest in different languages too offers opportunities for work. It is only through such services that many of scriptures and literary works are available in different languages around the world. In the same way, translations have made it possible for foreign literary works reach those who know Hindi or a regional language. Publishers that specialize in this field are on the lookout for good translators.

Business houses are also on the lookout for good translators to prepare instructional manuals, packaging, etc., for products that sell in non-English speaking countries.

Young people proficient in languages are required in foreign missions in India and abroad to serve as interpreters. Some of the government offices too have their need for people knowing foreign languages. Many features in newspapers and magazines in foreign languages need to be correctly understood for possible repercussions.

With many languages that can be learnt the greatest opportunity is that of teaching languages in schools, colleges and universities. Many courses are being introduced and teachers would be required to provide the necessary faculty. Besides a vocation the knowledge of other languages provides an opportunity to understand and know more about the nations where the language is spoken.

Educational Facilities

Young people interested in learning languages can begin learning them at school. However, all foreign languages are not available for study at school level. Most schools teach Hindi, English and the regional language. French and German can be learnt as additional languages.

The next step for gaining language proficiency is to opt for a language at the Bachelor's level after 10+2. Many institutions offer courses in languages. Jawahar Lal Nehru University's Centre for Language and Cultural Studies, New Delhi, offers courses both at Bachelor's and Master's level. Admission is on the basis of an entrance written test followed by an interview. One must check the admission requirements with the particular institution.

Making a Beginning

One can make a small beginning in the career even during one's studies. One can work part-time in one of the fields where language proficiency is required. On qualifying one can join the field of choice. Since additional knowledge is required in some of the fields pertaining to business and manufacturing, depending upon an individual's choice one can pursue additional knowledge. One settles in the work gradually.

Income from Careers in Languages

Careers in languages are at par with those in teaching. One will necessarily need to join at the lowest level, and rise gradually with ability and experience. Growth in such careers is slow. Many people have attained high positions with time.

Opportunities for Self-employment

Those who seek the security of a job join business and manufacturing units, government institutions and foreign missions or take up teaching assignments. Many prefer to be self-employed by taking up translation assignments, or work as interpreters when required.

Law

56

In any country one of the basic needs is that of providing justice to all its citizens. This requires an elaborate judicial set-up. Many laws need to be enacted to clearly define the responsibilities and privileges of the citizens, particularly in respect of their property, business, health, security, etc. In our country, there are hundreds of Acts enacted by the Lok Sabha to safeguard the interests of the citizens and the nation. Many more come within the scope of individual States. Vidhan Sabha in each State enacts them. Newer laws are enacted each year to ensure justice for everyone.

With human nature being what it is, and misunderstandings arising out of ignorance, or the wilful infringement of laws, peculiar situations arise that require a huge set-up of the legal machinery to find reasonable solutions. At each step, this gives rise to opportunities for careers in law. With increasing education and awareness amongst the weaker sections of the society, opportunities for service are growing. Young people interested in this field can use these to build up worthwhile careers in law for themselves.

Desirable Personal Qualities

To be successful in this field, a person must:

- be of high integrity and honour to enjoy the clients' confidence. A lawyer gets to know a lot of confidential details about a client's life and business.
- understand human nature well. Most disputes relate to lack of understanding between people.
- have a good knowledge of the basic laws and the field of specialization.
- be observant and analytical of a situation to understand

a legal case. Without such knowledge one cannot represent a client well.

- have excellent communication skills. A lawyer needs to present complicated situations in simple language.
- have good speaking skills. All cases need to be argued before a judge. Good speaking skills help represent a client's case well.
- be witty and humorous. Wit and good humour help ease many a complicated situation.
- be fond of reading. To keep up-to-date with the latest law, a reading habit is very important to a lawyer.
- be thorough and methodical in finding solutions to problems.
- be willing to spend long hours at work. One needs to spend the daytime in the courts, and mornings and evenings with the clients.

Opportunities in Law

To dispense justice to the citizens of the country, at the highest level we have the Supreme Court of India at New Delhi. At the state level, we have the High Courts. At the district level, District Judges ensure law and justice for all people. The District Judges are assisted by Additional District Judges, Civil Judges, Chief Judicial Magistrate, Judicial Magistrates, Munsifs and Additional Munsifs. Besides these officials, the Sub-Divisional Officers, Additional District Magistrates, Collectors and Commissioners also dispense justice besides fulfilling their executive responsibilities. To look after registration of property documents, wills, agreements, power of attorney, etc., there are Registrars and Sub-registrars.

To assist these custodians of law and justice in the country, there are lawyers, or advocates as they are popularly called who help and represent clients to plead their individual cases. To assist the lawyers there are assistants who help to do the less important duties, and typists who help type documents. For less important jobs, there are independent petition-writers that help draft and register documents. Lawyers working as

Notaries Public and Oath Commissioners assist in swearing affidavits and verifying documents. Stamp vendors sell court-fees stamps, paper, forms, etc. Lawyers who have specialized in taxation work, prepare returns of sales tax, trade tax, service tax, income tax, etc., and represent their clients in the offices of Sales Tax Officers, Income Tax Officers and others.

The field of practice of law is very large. Depending upon personal choice, lawyers specialize in one of the many fields open to them. With increasing education and awareness of the rights and privileges amongst people of all strata of society, there are increasing number of opportunities for young people interested in careers in law.

Educational Facilities

Many colleges and faculties of universities offer courses in law. Some offer a five-year course after 10+2 to offer a B.A. LL.B. (Hons.) degree. Graduates can join a three-year LL.B. course conducted by most universities in the country. These facilities are available all over the country. A two years' course after graduation in Arts or Science entitles one to a LL.B. degree. For professional practice, one needs to study for an additional year. Only then one is entitled to be called an Advocate. Before setting out in private practice, it is desirable to work as a junior advocate with an established senior lawyer practising the particular line of interest. Those interested in Taxation Law Practice need not do LL.B., but may pursue studies in the field of Accountancy. The details are given in the chapter: Accountancy.

Making a Beginning

One can make a beginning in a career in law at different levels. Some join a lawyer without any specialized knowledge of law or experience. They do petty jobs like filing papers, getting documents ready, obtaining copies from courts, and such other duties. In the same way, a typist interested in law work may get attached to a single lawyer who has enough work, or to several lawyers who can give him work to keep him occupied. He may also set out on his own, and work free lance for whoever comes to him. Those interested in petition writing learn the trade by attaching themselves to established petition-writers. They pick up the work gradually through experience and hard work. Assistants to magistrates and judges are promoted from clerical positions in the offices.

Those interested in the higher levels of work need to graduate in law after a Bachelor's degree in Arts or Science. On graduation one can join an established lawyer who is practising the line of one's choice, and work as his junior by helping to prepare documents, study case law, prepare arguments, etc.

Practising of law is divided into Civil Law Practice, Criminal Law Practice and Revenue Law Practice. Some go into the field of Taxation Law Practice. Even within these sub-divisions, lawyers specialize in particular Acts such as Rent Control Act, Land Acquisition Act, Labour Laws, Divorce Laws, Company Laws, Writing of Wills and Deeds, Criminal Law, etc. The choice depends upon personal liking and interest.

Lawyers who show merit and dedication are attached to business concerns, banks, schools and institutions as advisors. Those who have a flair for writing and interpretation of different laws can take to the writing of legal books that have a good demand, and one can live well off them.

The senior positions in the Judiciary are filled through promotions. Additional Munsifs are appointed on the basis of a competitive examination, followed by an interview. State governments appoint Oath Commissioners from amongst practising lawyers.

Income from Law

Lawyers who set out to practise independently do not attract immediate clientele. They do not possess the experience of their senior colleagues. Yet those engaged in careers in law do well. Lawyers are some of the most highly paid professionals. They normally charge for a case in a lump sum, or sometimes based on appearances in court. Ten to fifteen per cent of their charges are allocated for the assistant and miscellaneous expenses. Senior lawyers who have gained valuable experience charge exorbitantly for their work. The charges of petition-writers and typists in the courts are invariably fixed by mutual negotiation, or as directed by their own associations. The salaries of the Judiciary are at par with those of similar cadres in government service.

Opportunities for Self-employment

Except for the Judiciary that is a part of the government set-up, and some lawyers who may attach themselves to government departments and certain business houses as full-time legal advisors, the entire legal profession can be said to be self-employed. Many of the lawyers who are attached to business houses, banks and other institutions as advisors reserve their right to entertain clientele other than those for whom they work on a preferential basis. At all levels there are ample opportunities for young people to set out on their own in a career in law as soon as they have gained valuable working experience from a senior lawyer. The opportunities are there. It is for individuals to relate them to their personal needs, and build a lifetime career in the field of law.

Librarian

57

In the recent years there has been a big growth in educational institutions of all kinds. Every educational institution needs a library. Every library needs library staff. Earlier, a librarian's work was restricted in that libraries only had books and magazines. With the explosion in information technology and availability of computers and other devices, information is now available on records, tapes, films, microfilms, floppies, CDs and other audio-visual aids. It is the librarian's responsibility to ensure that a person can get a required information in the least amount of time with as little effort as possible. The librarian's work has become challenging.

Desirable Personal Qualities

To be successful in this field, a person must:

- love books. Books and book lovers surround a librarian all day.
- have the ability to handle a lot of information. There has been an explosion in the field of information. A librarian is expected to handle it all.
- have an interest in a wide range of subjects. Without a wide interest one cannot justify one's work.
- possess a good memory. That helps connect people and information quickly.
- have lots of patience. People who want information can be both, aggressive and impatient.
- have a good knowledge of the publishing industry. That helps procure a variety of books at competitive prices.
- have computer skills. Computers have made work easier and more comfortable for the librarian.

Opportunities as a Librarian

All good schools, colleges, educational institutions and universities need a good library. One or two people run the smaller libraries. The larger ones have separate departments looked after by several people. The larger libraries will have arrangements for user services, technical services and administrative services. They will have special departments like reference section, manuscript department, photo department and audio-visual section.

Besides libraries in educational institutions there are public libraries, government libraries and libraries maintained by embassies. Science and technology libraries, social science libraries, and media institution libraries also require qualified persons. Archives and national libraries too need library personnel. With a regular requirement for librarians, many educational institutions that train them require good teaching staff specializing in Library Science.

Educational Facilities

A person can get into this field after a bachelor's degree in Library Science. A large number of library schools are spread all over the country. They offer a one-year course leading to B.Lib.Sc. or B.Li.Sc. Many of these institutions offer a one-year course in M.Li.Sc. A few universities also offer correspondence courses with a study period of 4 to 12 months. Delhi University offers a M.Phil. course in Library Science.

Making a Beginning

One begins a career as an assistant in a library. The next step may be to become a deputy librarian and finally a librarian. The designation may vary from one institution to another, and also depending upon the responsibilities involved. One may be called Information assistant or Technical assistant, or something similar. At senior level one may rise to the position of Director of the library.

Income as a Librarian

A person working in a college library gets a salary that is in harmony with that of other college staff. There are steady increments. Salaries in private libraries are good, depending upon the kind of responsibilities handled.

Opportunities for Self-employment

By the very nature of the work one can appreciate that there are no opportunities for self-employment in this field. In smaller towns some people do run small lending libraries that stock a limited number of books, but depend specially on circulation of magazines.

Management

58

Specialization and competition in all fields is growing. With an interaction of several factors affecting the productivity and profitability of organizations, an important field of occupations that has emerged in the past few decades is that of management. In the present times, to ensure success of an organization one needs to understand the practical implications of the political, social and economic environment. One requires keeping pace with the changes, and in general promoting the concept of efficiency and productivity amongst workers.

This requires an understanding of subjects like psychology, politics, law, economics, commerce, production, human relations, etc. There is need to coordinate the many factors that affect the working of the organization. The detailed study of the subject constitutes the study of management techniques. Even those who are qualified as engineers, technologists, etc. are attracted to the study of management techniques as this ensures them important positions as managers in commerce and industry.

Desirable Personal Qualities

To be successful in this field, a person must:

- be endowed with leadership qualities. Managers need to show direction.
- have a good knowledge of people and places. One must be able to get along well with a variety of people.
- be observant. One must be able to assess a situation quickly.
- be capable of making good decisions. Success depends upon them.

- be completely dedicated to the work. One needs to keep going when others tend to slow down.
- know how to handle subordinates. Their work adds to make a manager successful.
- not be carried away by fair or unfair criticism. It is a part of a manager's work.
- be willing to take responsibility for failures. Successes come from learning from failures.
- know how to handle stressful circumstances. Stress is a part of a manager's work. One must know how to cope with it.
- not be discouraged when the going is tough. Management jobs involve individual responsibility. One may feel lonely in a senior position.
- strive to improve one's performance continuously. This is a dynamic world. One needs to be on the move all the time.
- be up-to-date with one's line of specialization. This is the only way to face competition.

Opportunities in Management

Good managers are required in all fields of business and commerce, and all other organizations that require management. Not many young people possess qualities to fill the exacting requirements of important positions in this field. A good manager is always welcome in any organization. It is true that those who go in for this field of work are capable. Therefore, the competition amongst them is stiff. Even in fields where only technical qualifications were required, specialization in management is being preferred. Engineers and technologists are finding it useful to learn the techniques of management for application in their respective fields of work.

Since experience is an important constituent of good management techniques, most of the important senior positions would not interest young people just emerging in a career in management. However, managerial positions, even at lower levels are very attractive. Companies are competing with each other to attract capable young managers, and go to important management institutes to pick the best. The positions generally relate to technical fields like marketing, finance, production, operations research, purchasing, advertising and other similar fields.

Educational Facilities

Young people interested in careers in management need to pursue postgraduate studies in management after graduation in a field of their choice. Many institutions and universities in India offer full-time and part-time courses in management. Several private institutions imparting education in management fields have come up in the recent past. Many of the bigger business houses have their own manpower development departments where they train their managers to suit the individual needs of their companies.

To qualify for admission to a postgraduate course in management, a person needs to be a graduate in the field of his specialization. There is an entrance examination. Those who secure necessary marks are invited for an interview/ personality test. The details of the courses offered can be obtained directly from the institutions. Many of them advertise in the national press for fresh admissions. Some of the important institutions offering courses in management are:

Indian Institute of Management,
Vastrapur,
Ahmedabad.

Indian Institute of Management,
Joka, Diamond Harbour Road,
Kolkata (24 Parganas).

Indian Institute of Management,
33 Langford Road,
Bangalore.

Indian Institute of Management,
Lucknow.

Jamnalal Bajaj Institute,
Mumbai.

Xavier Labour Relations Institute,
Post Box No. 46,
Jamshedpur-1.

College of Business Management,
Chikkadpalli,
Hyderabad.

Moti Lal Nehru Institute of
Research & Business
Administration,
University of Allahabad,
Allahabad (U.P.)

Besides the above-mentioned institutions, there are many colleges and departments of universities that offer courses in management studies, at both undergraduate and postgraduate level. The details of the courses and colleges can be referred to in the directories being published on the subject. Some institutions offer correspondence courses also.

The British Institutes, Mumbai-400023, offers postal courses in Management Accountancy, Business Administration, Personality Development and Human Relations, Sales Management, and also Industrial Administration and Management Course, Personnel Manager's Course and Management Executive's Course. Besides these, the Institute also prepares students for the A.I.A.M. examination of the Institute of Administrative Management, N-34, Jangpura Extension, New Delhi-110014, and for Diploma in Business Management examination of the Indian Merchants' Chamber, Mumbai-400020.

The International Correspondence School, Mumbai-400023, also offers Business Management Course, Personnel Management Course, Industrial Management Course, Sales Management Course and Marketing Management Course. There are no minimum qualifications laid down for the correspondence courses. Those who are already employed will find them useful to step to higher positions in their field of work.

Making a Beginning

Careers in management are very competitive. Only a selected few go into this field of vocations. Management positions are advertised in the national press, as one would want the very best candidates. Those in top management institutions are picked from the campus even before they pass out. Young people taking up careers in management may begin as management trainees, and after a period of on-the-job training in various departments of the company, may be appointed as assistant managers or junior executives attached to an established manager. Unless one is very highly qualified in a specialized line, few young people can join the senior positions in the management. Almost all of them require a high degree of work experience. However, in the field of management, ability matters. Those who are capable and hardworking rise swiftly.

Income from Management

Careers in management are well paid. Those who are well qualified can expect very high salaries even on starting in the career. Besides a good salary, many fringe benefits are offered to managers by way of house rent allowance, free vehicles, medical benefits for self and family, entertainment expense account and other such benefits. Good managers are always in short supply. A capable person can rise quickly if s/he can handle responsibility independently.

Opportunities for Self-employment

Since management positions aim at managing men and materials on a large scale, such a scope exists only in large undertakings. As a manager, one can use his capabilities in big companies. Therefore, one cannot hope to get self-employed as a manager unless one possesses other qualifications and resources to start a personal business concern. Managers at top levels can get self-employed as consultants to several companies. Such occupations would be beyond the scope of young people beginning a career in management.

Medical Transcription

59

Amongst the many careers based upon information technology, medical transcription and similar careers where computer literate persons need to process and give shape to important information and return it are important in a developing country like India.

Medical transcription involves the receiving of medical records and documents through telephones and satellites, processing them and returning without delay. This is a career suitable for persons who have medical knowledge and are computer literate. Language skills are also important. The careers in this field are the result of mandatory requirement in several developed countries to maintain different kinds of records not only for medical needs, but also to process insurance claims.

India is very suitably placed to provide service in this field. When it is day in the U.S.A., it is night here, and similarly when it is day here, it is night there. The information generated there in the day is sent to India. During the day in India (and night in U.S.A.) the information is processed and returned. The information as desired is in their hand the first thing the next morning.

What is Medical Transcription?

Doctors are highly paid in the developed countries. Their time is very valuable. To save on their time they use Dictaphones to dictate and record their medical observations about patients. These records include details of patient histories, pathological reports, details of surgical procedures and other important information. Since these records cannot be used in their audio form, they are transmitted to medical transcription centres. At the centres trained personnel use headphones and computers to transcribe the audio into text format. The text is returned to the medical centres where it is used to fulfil the necessary legal requirements.

Desirable Personal Qualities

To be successful in this field, a person must:

- possess good listening skills. The work is based upon hearing the correct message.
- have a good knowledge of English. Without language skills it will not be possible to prepare the correct text. It is important to write good English.
- appreciate that people in different parts of the world use different dialects when speaking English. One will need to get used to them.
- understand medical terminology. Doctors use medical jargon. Unless the professional understands it, the report may be incoherent.
- be willing to work for long hours on a desk job. Sometimes, the pressures can be high, and one may need to work for long periods.
- possess good typing skills. Accuracy is very important.
- be willing to work as a team. The work requires people to work in cooperation with each other.

Opportunities in Medical Transcription

Medical transcription is a new field of careers, and is based primarily on the fact that we have a large English knowing computer literate workforce. As compared to the developed countries, the workforce is willing to work at lower salaries. The difference in time zones helps provide efficient service.

Presently, there are about 200 medical transcription centres employing 5,000 to 8,000 persons. However, it is estimated that the work will grow. The projected need is estimated at 50,000 to 100,000 persons. The opening of the health insurance sector will make it necessary for hospitals and nursing homes to maintain greater documentation to process insurance claims. That too will add to the opportunities in this field.

Besides medical transcription there are similar services

required for correction of books and important documents. The field will gradually grow. Newer opportunities will come. Computer skills will be used in a variety of ways.

Other Related Fields

With a cheaper workforce of English knowing computer literate people available in India, there will be opportunities for similar work in other fields also. This is referred to as remote processing. This has the potential of becoming a big industry where people can work from their homes. Already people are getting involved in legal transcription, Tele-conferencing transcription, coding business and other such activities. We can look forward to additional employment opportunities in these fields.

Educational Facilities

With medical transcription growing as a field for careers for English-knowing computer literate persons, new institutions are coming up to train personnel through short-term and regular courses. Most of the institutes are new. To fulfil the need many personnel were hurriedly trained and provided jobs. One can join after 10+2, but it is preferable to do a bachelor's degree before taking a course in medical transcription. The course fees can be high. The course may be for 3 to 6 months.

With the training situation gradually stabilizing, when selecting an educational institution one should thoroughly understand the content of the course being offered. The curriculum must include details like study of diseases, pharmacology, laboratory terminology and details, medico-legal details, healthcare records and ethical considerations. It is also necessary that a part of the training must be on the job. The training must be thorough. The student must appreciate that there is no scope for making any mistakes.

Making a Beginning

A person joins the field as a trainee. With experience one becomes a medical transcriptionist. The responsibilities include transcribing a doctor's audio reports on the treatment of his patient into proper form. It may include converting a doctor's short technical jargon into proper medical language. This will involve formatting the document and checking on spellings and other inconsistencies.

With additional experience one becomes an executive and then a senior medical transcriptionist. The field of activity can include proof reading, editing, quality coordination, team leader, trainer and manager. As in all other fields those who are committed to their work rise quickly. Since this is a growing field, promotions can be fast for capable persons.

Income from Medical Transcription

Income from medical transcription in the developed countries could be as much as $ 25 per hour of work. In India it is at par with other computer-related jobs. Incentives in this field are performance-related. With great disparity between wages in the developed countries and in India, there is scope for increase in work and salaries.

Opportunities for Self-employment

Depending upon the nature of the responsibility and the set-up of the centre, a person doing a job will necessarily need to be accountable to the employer. However, there are persons who work from their homes on their own computers and are paid on the basis of the work they do. Opportunities for self-employment will grow with development of better telecommunications network.

Medicine

60

Many young people are attracted to careers in medicine because of the thrill and glamour attached to an occupation where a person is almost like God. One helps to alleviate pain and suffering and ensures health for everyone. The honour and prestige along with the financial gains also attract young people to this career. However, to be successful in a career in medicine, it is more important to understand the responsibilities involved. Careers in this field provide both challenges and rewards.

Next to food, healthcare is a primary need of all people. This has given rise to opportunities in many ways. Careers in medicine cover a very wide field of occupations. With increasing knowledge and experience specialization has grown in every field. In our country, besides the practice of the conventional system of treatment, there are several other systems of treatment such as Ayurveda, Unani, Homoeopathy, Nature cure and systems like Magneto-therapy, Acupuncture, Acupressure and Reiki. These are discussed separately in the chapter on Alternative Medicine. These have made it possible for a large number of people to find useful occupations in various positions.

Desirable Personal Qualities

To be successful in this field, a person must:

- possess a missionary zeal to serve. Conquering pain and suffering is an important element of careers in this field.
- have a thorough knowledge of the human mind and the body.
- appreciate the need to update knowledge regularly through continuous practice and study.

- have a keen observation and an analytical mind. This enables one to understand the patients well.
- be willing to work at odd hours. Emergencies are a part of this field of careers.
- personally enjoy good health. The work involves physical and mental involvement. The routine can be strenuous.
- have a genial temperament, patience and a good sense of humour. It will be necessary to keep the patients in a happy frame of mind.
- work with an open mind. The doctor treats. God cures the patient.

Opportunities in Medicine

The field of medicine is very vast. Wherever there are human beings, there will be need for the medical profession to ensure good health. With greater education and general awareness about sickness and disease, there is a greater health consciousness amongst all people. Rather than visit a doctor only in sickness, people are placing complete faith in the need for immunization of children against diseases, and for regular health check-ups, dental care, and eye care.

To most young people a career in medicine means working on their own as a private practitioner, or as a doctor in a hospital. Few realize that the field of medicine is very vast. Qualified persons are required at every step to look after the healthcare systems that are emerging as a result of specialization in every field. A general practitioner represents the typical person engaged in a career in medicine.

Specialization leads one to work not only as a physician, or as a surgeon. It leads one into fields like pathology, radiology, osteopathy, neurology, ophthalmology, dermatology, sexology, gynaecology, pediatrics, obstetrics, anesthetics, and cardiology. One specializes in diseases of ears, nose and throat, of the chest, or in diseases like tuberculosis, cancer, dysfunction of the ductless glands, etc. Surgery too leads to specialization of the brain, chest, heart, and other parts of the body. The field is fast growing into other areas of specialization according to need and interest.

In gauging opportunities in medicine and allied fields, we should not overlook that besides the main school of allopathic medicine being practised in our country, there are several other systems like Ayurveda, Unani, Homoeopathy, Nature cure and other alternate systems. Each one of these has its own importance. These are discussed in separate chapters on Alternative Medicine and Homoeopathy. Each system offers opportunities for gainful employment. There is a need for teaching of the systems in many colleges in the country, and to practice it. Each system has a need for medicines. This offers opportunities to prepare and market these medicines.

Besides the opportunities for becoming a practising doctor, there are many employment opportunities for manufacture and sale of all kinds of medicines, tonics and foods recommended by the doctors to the patients. We have a very large medicine manufacturing industry. It regularly needs qualified young people to fill in appropriate positions from time to time. The development in Ayurveda and other systems have brought in many useful medicines that can be shared worldwide, again opening newer opportunities for employment.

The manufacture of specialized equipment specially required by the medical profession in hospitals and nursing homes offers many useful opportunities also. Teaching and research opportunities in the field of medicine are always growing. These need to be brought to the notice of the practising medical profession through a vast number of medical journals. These offer many opportunities of employment to those interested in such careers.

At the lower levels in the field of medicine, we cannot overlook the need for nurses and attendants to look after the patients. Laboratory assistants, technicians, pharmacists, x-ray technicians, anesthetists, dental mechanics and hygienists all have important roles to play in the field of medicine. There is always a good demand for nurses in hospitals and dispensaries, and even as assistants to private practitioners.

Many people have found gainful employment as health visitors and family planning workers in the villages. Municipal services offer positions for sanitary inspectors, vaccinators, etc., who work under the supervision of qualified doctors. Physiotherapy is a growing field of service. Many physiotherapists are working under the supervision of qualified physicians and surgeons.

Dentistry is in itself a complete medical service. Besides qualified dentists, there is need for dental mechanics and hygienists to assist the dental surgeon in his work. This field of medicine is growing rapidly. Within dentistry, there is specialization into several fields like orthodontia, ceramics, etc. The subject is discussed in greater detail in the chapter on Dentistry.

The Medical Corps which serves the army, navy and the air force through the many military hospitals and health centres all over the country is a very large set-up. It has positions at all levels for young people interested in medicine as a career.

Young people who have a love for animals and are interested in medicine can become veterinarians. With a vast cattle population in our country, and with a general need to develop our cattle wealth, this field has many useful possibilities, particularly in the rural areas. Development of poultry farms too has created opportunities for veterinarians specializing in this field of service.

More than 70 per cent of our population lives in villages. Very little medical aid is available there. Most of the medical facilities in our country cater only to the urban areas. The specialists live only in the larger cities. With growing development and availability of better living conditions in the villages, doctors are gradually moving into rural areas. With this, more opportunities will open in the field of medicine. There is such a vast scope for better medical services in our villages that it will be a long time before we can say that we are self-sufficient in the medical field all over the country.

Educational Facilities

There are medical colleges in almost every state of the country. While the Central or State governments supervise the working of some, others are managed by private organizations. One can join a medical college after passing the Intermediate examination, pre-medical or pre-university examination, or passing the 10+2 examination with Physics, Chemistry and Biology as main subjects. Some colleges insist upon proficiency in English also. Students in Ayurvedic medical colleges need to know Sanskrit.

Admission to medical colleges is through a competitive examination. Some colleges observe domicile restrictions. Others do not. Most medical colleges provide education in the allopathic system of medicine. Some provide education in the integrated system that includes both allopathic and Ayurvedic systems. Several colleges provide education in Homoeopathy system of medicine. In most colleges, the courses are for four to five years, followed by a period of internship. The courses lead to a Bachelor's degree in Medicine and Surgery.

Most young people taking up a career in medicine do not immediately join on obtaining their Bachelor's degree in Medicine and Surgery, but proceed for postgraduate courses in a field of specialization. Almost all of the older medical colleges are offering postgraduate courses of specialization in various fields of medicine.

To obtain a complete list of medical colleges and the courses offered by them, please consult a directory listing the details.

Making a Beginning

To become a doctor one needs to qualify from a medical college, and join either a hospital or dispensary. One can also begin practice on one's own. The same is also applicable to Dental Surgeons, Veterinary Surgeons and other qualified persons. Many young people prefer to pursue a job for some time as this provides them valuable experience. Jobs are advertised in the national press, or one can apply directly if one is interested in serving in a private nursing home or hospital. Those who have received specialized education can set out as specialists in that field.

Many pharmacists and attendants attached to private practitioners have learnt the making and dispensing of powders, ointments and liquid medicines from doctors. However, law requires that a person who has passed High School should do such work after obtaining a Diploma approved by the Pharmacy Council of India. For manufacturing, dispensing and retailing of medicines, it is necessary that the work must be done under the supervision of a qualified person who has a Bachelor's degree in Pharmacy.

Laboratory assistants and technicians can take up responsibility only after obtaining a diploma in the particular field after High School or 10+2. Young people interested in careers as Dental hygienists and mechanics can qualify through diploma courses offered by Dental Colleges. The minimum requirement for these courses is High School or 10+2.

In some States if a person has the knowledge and experience gained through working with a qualified doctor over a period, registration as a medical practitioner can be obtained. This is not very common. It was done to encourage those with some medical knowledge to move to rural areas where no medical services are available. Some correspondence schools offer medical related knowledge through post, particularly in Homoeopathy. After completing the course, and appearing in an examination prescribed by the State government, one could be registered as a homoeopathic practitioner. With some individuals having taken undue advantage of some provisions, the government is adopting stiffer norms to restrict entry into this field through the back door.

Income from Careers in Medicine

Careers in medicine are well paid. At the lower levels when the young people are inexperienced, the salaries are negotiable. However, those who have gained experience are well paid. A qualified doctor can begin with a salary that is comparable with that of any other profession. Capable doctors earn good incomes. Incomes rise with experience. Private practitioners begin in a small way. Once established, they are known to earn much more than their salaried friends working in hospitals and nursing homes. There is really no upper limit of income for doctors as they earn large sums of money through private practice. Many doctors have their own nursing homes and clinics where they employ junior doctors to assist them.

Opportunities for Self-employment

Although there are no opportunities for self-employment for technicians, medical assistants, and other junior staff who would necessarily need to work under the supervision of qualified doctors in a hospital or nursing home, there are good opportunities for self-employment for qualified doctors. Doctors work on their own as general practitioners. Those with resources have opened their own nursing homes where facilities for surgery are also available. Many specialists work on their own. Some unite to form groups to establish a polyclinic where complete medical facilities are available. Doctors are known to supplement their income by running chemist's shops attached to their clinics, or by having a pathological laboratory, or a x-ray plant. Some are known to have established manufacturing units for medicines and other supplies.

Merchant Navy

61

With a vast coastline and a growing export trade with countries all over the world, one can well appreciate the importance of the merchant navy. With the development and growth of air services, passenger service by sea has reduced. However, a fair-sized merchant navy serving many faraway countries has developed over the years. The total tonnage of exports is on the rise.

It is a reasonable expectation that 50 per cent of exports must go through our own shipping companies. There is still a big gap to be covered. To this, if we could add the need for personnel in the merchant navy by the foreign shipping companies working in and around India, one can see the potential for careers in this vocation. This means growing opportunities for young people interested in careers in the merchant navy.

Desirable Personal Qualities

To be successful in this field, a person must:

- have a desire to move about in faraway places around the world.
- be willing to stay away from home for long periods. A single round of the ship may take 6 to 9 months to complete.
- accept living with a limited number of people on the ship. This can be a very lonely experience.
- enjoy swimming. One is surrounded by water most of the time.
- be physically strong and possess stamina for continuous work. The work can be very strenuous at times.
- be disciplined. One cannot afford to be careless. One must have neat working habits.

- be willing to work as a team. It is necessary to get along with others on the ship.
- have leadership skills and a good knowledge of one's work particularly when one aims at rising to higher positions.

Opportunities in the Merchant Navy

The merchant navy is a growing field of occupations. The government desires that the national exports must increase. At the same time, it is desirable that the quantum of goods shipped through our own navy should also rise to at least 50 per cent. This is a fair indication of the opportunities in the merchant navy. With greater allocations for the development of indigenous shipping, the opportunities will continue to grow. Besides jobs in various capacities in the shipping companies, the opportunities available in the merchant navy include the jobs offered by the Port Trusts and Port Commissions by way of Pilots and Harbour Masters, and in the Hooghly River Survey. Most of the opportunities exist on vessels and ships that serve the coastline and go out on the high seas to faraway countries all over the world.

On a ship there are opportunities for work at various levels. At the lowest level, there are the Ratings who are unskilled, semi-skilled and skilled workers on board. Their number varies with the type and size of the ship. The Ratings are responsible for duties on the deck, in the engine department, and in the catering and saloon departments. In each of these three sections of work, the Ratings are divided into groups each headed by a Rating designated as the Tindal. The head Rating in charge of a section is called the Serang. Besides the Ratings, there are storekeepers, sweepers, carpenters, fitters, wiremen, general servants, pantry boys, scullions, etc. Qualified electricians are responsible for the operation and maintenance of generators and fittings. Pursers are responsible for office work and account keeping.

At higher levels, there are radio officers who operate and maintain radio equipment, receive and transmit messages, decipher code messages, and do similar other work. Marine engineers are mechanical engineers with special reference to marine machinery. They are responsible for the operation and maintenance of all kinds of marine machinery on board. Depending upon the size of the vessel, there may be two to five engineers on the ship, each working turn by turn.

Besides these officers, each ship has three to five navigation officers designated as the Fifth Officer, Fourth Officer, the Third Officer, the Second Officer and the Chief Officer. Depending upon the division of responsibility, these officers are responsible for standing watch, helping arrange the loading and unloading of cargo, maintenance of lifeboats, safety and signalling equipment, winding chronometers, maintaining navigation equipment, etc.

The Chief Officer is in charge of all the operations on the ship. Finally, there is the Captain of the ship. He is overall in charge of the ship. As the representative of the owners of the ship, he is responsible for the safety of the ship, the passengers, the crew and the cargo. He ensures that there is discipline on the ship.

Opportunities for young people interested in careers in the merchant navy are not restricted to jobs in our own shipping companies. Shipping companies all over the world requires qualified personnel. There is also demand for qualified personnel in yards where the ships are repaired, and new ones fabricated. Those qualified as marine engineers have the option of working in other fields. They are basically mechanical engineers. In the same way, radio officers have opportunities of serving in other capacities in related fields of work.

Educational Facilities

Those interested in working as Ratings should apply to: The Director, Seamen's Employment Office, Nicol Road, Mumbai, or The Director, Seamen's Employment Office, "Marine House", Hastings Road, Kolkata, or The Principal Officer, Mercantile Marine Department, Chennai. Selected candidates are sent to any one of the three training ships: T.S. Bhadra at Kolkata, T.S. Mekhla at Visakhapatnam and T.S. Naulakshi at Nauakhi.

To qualify as a radio Officer, one can write to:

The Advisor, Wireless Planning & Coordination,
Ministry of Transport & Communication,
(Department of Communications),
Block no. 2, Brassey Avenue, Church Road,
New Delhi.

Young people interested in training on the T.S. Rajendra should write to:

The Captain Superintendent,
T.S. Rajendra,
Off Mazgaon Pier,
Mumbai-400010.

Those interested in marine engineering may write to:

The Director of Marine Engineering Training,
Marine Engineering College,
14 New Taratolla Road,
Kolkata-700027.

He can arrange for apprenticeship in a qualified marine workshop, and provide full-time training to qualify to appear for Part A of the Transport & Communication Ministry's Certificate of Competence as Second Class Marine Engineer.

Post-sea training courses for the Part B of the examination are offered by:

The Nautical and Engineering College,
Azad Maidan,
Waudby Road,
Mumbai-400001.

This institution also trains candidates for the Transport & Communication Ministry's Certificate of Competency as Second Mate (Foreign-going), or Mate (Home-trade). The details of the examination can be had from the Principal Officer, Mercantile Marine Department, Commerce House, Ballard Estate, Mumbai, or The Principal Officer, Mercantile Marine Department, Marine House, Hastings Road, Kolkata.

Making a Beginning

Young people interested in working as Ratings must be 18 to 25 years old, be of good health and physique, belong to a family of seafaring men, and must have completed the training course for Ratings on one of the training ships. Employment is rotational, and one works one's way up. On qualifying, one should register oneself with the Director, Seamen's Employment Office, Mumbai/Kolkata. One is placed on a ship as and when demands are received from the shipowners.

Those interested in working as electricians must possess the qualifications for an electrician. Pursers must possess a degree in Commerce. To be a Radio Officer, one must have the Transport & Communication Ministry's Second Class Certificate of Proficiency as Wireless Operator (Radiotelegraphy).

To qualify as a Marine Engineer, a candidate must obtain the Transport & Communication Ministry's Certificate of Competency as Second Class Marine Engineer. The Mercantile Marine Department holds examinations for this certificate. To be entitled to appear for Part A of the examination, a candidate must have served for four years as an apprentice in a marine or mechanical workshop, or possess the Final Passing Out Certificate of the Marine Engineering College.

For Part B, one must have served on a regular watch for 18 months as a Watch-keeping engineer. The Certificate can be either for motor or for steamships, or can be a combined Steam and Motor Certificate. A Second Class Marine Engineer, after obtaining the Certificate can find employment as a Fourth, Third or Second Engineer on a ship, depending upon the size of the ship.

A Second Class Marine Engineer can appear for Part A of the Certificate as a First Class Marine Engineer after he has obtained the Second Class Certificate, and for Part B after a sea service in full charge of a vessel for 18 months. The holder of a First Class Certificate is entitled to work as the Chief Engineer of a vessel.

To become a navigating officer in the merchant navy, sea service as an apprentice is necessary. Some join directly as apprentices on just free board and lodging, and gain experience. Some companies also pay their apprentices. If a young man has passed high school, is 16 to 18 years old, and enjoys good health, he can apply for the qualifying examination conducted by the Captain Superintendent, T.S. Rajendra. Those who qualify are called for an interview. They are then admitted to a two-year training course. On completion, one can join some of the services available directly, or join a shipping company, gain experience as an apprentice, and finally qualify for higher positions. Candidates who have successfully completed the course on T.S. Rajendra are entitled to one year's reduction in the sea service experience necessary for higher positions.

To qualify as a Navigating Officer, it is necessary to obtain the Transport & Communication Ministry's Certificate of Competency as Second Mate (Foreign-going), or as Mate (Home-trade). The Mercantile Marine Department at Mumbai and Kolkata holds examinations for these certificates. To be entitled to appear in these examinations, candidates for the Foreign-going Certificate must be 20 years old, and must have served at sea the equivalent of four years in foreign-going steamships, or six years in home-trade steamships. For the Home-trade Certificate, the sea experience desired is four years. An officer holding the Master's Certificate, Foreign-going or Home-trade is entitled to become the Captain of a ship.

Income from the Merchant Navy

Jobs in the merchant navy are well paid. Almost the entire sum is like pocket money because while on board, the living expenses are paid by the company. Besides the salary, several other benefits are offered to the workers. Foreign companies pay their employees in foreign exchange. The salaries at the lower levels are attractive. As one rises in experience and position, the increments are substantive. The promotions are steady, and capable persons rise quickly in their careers. The Captain draws the highest salary, the amount depending upon the size of the vessel in command.

Opportunities for Self-employment

Strictly speaking, there are no opportunities for self-employment in careers in the merchant navy. However, radio officers and marine engineers can find alternative employment. They can also become self-employed in a field related to their work. Having gained much experience from travels around the world, and saving enough money, many young people retire early to start their own work in a field of their choice. This also enables them to be closer to their families.

Multi-level Marketing

62

Multi-level marketing has existed for a long time. However, it was only in the mid-nineties that it caught the imagination of a lot of young people in our country, and it gained significant importance. Much of the enthusiasm was short-lived. This was particularly due to two reasons. Firstly, most people did not understand the concept of multi-level marketing. Many thought it was just a way to some quick and easy money. Secondly, many unscrupulous operators jumped on to the bandwagon to take advantage of the gullible people to make a fast buck.

For any vocation to entrench itself as a source of livelihood, it is essential that it must be based upon sound principles of fulfilling a human need. It must be based upon ethics and ethical behaviour. Only those companies progress that provide value for money. As in other vocations there are no shortcuts to success. There is no substitute for hard work.

Although several people made an attempt at introducing multi-level marketing in India, it was Amway, an international operator, which aroused the imagination of those interested in this field of work. Avon and Oriflame had existed for a long time, but their operations are limited. Modicare was the first Indian Company to build a national network of consultants, supported by a wide range of products and service. Several other Indian companies followed, but the enthusiasm has cooled down, particularly due to the negative influence of the unscrupulous operators through who people lost money. One must understand the concept of multi-level marketing before taking it up as a vocation.

What is Multi-level Marketing?

To appreciate multi-level marketing, one must understand three important concepts:

1. That it is a business. Like any other business it will require time and personal involvement. It can be a part-time business, or a full-time one.
2. That it is a business of selling products. It is, therefore, necessary that one will need to understand, use and promote these products amongst friends and relatives.
3. That it is a business of selling products through networking. Multi-level marketing is different from conventional marketing in that the profit comes not only from personal selling, but mainly from the network that one needs to build up gradually.

Is multi-level marketing worthwhile? Certainly, if one knows how to go about it. Perhaps no other business with almost an insignificant investment can give as much money as multi-level marketing. One must pick up the correct company and work sincerely.

Desirable Personal Qualities

To be successful in this field, a person must:

- be well acquainted with the principles of multi-level marketing. Without that one cannot achieve continuous success.
- use and understand the products offered by the company. One cannot sell what one does not know about well.
- be able to make friends quickly. It is not possible to build a network without being friendly.
- be sincere, honest and caring in one's dealings. One cannot sustain a network without these qualities.
- possess leadership qualities. Building and sustaining a network requires able leadership.
- be able to communicate well. To sustain a good network it will be necessary to be able to communicate fresh ideas effectively.
- be persistent. Perhaps no other work requires as much persistence as multi-level marketing.

Opportunities in Multi-level Marketing

In no other vocation can a person earn good amount of money in a short period with almost an insignificant investment as one can through multi-level marketing. However, it is important that the company one is dealing with must have products that offer value for money, and also the services of the company must be prompt and above doubt. With the vast opportunities that exist in this field, many companies were launched. However, they failed to provide the service that is expected in this field. One of the greatest opportunities that exist is that of launching new companies with innovative products offered at competitive prices. Since many small-scale industries have spare production capacity, outsourcing new products should be no problem. With millions of young people searching avenues for self-employment, building networks too should not be difficult.

Educational Facilities

To be involved in multi-level marketing one only needs to be reasonably educated. There are no educational institutions that provide formal specialized knowledge in this field. In this field one learns through consultants' meetings organized by those who are already involved in the work. The emphasis in the meetings is on two things. Firstly, to use and know the products well. Secondly, to understand human nature and use leadership techniques to build a responsible network.

Making a Beginning

One makes a beginning in this field by being sponsored as a consultant/distributor/member by an existing consultant of a multi-level marketing company. On becoming a member one is provided a kit that includes instruction manuals along with some sample products for personal use and demonstration to others.

Becoming a consultant entitles one to make purchases at special prices. The normal discount offered is about 20 per cent. This also entitles one to sponsor new members and create a network. All business transactions carry business points that are credited to a member. At the end of the month cash incentives are given on the basis of these points. The greater the points, the higher the incentive. Beginning with 3 per cent the incentives rise to as much as 21 per cent on the basis of the business points.

At higher levels additional incentives in the shape of royalty, leadership incentive and annual incentive are given. Differential incentive also adds to the income. Many companies also offer free holidays as incentives to their high performers. The secret of success lies in using and selling some products every month, building a good network, and sustaining the network through regular contact and meetings.

Income from Multi-level Marketing

The income from multi-level marketing is in direct proportion to the amount of time and effort one puts into the work. Retail income is immediate. Although about 20 per cent discount is allowed, most people pass a part of this to the consumer. The incentive income depends upon the network. If the network is developed on ideal lines, and is provided regular care, one becomes entitled to other incentives that can be very substantial.

Opportunities for Self-employment

No other field of work offers as many opportunities for self-employment (part-time or full-time) as does multi-level marketing. In this field everyone except for the company executives who supervise the work, or run the supply depots, are self-employed. This field needs to be developed to absorb the vast unemployed population of the country.

Nursing

63

Few careers are as service oriented as nursing. If doctors are greatly appreciated for their service to eliminate suffering and pain, it is not possible without the active service support of efficient nursing staff. The doctors provide the medicine and directions, but it is the nursing staff that helps comfort the patients through continuous care.

Nursing is a noble profession in that it aims at not only providing care and service to a patient, but also respects human dignity and the need for privacy in unique circumstances that are beyond control. It aims at a high level of competency. It also takes on the collective responsibility of a healthy society.

There is a great demand for efficient nursing staff by nursing homes and hospitals. With the rapid growth of medical services, the need for nursing staff has grown proportionately. As with other services, the medical services in other countries have an eye on India to supply good nursing staff. The opportunities for work are growing. With greater penetration of medical services to the rural areas, one can look forward to a steady demand for qualified nursing staff.

Desirable Personal Qualities

To be successful in this work a person must:

- be sensitive to human suffering. Without the sensitivity one cannot be caring.
- be service-minded. The patients desire great attention.
- be well acquainted with diseases and their treatment. It makes it easier to follow doctor's directions.
- be well acquainted with the use of modern medical equipment. There is much to their use.

- be observant. Good observation helps the doctors treat better.
- have good manners and etiquette. Patients appreciate them.
- be willing to work as a team. Many people work together to treat a patient.
- be a stickler for detail. It can be a matter of life and death. There is no scope for approximation.
- be willing to work at odd hours. Sickness does not send signals before coming.

Opportunities in Nursing

The opportunities for the nursing staff are in proportion to the need for medical services. The entire medical care and follow-up depends upon the nursing staff. Opportunities exist at all places. Good nursing staff is required in the rural area, in the smaller towns, the district towns and the metros.

In the rural area with shortage of doctors the role of the nursing staff becomes wider. They serve as midwives and family welfare counsellors. In the larger towns the services become specialized in that besides the care of the patients in the hospital rooms and wards, they also help provide support services in the pathological labs, investigation centres and also during surgical and other procedures. Many specialize in the fields of anaesthetics, surgery, paediatrics, obstetrics and psychiatric care.

Besides the medical institutions, nurses also fulfil important responsibilities in private clinics, assisting the doctors. Nurses are also required to provide useful service to the elderly and the sick at home when resident treatment is not essential. Nurses are also employed by resident schools for maintaining health records of the children.

With efficient nursing staff being trained in India, many opportunities for jobs in this field are opening up in foreign countries. That does entail the hardship of living away from the family, but the remuneration is attractive.

Educational Facilities

To be a nurse one needs to be educated and licensed in the practice of nursing. The word: educated strictly means the obtaining of a bachelor's degree in Nursing. There are hundreds of colleges offering the bachelor's degree after 10+2. It is a three-year course. Most of these colleges are attached with hospitals and the education involves practical training. Most join a nursing home or a hospital after completing the course. A few go on for specialization in one of the many options available in this field.

Making a Beginning

For a career as a nurse, one can start right away after obtaining the degree in Nursing. Nursing homes and hospitals need nursing staff.

However, there are many that learn the work through sheer hard work and experience while working with a doctor. They do not strictly qualify as nurses, but have found positions with private practitioners as support staff. Many women who have some knowledge of First Aid, elementary nursing, midwifery and family planning are absorbed as auxiliary nurse-midwives in the State Health services after they have been given some training. They are assigned responsibilities to work in the rural areas.

By the very nature of the work the scope for growth is very limited. One may move from a nursing home to a large hospital. In the larger hospitals where a group of nurses serve a ward, one may become the head of the group. At the higher level there is the Matron who oversees the work of the nursing staff.

Income from Nursing

Qualified nurses earn as much as those starting on any similar career that requires technical knowledge. They earn more than other support staff. Beginning as a staff nurse, one can rise to work as a Sister, Assistant Matron and Matron. Efficient nurses, working freelance in the larger cities, are earning high incomes. Many nurses are connected with hospitals and nursing homes, but work on their own in private homes under the supervision of doctors. They are well paid for such work.

Opportunities for Self-employment

By the very nature of the work the nursing staff needs to work under the directions of qualified doctors. This is possible in the nursing homes and hospitals. Therefore, the nursing staff is part of the hospital staff. A few who are capable and experienced work in private homes under instructions from the doctor looking after the patient. In the rural areas and also amongst the poorer sections of the society many work as midwives.

Ophthalmology

64

Ophthalmology is yet another important field of medical practice. This branch of medical science deals with the study and treatment of the functions of the eye. It also includes the care and treatment of injuries and diseases of the eye. The ophthalmologist is a physician and surgeon who prescribes treatment and also conducts surgeries to remove cataracts and other problems. Although this field of medicine deals with a small portion of the human body, it is a vast field. There are several non-medical areas of specialization.

The World Health Organization recommends that for every one ophthalmologist there must be four optometrists, eight each of eye care workers and ophthalmic assistants and sixteen ophthalmic nurses. At this standard there is a gross shortage of qualified staff in every area of work.

Fields of Specialization

Amongst the several non-medical areas of practice pertaining to eyes, one could take up any of these lines:

Optometrist: an optometrist is responsible for visual screening, testing the eyes for refractive conditions and prescribing remedial treatment and corrective visual aids by way of spectacles or contact lenses.

Optician: an optician fits glasses or contact lenses in accordance with the prescription from an ophthalmologist or an optometrist. Many optometrists fulfil this responsibility also.

Ocularist: an ocularist is responsible for designing and fitting artificial eyes.

Desirable Personal Qualities

To be successful in this field, a person must:

- have a good personality. That helps win the confidence of the patient.
- be a person with good etiquette and manners. This enhances the individual's personality.
- be a stickler for precision. There is no scope for inaccuracies.
- be service minded. That helps win the confidence of the patients.
- have good communication skills. This is important if you want to understand a person, or be understood yourself.
- be well acquainted with the line of specialization.

Opportunities in Ophthalmology

India has the largest number of blind people in the world. And what is worse is that the number is growing. Unfortunately, what makes this shameful is that the vast majority suffers from avoidable blindness. These facts alone should enable one to appreciate the opportunities that exist in pursuing ophthalmology as a career.

Seventy per cent of India's population lives in the rural areas where the medical facilities are very limited. Specialized treatment through ophthalmology is unknown. The only treatment available is through eye relief camps organized by service organizations. Many times the purpose of these camps is to do cataract surgery enabling the persons to see once again. It will still take a long time before ophthalmic services will be available in the rural areas.

Since malnutrition is a common cause for avoidable blindness, many service organizations are regularly organizing awareness eye check-up camps in schools. Although the latest surgical procedures are available in the metros and the larger cities, the smaller towns and the vast rural areas are still without them. There is indeed a great need for specialists to be working in these areas.

Optometrists and opticians too are restricted to the towns, cities and metros. The vast rural population still needs to go to nearby towns to meet their needs. This is by no means a small need because many people need spectacles for proper eyesight. Almost all elderly people need reading glasses. With growing literacy the number of people who will require reading glasses will continue to increase.

The use of sunglasses both as a means of sight protection particularly in the hot weather and for purposes of fashion is also on the increase. With the introduction of prime brands from overseas this need has been fulfilled in the upper strata of the society. However, there is a big gap in the lower and middle strata for reasonably priced good sunglasses. This offers challenges to the opticians.

Educational Facilities

Ophthalmology is strictly a medical specialization and one must qualify in a medical college. However, optometrists and opticians are not medical people. One can join an institution that provides education in this field. Both degree and diploma courses are available. One can join after 10+2 with science and mathematics. Knowledge of Biology is an added advantage. Some institutions conduct entrance exams followed by an interview. Details can be obtained directly from the institution concerned.

Making a Beginning

Soon after qualifying most ophthalmologists join a hospital as an assistant or join a private practising eye specialist. This enables one to get on the job practice, and perhaps later set out on one's own as a private practitioner. Eye surgery is intricate and gradually one is acknowledged as an expert eye surgeon.

Optometrists often play the role of both the optometrist and the optician in not only checking the eyesight for corrective spectacles, but also supply them as opticians. For this purpose they stock a variety of frames and have arrangements for grinding and fitting lenses. Most young people join established optometrists and later set out on their own to establish personal work.

Income from Ophthalmology

An ophthalmologist is a medical specialist and the income is similar to that of other specialized medical personnel. Ophthalmologists who do optometry charge their usual fee. However, many optometrists do not charge a fee, but include it as a part of the charges for the spectacles they supply as opticians. Most opticians are optometrists-cum-opticians, and the value of their services are included as part of the spectacles that they sell.

Opportunities for Self-employment

Except for those who take up work in hospitals being run by the government, the defence services or by private organizations, most of the ophthalmologists are self-employed running their own nursing homes. They may have junior doctors or nursing staff to support them in their work. Most of these doctors perform the responsibilities of the optometrists also.

Optometrists-cum-opticians are invariably always self-employed running a store where they stock a variety of frames and have facilities for lens grinding and fixing. They also stock sunglasses and provide repair facilities for spectacles.

Pharmacy

65

Many young people aspire for a career in medicine, but fail to get admission into a medical college because of high level of competition or poor academic background. A career closely related to that of a doctor is that in pharmacy.

Pharmacy is the science or practice of preparing and dispensing medicinal drugs. It also refers to the place where medicinal drugs are made and sold. Since making of medicinal mixtures is outmoded, and doctors depend upon branded preparations, in everyday use pharmacy refers to a place where medicines are sold. Under national law it is necessary that only a qualified pharmacist can operate a pharmacy.

Pharmacology is a subject closely related to pharmacy. It is a branch of medicine concerned with the uses, effects, and action of drugs.

Desirable Personal Qualities

To be successful in this field, a person must:

- appreciate the need for accuracy and detail. There is no scope for approximation in these matters.
- be well acquainted with drugs and their use. Effects and side effects of drugs are very important.
- have a good knowledge of diseases. Unless one knows enough about the disease, it becomes difficult to relate drugs for it.
- be creative and analytical in his approach. Without an analytical approach it is difficult to critically understand the effects of drugs.

Opportunities in Pharmacy

In a country where more than 70 per cent of the population lives in the villages, and medical care is slowly moving in, one can well appreciate the need for better health care. Careers in Pharmacy are closely related to it.

There are more than 20,000 registered units that manufacture pharmaceuticals. Some of these work on large scales and not only supply the national market, but also export medicines to developed countries. Besides these, there are units devoted to manufacture medicines for other fields like Ayurveda, Unani, Homoeopathy, etc. All these need personnel who can help in the manufacture, research and marketing of medicines.

Law requires that medicines can be dispensed only at retail pharmacies that are manned by qualified pharmacists. There are hundreds of thousands of such outlets around the country. New ones are added everyday. Young people interested in starting a retail outlet of medicines must be qualified pharmacists.

The drug control departments that run at district level also require qualified pharmacists. Those who pursue research and are highly qualified devote time to teaching in Pharmacy colleges. There is a good demand for pharmacists abroad, in both the developed and underdeveloped countries.

Educational Facilities

There are several universities and institutions offering courses that lead to the Bachelor's degree in Pharmacy (B.Pharm). Admission is open to those who have done 10+2 with science subjects. Some institutions require Graduate Aptitude Test for Engineering (GATE) score for admission to the M.Pharm courses. One could follow this later with Ph.D. in Pharmacology. Some institutions conduct written exams followed by an interview for entry into M.Sc., Ph.D. and M.D. courses in Pharmacology. Some require a MBBS degree before one can pursue for M.D. in Pharmacology.

Making a Beginning

Several good institutions have placement services through interviews prior to one's leaving the college. Leading pharmaceutical companies are always on the lookout for brilliant students in this field to help in their manufacturing and research units. One can also join a manufacturing unit in the field of specialization. Those who do not specialize may opt for opening a pharmacy or retail counter dispensing medicines. Those who work hard in this field rise quickly. There is great scope for newer formulations and drugs.

Income from Pharmacy

Income from careers in Pharmacy is good. One can find employment in a good pharmaceutical company. With the right qualifications like a M.Pharm one can begin with a five-figure salary rising swiftly with hard work and experience. Income rises with additional qualifications. Some institutions offer research stipends while pursuing for M.D. in Pharmacology. There is a good demand for senior positions in the developed countries. They offer very attractive salaries.

Opportunities for Self-employment

Self-employment opportunities in this field are restricted to starting one's own pharmacy or a pharmaceutical manufacturing concern. One can have a retail-dispensing counter from where drugs and medicines from a number of leading manufacturers can be sold. Wholesale suppliers make purchasing easier. In the manufacturing field, people restrict themselves to a small range of products, selling them in nearby areas through personal contacts. Popularity of herbal preparations has opened a wide field for manufacturing medicines.

Photography

66

There never was as good a demand for good photographers as we see today. Everybody needs to be photographed. It is mandatory to have photographs on identity cards of all descriptions, on election cards, bank account opening forms, on legal documents and in a variety of other places. Photography at birthday parties, social functions, inaugurations and of course at weddings has become an important need. Today we have more newspapers, house journals, magazines and books that need photographs. A good photographer is in demand by everyone.

Desirable Personal Qualities

To be successful in this field, a person must:

- be observant. A good observation differentiates a good photographer from an ordinary one.
- be creative. Photography is an art form. Without creativity one cannot shine.
- have the ability to visualise a picture. A photographer sees a picture where others do not.
- have a strong sense of aesthetics. Art forms must appeal to the eye and the mind.
- understand composition and colours. A well-composed picture with balanced colours is always attractive.
- be willing to work hard and at odd times. Assignments will require working till late at night.
- have an understanding of equipment. New equipment is being marketed everyday.

Opportunities in Photography

Opportunities in photography abound everywhere. Earlier, good photographers were available only in cities. Today you meet them even in rural areas. This is particularly because of growth of amateur photography, and the need to have films processed. Besides photographs are required for a variety of purposes in our everyday life as in identity cards in schools and colleges, on application forms for exams, and at the workplace. Photography is popular at social functions, birthday parties and during weddings.

The commercial use of photography in advertising, in newspapers and magazines and by industrial houses has opened a wide area of application. The introduction of cheaper movie and video cameras has made movie making easy and popular. All this has given rise to the need for retail outlets, commercial photo labs and photographers who can fulfil the variety of needs that have been generated.

Specialization in Photography

Most people in this field run a retail store selling films, albums, frames and other photographic equipment along with a studio where indoor work is done. Many people have moved out as loners to specialize in fields like outdoor photography in tourist spots, function photography, marriage photography and video photography. Many are connected with newspapers, magazines, advertising agencies and industrial houses. Some specialize in photography for calendars and greeting cards.

For those who are well established in the field, there is no limit to their work. They sell their photographs all over the world. Many are freelances. They may specialize in portraits, nature photography, advertising photography, fashion photography or a very wide and challenging field of industrial photography.

Operating a Colour Lab

Individual photographers handle black and white photography in their own studio labs. However, colour photography has become popular because of fast film processing in colour labs that are swift and efficient. These labs can be fitted in a room and can be operated after little training, but require heavy initial investment on the equipment. Those who operate these labs depend upon job work from photographers.

They rarely do photography themselves. They operate more as a cottage industry than as a photo shop.

Changing Trends in Photography

With computers invading every sphere of life, photography is no exception. The conventional cameras are giving way to digital cameras. Rather than films being processed with chemicals, the floppy disks used in cameras are loaded on to the computer. The pictures are edited as desired and printed right away on reasonably priced printers used with computers. The procedure is swift, allows a lot of editing and can be done at home on a personal computer.

Educational Facilities

Most people start as amateurs and gradually enter the field with someone who is already established. Few people learn photography in a school. However, it is felt that those who have studied photography have a stronger foundation to build a career on. The growth in the field does not come from academics, but from a personal concept of framing a picture and through hard work.

Until a few years ago people were learning photography on the job, but presently several leading institutions are offering courses. Some offer diploma courses. Others are offering bachelor's degree in photography.

Making a Beginning

One can make a beginning as a lab or studio assistant and gradually take up solo assignments. Many have begun careers with as little as a camera and a flash-gun. They started with assignments at schools, colleges and other institutions, taking marriage photographs, or even freelancing as an independent photographer. Many have started by taking single shots at restaurants or places of tourist interest, and gradually grown. Selling photographs for picture postcards, greeting cards and calendars, or to newspapers and magazines in one's own country and abroad offers remunerative openings. Eventually most people aim at having a photography retail store with an indoor studio.

Income from Photography

Unless one has some knowledge one may need to begin work on a small salary, and gradually move up. Those who are established make good money. A photo retail shop can be likened to any other similar business giving a reasonable return. Once a photographer is recognized for his ability, he can charge his price. Specialized work is well paid for.

Opportunities for Self-employment

Besides a few photographers who are permanently employed with institutions and departments, and others who are working as assistants and apprentices, most of them are self-employed. All that one requires is a reasonably good camera and a flash-gun and one can set out on one's own as a self-employed photographer. To be successful one needs to be physically and emotionally involved in the work. It is a lot of hard work. However, experience has shown that those who dedicate themselves to the work can rise to great heights.

Police Service

67

The police service is responsible for security in the towns and cities. The rural areas are connected to nearby town areas for the purpose. All civilisations depend upon discipline, upon law and order. To make it possible the governments enact rules and regulations through Acts enacted both at the Centre and by the State governments. The police force maintains law and order by enforcing the rules and regulations made through these laws.

Desirable Personal Qualities

To be successful in this field, a person must:

- have a high sense of patriotism. The love of one's nation is an important motivating force.
- be sturdy and courageous. One will need to face criminals.
- enjoy good health. The work requires one to face difficult situations at odd hours.
- have a friendly disposition. One must enjoy the confidence of the public in general to achieve one's purpose.
- be willing to work hard at odd hours without a break. It can be difficult.
- have a good understanding of human nature. One needs to differentiate between the good and the bad people.

Opportunities in Police Service

With ever increasing law and order problems, the police service continues to be expanded. New personnel are required to fill in the positions. The responsibilities are not restricted to just maintaining law and order in the towns, as most people understand. There is the need for guiding the traffic, securing life and property, providing security cover to important people, guarding important sites like water and electricity installations, bus terminals, airports, railways and government property, looking after the jails, and apprehending culprits who break a variety of laws. Both men and women make up the police force.

Educational Facilities

Every state has its own police force and enacts its own rules and regulations. It maintains its own training institutions. At the lowest level in general it is necessary for a constable to have passed the 10th class. The selection is through a recruitment board. For joining as a Sub-Inspector it is necessary to have a bachelor's degree. Entry at the higher levels is through exams conducted by the UPSC. IPS officers are a part of the IAS and Allied Services.

Making a Beginning

In general, there are three levels of entry into the state police service. First, one can join at the level of a Constable. Second, at the level of an Assistant Sub-Inspector. And third, at the level of Deputy Superintendent of Police (DSP) or Assistant Commissioner of Police (ACP), depending upon the nomenclature followed in a state. The training is imparted at the training institutes maintained by the government.

One grows in the Police Service in this order: Constable—Head Constable—Assistant Sub-Inspector (ASI)—Sub-Inspector (SI)—Inspector—Assistant Commissioner of Police (ACP)—Deputy Commissioner of Police (DCP)—Additional Commissioner of Police—Senior Additional Commissioner of Police—Special Commissioner of Police—Commissioner of Police. Ranks of ACP and above are gazetted officers.

Income from Police Service

The state government controls careers in Police Service. Pay scales are controlled and periodically revised as per prevalent rules.

Opportunities for Self-employment

There are no opportunities for self-employment for people working in active police service. However, on retirement some people join private security services, or may establish a security agency, providing security personnel for private needs. Some may start an investigating agency. A few with writing skills are known to have got down to writing about their experiences with crime and criminals.

Printing

68

Everyone needs to communicate through the printed word everyday. The news from all over the world comes through newspapers. Our children read textbooks on different subjects. We use printed letterheads on our business stationery, read magazines to be informed and entertained. We use the printed word in several other ways. It plays a significant part in our everyday lives. It is difficult to imagine life without it. Everything would come to a standstill. With increasing knowledge and business activities, the need for the printed word is also growing.

To fulfil the need of printing there are thousands of printing presses of varying sizes in the country. While most of these presses are in small towns and cities, and employ less than ten persons each, the bigger ones provide comprehensive printing services. They are big employers, and provide a variety of printing services. They are based in the larger cities. Computers and a variety of small and big printing machines in our offices have revolutionized the field of the printed word. There are growing opportunities in the field of printing. It is for young people interested in this field of work to develop these opportunities to provide them satisfying work.

Desirable Personal Qualities

To be successful in this field, a person must:

- have artistic abilities. One must look at every page as a piece of art.
- possess an aesthetic sense to compose words and illustrations.
- have a good knowledge of computers and related software. Computers have revolutionised the field of printing.

- be able to work under pressure. Work pressures in this field are high.
- possess the stamina to face the strenuous work.
- have good eyesight. It may be necessary to do very fine artistic jobs.
- have knowledge of photography. That helps produce good work.
- have knowledge of different kinds of printing machinery. Keeping them running in good order is important.
- not be shy of working personally. Handling printing inks can be messy at times.
- be willing to work as a team. Many people contribute to produce good work.

Opportunities in Printing

Printing has always offered innumerable opportunities for careers. There are small printing presses in every town. As the towns become larger, the size of printing machines becomes bigger. The larger cities can boast of large multi-colour printing presses. They depend upon publishers and the larger business houses for continued work. Most newspapers and magazines have their own printing presses. The government owns large printing presses where they do various printing jobs for different departments of the Central and State governments. Many rely upon private presses also. While new printing machines are being installed, the older ones are expanding with newer equipment and processes.

The printing business requires people to do a variety of jobs. It involves preparing the matter, creating illustrations, composing the matter, preparing the printing plates in colour, or black and white, printing the matter, binding it and finally trimming it to prepare the final publication. This has led to specialization in each sphere of activity. The larger printers would have all the activities available under one roof. However, the smaller printers may depend upon freelance operators specializing in a particular activity of work. DTP personnel would compose the necessary matter. Machine operators are required to work and maintain printing machinery. The office staff looks after the procurement of work, billing, collection and general office work. An executive would supervise the entire work.

The need for printed work is on the increase. New newspapers and magazines are being launched. A variety of textbooks are required for an increasing number of schools and colleges. There is a huge publishing industry that produces books in many languages. Besides these bulk needs, there are smaller needs of printing business letterheads, catalogues, sales promotion literature, price lists, bill books, account books, and similar other needs of business and trade. There is the need for printing handbills, invitation cards for weddings and other occasions, greeting cards, etc.

With growing education, business and trade, the printing needs continue to increase. The need for attractive packaging for products in itself creates a massive need for printing cartons, containers and other forms of packaging. This need includes printing of labels, cartons, plastic bags and packaging, metal containers and other kinds of packaging. This has given rise to a specialized packaging industry.

Besides the need for printed work, the printing business has given rise to the need for suppliers of different kinds of paper and printing machinery. The printing industry requires a variety of small and big machines. These need to be kept in good order, creating opportunities for maintenance services. Composition of matter is done on computers. Even the binding is now done by machine. All these add up to create opportunities for useful work.

Educational Facilities

Several computer institutions offer courses in desktop publishing. Along with training, they also offer opportunities for small working assignments. Industrial Training Institutes offer courses in proofreading and press operation. The bigger printing presses take in apprentices for training in various printing responsibilities. For jobs as machine operators, a pass in high school or 10+2 may suffice, but for composing matter on a computer, besides knowledge in computer application software, a good knowledge of the languages is useful. For specialized training in printing technology, after 10+2, or an equivalent examination, one can apply to one of the following institutions:

Regional School of Printing,
Chennai.

Regional School of Printing Technology,
Allahabad.

School of Printing Technology,
Jadavpur, Kolkata-700032.

School of Printing Technology,
Dr. D. Naoroji Road,
Mumbai-400001.

Spicer Memorial College,
Aundh Road, Ganeshhind,
Pune-7.

Government School of Printing Technology,
Sharanm-2, Kerala.

Kala Niketan,
Jabalpur (M.P.)

Shri Jayachamrajinder Polytechnic,
Bangalore.

Maharashtra Mudran Shala,
1786, Sadashiv Peth, Pune-2.

National Institute of Design,
Paldi, Ahmedabad-7.

M.H. Saboo Siddik Technical Institute,
8, Shepherd Street
Mumbai-400008.

Making a Beginning

Many of the smaller presses employ workers who have learnt their work by working as assistants and apprentices in printing presses, gradually learning the tricks of the trade. The larger printing establishments insist upon qualified personnel for working various kinds of printing presses and other machinery.

Many Industrial Training Institutes offer courses for personnel for the printing industry. Several government presses also offer apprenticeship courses for training workers in various printing trades. The Regional Schools of Printing and some other institutions provide full-time courses in printing technology after 10+2. Some courses are open for graduates. The training is followed by one year's practical work in a big printing press. This opens opportunities for rising to higher positions in careers in printing. Without this specialized training, promotions in this profession are very restricted as each worker keeps doing one kind of work only.

Income from Printing

Income from careers in printing varies with the kind of job one does. As an apprentice, one may receive a nominal income. However, as one learns the trade, one can expect a reasonable income. Many of the jobs like composing, printing and binding are on job basis. Those who are creative and do a fine job can do well. Since each job is typical in itself, promotions within an organization are slow. Only those who are well educated with specialization in some field rise to high positions. Individuals or groups often own printing presses. As a business, it is a lucrative work provided one gives good service. Owners of large printing presses earn very high incomes.

Opportunities for Self-employment

Keeping in view the high cost of printing machinery, few workers in the printing presses can expect to establish their own printing presses. However, young people who have done a course in printing technology and can arrange for some capital, can establish a small printing press to be profitably self-employed. With computers playing an essential role in composing matter to be printed, many young people are finding useful self-employment through links with printing presses.

A career in printing opens up opportunities for starting a local newspaper, a publishing concern, printing greeting cards, business stationery, etc. Printing of thesis, project reports, legal documents, and similar items in black and white, and even in colour, has become easier through computers and connected printers and duplicating machines. Many young people have found useful self-employment in these fields, particularly near big educational institutions. Rapid technological developments are making printing easier, swifter and better. Young people interested in this field can make a career for themselves through self-employment.

Public Relations

69

All organizations have a definite purpose—to fulfil the need for a particular product or service. However, the ability to provide a product or service is never enough. There are a large number of organizations providing similar products and services, creating competition for each other. To be effective, the product or the service must reach the public for which it is provided. Even when there are similar products and services available, the public must get to know what choices are available to them.

The most obvious way to inform the public about particular products and services is to advertise through the various media that reaches the targeted public. Since this can be expensive, experience has given rise to a new activity—building good public relations! The need to advertise is not altogether omitted. But with good public relations, the need is substantially reduced. Many organizations including those in the commercial and government sectors are now maintaining public relations departments. The aim of this department is to create a good public image for the organization.

Desirable Personal Qualities

To be successful in this field, a person must:

- have a presentable personality with a smiling face. That helps draw immediate attention.
- be well educated, cultured and have good manners. That helps enhance an individual's personality.
- be imaginative. Good public relations is intelligent advertising.
- have the ability to appreciate other people's views. Without it the other people can take offence.

- have a good rapport with every department in the organization. One cannot promote an organization unless one is well informed about every aspect of the work.
- understand the public to which the organization caters. They are your ultimate target audience.
- have good communication skills. Without them you cannot tell others what you need to.
- have good relations with media persons. They can make your work easier.
- understand the need to work as a team. One cannot achieve much by oneself.
- have the ability to handle difficult situations. If things can go wrong, they will.
- be willing to work long hours. Good public relations are a full time responsibility.

Opportunities in Public Relations

With greater awareness for the need for good public relations more organizations are opening departments catering to this specific need. It is important to understand that good public relations is not talking good about one's products and services. It aims at initially providing the best products and services and then talking a little about it. Doing good work represents 90 per cent of the job, and the other 10 per cent is to highlight the good work done.

The importance of good public relations is being realised not only by commercial concerns that think in terms of profits, but also by government departments and important service organizations. Even departments like Income Tax feel that good public relations is important to tax collection. The police claim to be 'friendly'. Political parties too have felt the need for public relations professionals. Good public relations help develop the image of an organization, gradually converting a name to a brand that offers reliability. Brands carry huge value, and everyone strives to create these through good public relations.

Educational Facilities

A public relations person is an all-rounder who serves as the mouthpiece of the top management, projecting the aims, objects and policies of the organization to both the people within the organization and the public for which the organization works. Some institutions are offering specific courses in public relations, but since the work involves good communication skills, many people prefer to specialize in journalism and mass communication. Many people also move from the field of advertising to public relations.

Making a Beginning

Public relations is comparatively a new field. Tools of public relations include good relations with the press media, advertisers, direct publicity through word of mouth and literature, and at exhibitions and trade fairs. Most people have moved in from other areas like journalism and advertising, or even from a department within the organization. Those joining directly would begin as assistants in the public relations department, and after gaining experience on the job move to higher positions in the department.

Since the public relations department projects the views of the top management it is very important that the persons involved must be very responsible, must understand the situations well and must know how to handle delicate situations. The work in the public relations department is very much like that in an embassy where a person must be well acquainted with one's own country and the host country. One cannot afford to accept any kind of misunderstanding.

Income from Public Relations

Entry level jobs in this field are similar to those in other fields. Salaries are also similar. However, with time those who are capable earn a good income. Since the department works directly under the top management, the staff is always in close proximity with those who matter in an organization. This can be a difficult situation, but at the same time it can be beneficial in securing special favours.

Opportunities for Self-employment

Strictly speaking, by the very nature of the work there are no opportunities for self-employment in this field. However, with the connections made with a variety of people and organizations, one can always secure other avenues for self-employment.

70

Publishing

We have one of the largest publishing industries in the world. We have Hindi and English as principal languages, but every region has a different language, and in each language we have newspapers, magazines and a big variety of books. We have national newspapers and magazines, and also some that are exported to other countries particularly for Indians settled abroad. Besides these, there is a very big book publishing industry publishing books on almost every subject you can think of.

The publishing needs of a country bear a close relationship to the population, levels of literacy and development. Radio and TV play a significant role in keeping people informed, but unless supplemented by education and reading, their value is considerably reduced. Good books inspire, inform and entertain. With steady development of the country, there is a marked increase in the need for books and magazines on a variety of subjects.

Specialized Publishing

It is not practical for a publisher to delve into the publishing of any book that he likes. Publishing is a competitive field. Selection, preparation and publishing of a book are just one part of the publishing process. For the work to be profitable it is important that the published magazine or book must be sold within a particular period. Therefore, marketing is important. To make the operation profitable, most publishers have specialized in particular fields. Some of the publishing fields include:

- Newspapers of regional or national interest.
- Magazines that interest a particular audience.

- Textbooks in different subjects.
- Books of general interest.
- Children's books.
- Technical books as on medicine, engineering, law, etc.
- Travel books.
- Religious books and literature.
- Fiction.
- Reference books.
- Audio-visual publishing.

Steps in Publishing

There are several steps in producing a book or a magazine. The important steps include:

1. The author who conceives the idea of the book himself, or at the suggestion of a publisher, an institution or a friend. He collects the relevant data and writes the book preparing a typescript for the publisher.
2. The publisher examines the typescript and passes it on to the editor who may go through the typescript personally or through a specialist in that field. When satisfied, the editor consults the production department for costing and the sales department for the sales potential, and presents the report to the publisher for a final decision.
3. If the book is approved, an agreement is executed between the publisher and the author.
4. The editor passes the typescript to his assistant for preparation of the final typescript for the printer. Simultaneously, the artwork is prepared for the cover, inside cover and the back of the book.
5. The printer prints the book as per the publisher's instructions.
6. They announce the book to the prospective stockists who place orders for the copies required.
7. The reader for whom the book is intended buys the book from the bookseller, or through direct mail.

Desirable Personal Qualities

To be successful in this field, a person must:

- be a visionary in that he can grasp ideas for new publications. The reader is forever on the lookout for new ideas.
- be educated and have good literary judgement. Readers are intelligent people.
- have the knowledge in a variety of subjects. Variety is the spice of good publishing.
- have the sensitivity to know what the reading public wants. A good knowledge of the target audience is important.
- be able to get along well with a variety of people like authors, editors, printers, booksellers, critics and readers.
- have an eye for financial detail. Every publication is an independent project.
- understand the market. Market trends keep changing for several reasons.
- be computer-literate. Most of the publishing work now is computer-based.

Opportunities in Publishing

For a career in the publishing industry, one rarely sets out as an independent publisher. One necessarily needs to begin in one of the departments in a publishing house.

The publishers in India can be divided into three categories:

1. Central institutions like The National Book Trust, N.C.E.R.T., etc.
2. State level institutions that primarily publish textbooks.
3. The private sector that includes about 10,000 publishers. Unfortunately, less than 500 of them are of the optimum level.

The openings in the first two categories are limited. It is the private sector that provides opportunities for careers in this field. Most start in the editorial department as sub-editors working under the senior editor. With typescripts now being prepared in the electronic media, there is need for good desk-top publishing assistants who know how to operate some of the popularly used computer publishing software. Most publishing houses get artwork done on piecework basis, but the larger publishing houses may need art assistants.

Magazines need to work on tight time schedules, and the work of different departments is specifically assigned. In the past decade many new magazines serving different groups of people have come up, and have given employment to writers, sub-editors, layout artists, photographers, marketing personnel and those who are assigned the responsibility of collecting advertisements.

With literacy levels rising, and with the development of new educational institutions, the demand for good publishing is bound to increase. Many new opportunities will be generated. Although we can boast of one of the largest publishing industries in the world, it is interesting to note that as compared to developed countries, we are way behind when we compare population figures and published works.

The business of electronic publishing is still in infancy, but with time it is bound to grow, offering many opportunities for careers in publishing.

Educational Facilities

Most people join publishing houses for specific assignments for which they may have received the necessary training. Prior to joining, it may be preferable to gain proficiency in languages, journalism or art. However, courses specifically devoted to publishing as a career are available. Those who are interested in making publishing a full-time career, or hope to start a publishing house on their own would greatly benefit by undergoing training in the field. The training gives them an overview of the responsibilities involved in the work, and provides a strong foundation to grow on in the field.

Making a Beginning

One makes a beginning in this field by joining a department in a publishing house. Beginnings are invariably small, and one develops skills through work experience. Growth within a publishing house is bound to be slow. Those who are capable change jobs to move to bigger publishing houses after they have gained the requisite experience.

Income from Publishing

Publishing is a very competitive business, and income at the lower levels is just at par with those of similar work. Growth in the career is slow. Those who reach senior positions enjoy good salaries and perks. Well-established publishing houses earn well.

Opportunities for Self-employment

One is free to establish a publishing house. However, without sufficient experience the risks in the business are high. It is better to work in an established publishing house for some time, and only then get into business individually. The self-employment opportunities in different fields associated with publishing are discussed separately in appropriate chapters.

Railways

71

The Railways are referred to as the lifeline of the country. The needs of the people are transported through it even to the remotest corners. Transportation of goods by truck, and of passengers by bus, has acquired great importance in the country. However, the Railways continue to be most convenient and competitive.

We have one of the largest railway networks in the world. The Ministry of Railways, New Delhi, directly supervises it. It is divided into several sectors like Northern Railway, Western Railway, Southern Railway, etc., for convenience of operation and administration. The development of the Railways has come a long way since the country became independent. The network is being further developed. New trains are being introduced. The trains are becoming faster. Newer facilities are being provided.

With greater development of tourism, and of industry all over the country, both the passenger and the goods traffic is on the increase. Besides, with the Locomotive Works at Chittaranjan, and the Integral Coach Factory at Perambur, and workshops spread over the country, we can look forward to continued development in the Railways. There is a regular flow of opportunities for young people interested in working for the Railways as a career.

Desirable Personal Qualities

To be successful in this field, a person must:

- be especially aware of need for safety. There is no scope for any mistakes.
- be time conscious. Every minute matters in this field. Trains move to a strict timetable.

- be willing to travel all the time. The work involves a lot of movement between places.
- be willing to work at odd hours. The Railways operate round the clock.
- be able to adjust sleeping time. One may need to work at night, and sleep in the day.
- be willing to make family adjustments according to need.
- be proficient in the line of specialization. There is a great variety of work that needs to be done in the Railways.
- be willing to work as a team. One needs to work with others all the time.
- have good etiquette and manners particularly when dealing with passengers.

Opportunities in the Railways

The Railways provide an opportunity for work at all levels. There is great variety in the kind of work offered. Beginning at the lowest level where a vast working taskforce keeps the Railways moving through maintenance operations, there are assistant guards, guards, carriage assistants, conductors, ticket collectors, booking clerks, goods clerks, engine drivers, signallers, assistant station masters, station masters, etc.

Gang men, supervisory staff, permanent way inspectors and engineers involve a very huge staff in maintaining the tracks. The rail crossings and bridges need to be guarded. The engineering staff at the workshops helps maintain the locomotives and the carriages. The civil engineering staff looks after the maintenance of the bridges, railway stations, buildings, etc. A medical force looks after the railway hospitals and dispensaries established at various important points.

We have a vast network of railways spread all over the country. Further extensions are being made into new areas. Metre-gauge lines are being upgraded to broad-gauge lines. New and swifter trains are being introduced to cope with increased traffic. In view of the weather conditions, air-conditioned coaches and trains are operational on busy routes. More will be added.

Besides the regular maintenance and administrative staff in the Railways who draw a regular salary, a large number of people have found self-employment at the railway stations by managing tea stalls, book stalls, restaurants, etc. There is a vast taskforce of porters who do the work of carrying luggage and goods. Since millions of people pass through the railway stations each day, there is great scope for exposure of advertising messages. Therefore, there is a big advertising trade in the Railways. To guard goods and property, there is the Railway Protection Force that looks after the security and operates like the police.

Educational Facilities

Young people selected for working in various branches of work in the Railways are provided the requisite training in their own establishments before being assigned to take up their responsibilities. For the lower levels 10+2 will suffice, but graduation is important for higher positions. A degree in a particular field of engineering will be necessary for specialized careers.

Making a Beginning

There is direct recruitment for the clerical and subordinate posts by the Railway Service Commissions at Mumbai for Western Railway, at Kolkata for Eastern Railway and the Chittaranjan Locomotive Works, at Chennai for Southern Railway and the Integral Coach Factory at Perambur, and at Allahabad for Northern Railway.

The Railway Service Commission at Allahabad conducts an examination through a single written paper in English, Arithmetic, Geography and General Knowledge for recruiting assistant station masters, guards, ticket collectors, signallers, clerks, bridge inspectors and other staff for the administrative control of the Railways.

If one is 16 to 19 years old, and has passed the 10+2 or an equivalent examination, one can join the Railways through the Special Class Railway Apprentices examination. The Union Public Service Commission conducts this examination. It consists of a written examination followed by a personality test constituted of psychological tests to assess basic intelligence and mechanical aptitude, and an interview. Successful candidates join the Indian Railway Service of Mechanical Engineers after receiving the necessary training.

Young people who possess an engineering degree can join the Railways by appearing for the examinations conducted by the Union Public Service Commission for the Indian Railways Stores Service, or for the Engineering Services through which one can join the Indian Railway Service of Engineers, the Indian Railway Service of Mechanical Engineers, the Indian Railway Service of Electrical Engineers and the Indian Railway Service of Signal Engineers.

Graduates who are interested in working for the Railways can appear for the examination conducted by the Union Public Service Commission for I.A.S. and Allied Services to join the Indian Railway Accounts Service, the Indian Railway Traffic Service, and the Railway Board Secretariat Service, Class II.

Income in the Railways

Income from jobs in the Railways is at par with similar jobs in the government departments. Besides the salary there are additional benefits like housing, medical facilities, free travelling by the Railways, etc. Senior positions carry great honour and prestige.

Opportunities for Self-employment

There are no opportunities for self-employment except for those available to qualified engineers who can use their capabilities in other fields of work. The people who operate the different kinds of stalls at the railway stations are of course self-employed. The contractors providing services to the Railways are also self-employed.

Real Estate

72

More people have earned their millions from real estate than from any other vocation. By the very nature of the work, the situation will continue to be the same. However, it is not that everyone who deals in real estate, or takes up a vocation related to real estate becomes a millionaire. Like other vocations one needs to understand the work and persevere.

With rising population there is bound to be greater pressure on land and buildings. The towns and cities are going to expand. The metros are already bursting. The suburbs will become a part of the city, and the adjoining agricultural area will become land for suburban homes. With more homes there will be need for markets, schools and hospitals. As the demand grows the opportunities too will grow. There will be the need for people to buy and sell land, build homes and other institutions and provide rental services.

Desirable Personal Qualities

To be successful in this field a person must:

- be well acquainted with local laws pertaining to land and buildings. Without this knowledge one can get into problems.
- have the imagination and insight for converting land into colonies.
- understand the principles of building construction. One cannot totally depend upon outside help.
- be honest and straightforward. Many people have lost their reputation through unethical practices.
- appreciate good time management. Irresponsible behaviour can cause resentment and problems.
- deliver what one promises. Broken promises have cut short many a promising career.

Opportunities in Real Estate

Opportunities in the field of real estate have always existed. They will continue to grow. There is a regular demand for plots of land, for flats and readymade buildings. To fulfil this need people are required to seek fresh land, develop them into colonies. Then sell plots or built-up houses. Where the pressure on land is great there is the need to build multi-storeyed buildings and sell portions as individual flats.

Just as there is the need for residential colonies, there is also the need for industrial estates. The Department of Industry is developing these estates in certain areas. However, many people develop private industrial estates at strategic points and either sell the industrial plots and sheds or give them on lease or rent.

Work in real estate is not restricted only to buying and selling land and buildings. Many people earn large sums in brokerage when they help sellers and purchasers to buy and sell property. This work entails great responsibility towards both the sides. Brokers earn commission from both. A broker must ensure that both are satisfied.

Rental services are also a part of the real estate work. Real estate agents maintain lists of houses, flats, shops, etc. that are available on rent. This way they help a landlord meet prospective tenants. For this service the agents charge a commission on the basis of the rent and period of tenancy.

Many real estate agents are also acquiring old built-up properties, demolishing them, and building larger houses where they rehabilitate the original owner and also build additional space that compensates them for the building expense and their profits. This is possible in areas where the price of land is prohibitive, and the additional expense on a new building is justifiable. These transactions need to be completed swiftly and efficiently.

Since the development and building of new buildings is being conducted by the bigger operators in this business, most of the young people entering the field serve to contact prospective customers, show them the sites, and after convincing them of the bargain complete the sale.

Educational Facilities

There are no formal courses that teach real estate work the way it is practised. The knowledge that is required is mostly acquired through experience although many of the things are taught as a part of the courses in architecture. Graduates in architecture would find their knowledge useful in promoting colonies, buildings and estates. They generally support real estate agents who spend the majority of their time in building contacts with sellers and buyers rather than on technical details. Real estate promoters are basically entrepreneurs who have money that is invested in real estate. Architects do the technical work. The purchasing and selling is done through brokers. Contract staff provide supporting services.

Making a Beginning

One makes a beginning in this field of work as an assistant to an established real estate agent or promoter. One learns the work on the job. Those who are outgoing and can build good contacts rise fast in the career. Honesty and ethical behaviour is important if one wants to grow in this line as many opportunities arise where easy money puts one's honesty to test. One also needs to be careful about the large number of unscrupulous people in this trade.

Opportunities for Self-employment

Except for those who are employed by real estate promoters, most of the people involved in this field work independently. They are self-employed. Many people work individually, but develop small groups that help each other in time of need. Most of the people who are on contract with the bigger groups are self-employed and work on commission basis.

Religious Services

73

Religion means to believe in and worship of a God or gods. It also signifies a particular system of faith and worship. When one belongs to a particular religion, it becomes necessary to follow certain rites, rituals and customs recommended by the religion. Most of these are conducted and supervised by individuals connected with the religion. The services offered by these individuals could be referred to as religious services.

A religion or any religious ceremony is something personal to an individual. However, it is a valid need of almost all people irrespective of the religion they follow. Individuals closely connected with the religion fulfil the need, and since the fulfilment of the need is paid for in one form or another, it is a valid vocation for the people involved in it. A very large number of people have been providing these services, and will continue to do so in the future. Opportunities for such careers will continue to grow, and are worthy of consideration by those interested in this field of activity.

Desirable Personal Qualities

To be successful in this field a person must:

- know the religious scriptures well. Incomplete knowledge can be dangerous.
- be well trained and acquainted with the rites, rituals and customs involved. One will need to conduct them from day-to-day.
- be truthful, honest and thoughtful of others. This way one exemplifies the religion.
- have an impeccable character. All religions aim at character building.
- live a simple life. It should be a model for others to adopt.

- not be critical of other religions. That would be counter-productive.
- be able to communicate well. One will need to do public speaking on many occasions. Much is achieved through the spoken word.
- be social and outgoing. It is necessary to have a large clientele.

Opportunities in Religious Services

India is a vast country with people who have adopted almost all the principal religions of the world. There are custodians of all the religions. They look after the followers of their respective religions, maintain the religious institutions and also try to promote the religions in whatever way they can. Each religion has its need of continuity.

India is basically a Hindu nation with the largest number of people who follow Hinduism. In this religion or way of life rites, rituals and customs predominate from birth until death. At every step there is the need for religious services. There are thousands of temples, *ashrams* and *vidyalayas* spread all over the country that would come to a standstill without proper religious services.

Even within Hinduism several sects that maintain their own religious institutions require these services. Jainism, Buddhism and Sikhism were founded in India, and have major shrines and institutions that attract the attention of not only the national population, but also of those living abroad. There are many lesser-known sects, but they are all important in that they need people to keep them going.

Muslims, Christians and Parsis too have their places of prayer, teaching and promotion that need to be serviced. Directly or indirectly, religion touches everyone, and it cannot be without support.

All religions need promotion, and in the modern context are preparing programmes for the television. Some also operate TV channels. The different religions also have the need for publishing religious literature, and this too has provided innumerable opportunities for work. Audio and videotapes and CDs too are the work of religious service providers.

Those who have musical abilities and are interested in religious services have a significant role in that every religion has its requirements of performers. Many provide their services during prayer time. Others are recorded on tapes and CDs for promotion purposes. Religious music is big business. The turnovers are very large. Some religious publishers are in big business too.

Educational Facilities

Every religion has its own educational facilities. Those who are interested in this field of work enter at a very young age. The Hindu scriptures are in Sanskrit. Many join Sanskrit Vidyalayas as youngsters. Gradually they master the study of the Vedas and the Upanishads, and learn about the rites, rituals and customs. A few study Sanskrit in colleges at Master's level and above, but that is more for academic purpose than to provide religious services.

In the same way, Muslims interested in this field send youngsters to *madrasas* followed by institutions of higher learning that are run for their own religion and purpose. They train the people who ultimately provide the religious services. The other religions too have similar arrangements.

There are some that do not follow the conventional system of training, but may join an institution being run by a religious head. It is a hands-on training there. One learns the work gradually. Many of these people perform limited functions only.

We cannot overlook the religious requirements of the large number of Indians that are settled abroad. In places where the number is large enough, they have built religious institutions that are looked after by people specially trained to provide religious services. The need for such personnel is also growing.

Making a Beginning

All religions have their own procedures for inducting the service providers at different levels. Most join at a very young age. They learn the basics and then serve as an assistant to a person already involved in providing a particular service. With time one begins to operate individually.

Those who can communicate well and are able to speak in public convincingly progress fast. Those who can sing or play a musical instrument join a religious group of singers, and grow with time. Many young people who joined religious groups in their younger years rise to important positions in their own religious institution. Later they may even be able to influence religious opinion at higher levels.

Income from Religious Services

More people join this field of vocational activity out of missionary spirit than for financial considerations. In this field there is great uncertainty in that no rates are fixed for particular activities. Those who live within the institutions are provided free boarding and lodging. Some pocket money comes their way through amounts paid by the people who visit the institutions. The salaries that are paid to priests are meagre. Those who have a genial temperament and are able to build a good lot of regular followers are able to earn well. The Hindu priests make additional money by making horoscopes, doing palmistry and helping the followers fix appropriate auspicious days for special functions.

Opportunities for Self-employment

Initially all people involved in providing religious services prefer to be part of an institution because of uncertain income. Only later when acclaimed as learned in the art of performing the rites and rituals well does one work independently. Many young people have succeeded in establishing important religious centres through personal knowledge and proficiency.

Retail Selling

74

Selling goods in retail is one of the oldest professions in the world. It still continues to hold interest for young people who want to be self-employed.

The pre-historic man met his own needs. When he had a surplus, he would barter it for other goods. However, when transactions became too complicated to be practical, money in the form of gold and silver coins took over as a common medium of exchange. This gave rise to the business of retail selling. Over the years the business has undergone substantial refinement. It has gone a long way from selling surplus goods in the marketplace to organized superstores selling a variety of items at fixed rates.

Even today we see vendors selling on the roadside, in pushcarts, in baskets and also in small stores, or in the large superstore that is like several retail stores put together. The purpose in each case is the same—to sell goods to the public to earn a little extra over the cost price.

Desirable Personal Qualities

To be successful in this field a person must:

- be willing to work for long hours waiting for customers. One never knows when a customer will come.
- be service-minded. Retail business is based upon good service.
- have a friendly disposition. Customers like to visit shops where they are welcome.
- be aware of market trends. Excessive purchases can eat into profits.
- possess good communication skills. People buy what sellers convince would be good for them.

- maintain financial discipline. Only a part of the money that comes in is profit.

Opportunities in Retail Selling

Retail selling was one of the first business forms in this world. Even today retail selling continues to be the choice of people who have some capital, or can arrange some, and are willing to work hard to provide good service to the customers. Opportunities exist in the villages, in small towns, in the larger cities and metros. Wherever there are people, they will have needs. To meet these needs, there will be the need for retail selling to them. Only the size of operations will vary from one individual to another, or according to need of the area and community.

Retail selling can be done at as small a scale as carrying a few products in a bag, and selling them from home to home. It can even take the form of a person carrying vegetables in a basket selling them from one place to another. On a larger scale it can be in the form of a retail store specializing in one kind of products or even a department store that stocks hundreds of items of consumer interest. Selling of refrigerators, TVs, household equipment, scooters and motor cycles, and even cars and trucks comes within the scope of retail selling. Each one must decide the kind of work that one likes.

Educational Facilities

Few people take up a career in retail selling after a specialized course in the subject. Most learn the business at work. Only at higher levels where one is in specialized retail business one may enter after training in the related field like engineering, medical equipment, computer science, automobile engineering or even a career in marketing management. Specialized courses in retail selling are not available. Some companies that sell consumer products promote short-term programmes pertaining to their products and to ensure better service to the customers.

Making a Beginning

Most people make a beginning in the retail selling business at a small scale depending upon the kind of products for sale, the size and location of the outlet, and the category of the town or city where one lives. One can as well make a beginning in the rural area.

Beginners need to be particularly careful about the products they choose, and the initial quantity they order to start the business. Very few people are fully aware of the consumer demand, and may stock items more than what would have been appropriate. The leftover stocks discourage newcomers to the business. Another aspect that all beginners need to be aware of is that retail business depends greatly upon merchandising of stocks in the show windows. Many people choose items on the recommendation of the shopkeeper. To build goodwill, one would do well to suggest the best brands and not those where the retail margins may be greater.

Most manufacturers support retailers through advertising in the press and on TV. Besides, the manufacturers also support the retailers with a policy of replacement of defective goods. This does sometimes create added responsibilities for the retailer, but it helps generate goodwill. Extending credit is not a good policy because the cost of the credit reduces selling margins, and may also end up as bad debts. In the best interests of the business, one should study local market trends.

Income from Retail Selling

National laws require that all consumer products must bear the maximum retail price (MRP). No retailer can sell above this price. Even consumer durables bear a MRP, but often the prices are negotiable on account of company pressures on one side and the retail competition on the other.

Retail margins on consumer products vary from 5 to 10 per cent. Products that sell at a slower pace carry a higher margin. Initially, wholesalers supply goods to retailers against cash. When a party has established itself, credit facilities are available. The credit may vary from one to four weeks depending upon the product and the brand name. In some fields longer credit is also available.

Creating creditworthiness should be an important target for those involved in this field. The ultimate income that one derives is directly dependent upon the volumes one can generate and also the credit one can get. With experience most retailers create a balance between products that carry a lower commission and those that carry higher margins.

Opportunities for Self-employment

Besides the salesmen and support staff employed at retail outlets, all those involved in this field are self-employed. In fact, it is the freedom of being self-employed that attracts most people to retail selling.

Selling

75

Selling is perhaps one of the earliest vocations taken up by mankind. At that time, it may have been no more than bartering one commodity for another. However, as human needs grew, and the transactions became too complicated to be practical, money became an equitable and acceptable medium of exchange for everyone. Selling became a vocation, as we know it today.

Selling continues to be the most elementary of vocations. All other businesses, trades and professions depend upon it. All commodities and services must be sold to people to bring in profit. With time, it has become a highly complex and competitive vocation. It requires both skill and perseverance. Those who have reached the highest levels in this profession are admired and respected. Many a rich man today has made their fortune from selling. Many more will continue to do so for all times to come.

Desirable Personal Qualities

To be successful in this field, a person must:

- have a good knowledge of human nature. Selling aims at providing for their needs.
- know all that there is to know about the products or services. Without this knowledge failure is certain.
- know the market well. It is not enough to sell what people want. It is equally important to create demand for new products.
- be observant. One must understand what the customer desires.
- have a good imagination and be creative.
- have a pleasing personality. That helps in drawing the immediate attention of a prospective customer.

- observe good etiquette and manners. Customers find crudity repulsive.
- have the ability to converse and communicate effectively.
- have a good memory for names and faces. Customers feel happy at being addressed by their names.
- have lots of enthusiasm and initiative to provide service.
- be persevering till a sale is closed. Giving up halfway would be disastrous.
- be willing to travel, eat and stay away from home. Selling jobs require extensive travelling.
- be patient and tolerant. Many customers can be very demanding and also unreasonable.
- be able to get along well with a variety of people. Few persons meet as many people as salesmen do.

Opportunities in Selling

Opportunities in selling exist everywhere. At the lowest level in this vocation, besides the many self-employed persons selling their services, we find people selling their own produce in the villages. Perhaps the first attempt to organized selling came in the shape of the weekly village market. We still see it in our villages. The village market is a common sight in the rural areas.

The inability of producers to sell their own produce has given rise to the need for professional salesmen. They may sell on a commission basis, or even purchase small quantities from the producers and sell the goods collectively at more attractive prices. With growing human needs selling as a vocation has become rather specialized. Professional salesmen not only fulfil obvious human needs, but very often create their own opportunities by making people aware of newer needs, and then set out to fulfil them.

In the present age, selling is an organized profession. We find persons involved at all level. Every individual offers services for certain remuneration. At the village level, we come across people who buy commodities directly from the producers.

They may buy produce as a business opportunity, or on a commission basis for onward sale. The produce is passed on to wholesalers who, in turn, either sell them to processing and manufacturing units, or even sell them to retail outlets.

Even in the industrial field, selling plays its role first at the primary stage of assembling the raw material, and then in a more sophisticated manner after the finished product is ready. At each step in every industry, these transactions mean opportunities for those who have the right commodity to sell.

A large industrial output and a high degree of competition in every field has made it necessary that the industrial produce must be sold regularly and swiftly. This has resulted in organized selling at all levels, making way for those interested in selling as a career. At the top level, there is a complete marketing department that maintains its regional offices and warehouses, and supplies goods to wholesalers or directly to retailers.

Those who prefer to sell goods to wholesalers have them pass on the products to the retailers, and eventually to consumers. Even when companies rely upon wholesalers, they still maintain a full-fledged sales office along with field staff to supervise the marketing operations. This is important because one little mistake in the entire set-up resulting in failure of the marketing process can bring the entire manufacturing process to a standstill. Since consumer preferences continue to change, an important role of the marketing department is to keep abreast of these through regular market research. This may be about one's own products, or even about those of one's competitors.

The selling profession that helps assemble food and other commodities for processing and manufacturing industries has reached out to the rural population in our country. However, the selling of finished products and consumer items has yet to be fully developed in these areas. These opportunities are yet to be exploited. Young people who may like to serve the rural market in the country can develop these opportunities into useful careers.

One may argue that at least theoretically a stage will come when there will be no more opportunities in selling. In reality, this can never happen. In fact, the selling profession keeps an eye on the changing trends and responds with new products to keep the demand high, and even create new needs. New products are always in demand in new markets. With rapid development of export marketing, the whole world has become a market for all kinds of things.

Keeping in view the growing complexities of human needs, the selling network also continues to grow in every direction. To fulfil the needs of people, there is organized selling at every level. The government agencies sell food grains and other necessities through fair price shops. Super markets and co-operative stores may sell anything ranging from common everyday necessities to seeds and fertilizers for farmers. Through private efforts, we see thousands of shops bringing the everyday needs close to people. Competition in the field has even made it possible for many needs to be supplied at the very footsteps of consumers. People will continue to think of new ways to sell products and services to others. There will be a growing number of opportunities in every trade. A career in selling can be both challenging and profitable.

Responsibilities Involved

Different kinds of selling jobs involve varied kinds of responsibilities. The work of a sales assistant or a counter attendant requires standing throughout the day. Besides selling goods to customers, his responsibilities include proper display and storage of goods. He will need to be gently persuasive to encourage the customers to buy more, or try new products. Issue of cash or credit vouchers, packing of sold goods, and stock taking or ordering fresh supplies will also claim his attention regularly. Courtesy to customers helps build a lot of goodwill for the business, and a good relationship between the store and the customers.

The job of a sales representative of a business concern entails extensive travelling with samples, descriptive literature, etc. to meet and take orders from customers. He is required to look into the customers' requirements of established products, and to introduce new products. As a part of his regular work, he will need to guide and help wholesale and retail outlets to develop the sales of the company's products. Display and promotion of products will also need his attention. He will need to keep track of the stock and sales situation of various sales outlets. He will need to be aware of the competitors' products and policies in the market. In brief, he is the most important link between the company and the retail outlet or customer. At times, he will need to sell directly to consumers, or even otherwise to note the views and reactions about his company's products and services. When the representative's income is linked to sales, he will need to look for new avenues to promote sales. Amongst other responsibilities, he will need to keep the company informed about his work, sending the orders procured each evening so that the same may be complied with at the earliest moment.

At a still higher level, sales supervisors look into the work of several sales representatives. Since they are promoted from the position of a sales representative, they know the pitfalls of the job. They are responsible for helping the sales representatives under their charge to improve upon their performance, and build a better image of the company.

The responsibility of the entire sales network of the company is that of the sales manager who is stationed at the company headquarters. He is assisted by a complete department, which keeps track of sales in every area. The office set-up will depend upon the magnitude of the company's sales and services. In smaller companies, an office supervisor and other clerical staff may assist him. In a larger company managers who may supervise the sales for particular products, or types of products may assist him. In some companies, the sales manager looks after export sales also, whereas in others the responsibility may be that of an independent export manager.

Educational Facilities

Until a few years ago, few educational institutions were offering undergraduate courses in selling. However, presently institutions spread all over the country are offering both undergraduate and postgraduate courses in management. Many of them lead to specialization in marketing. An undergraduate course is of three years duration, and leads to a B.B.A degree. The specialization is at the postgraduate level. Diploma courses are of shorter duration, depending upon the subjects covered. A course in Export Marketing may be of six months, or more. In the recent years, a large number of private institutions offering a variety of courses have come up. Many offer courses affiliated to foreign universities. These institutions advertise in the national press. For a complete list of institutions offering courses in marketing, please refer to a directory listing names of these institutions.

Making a Beginning

Most of the people engaged in selling as a vocation at lower levels are self-employed. They made a beginning in a small way with a little capital to purchase small items, and backed by their determination, began selling on the roadside. Many did it more out of necessity than out of choice. Finding it remunerative enough to make their ends meet, they have continued at that level. Some are able to save enough to move into a retail outlet of their own.

Self-employed people own almost all retail outlets. They select their lines depending upon their personal knowledge and experience, or by assessing the needs of a particular area. Their knowledge of selling is self-acquired. The sales assistants employed at some of the larger retail stores have always had humble beginnings, learning whatever they do know from their employers, or from senior sales assistants.

Many of the wholesale dealers have also graduated to their higher positions in the field of selling by gaining experience at lower levels. They do not have much to claim by way of formal training or education in selling as a career. However, the children of many of the established self-employed people engaged in selling are finding it useful to graduate in subjects like economics, commerce and accountancy. Some have even preferred to get some formal education in the field of specialization.

When it comes to taking up a career in selling at higher levels in a company, it is a different thing. Besides a bachelor's degree with subjects that provide the foundation knowledge of the products a company deals in, some specialized training in selling and organizational skills is important. Young people who have diplomas and degrees in management get preference over others. Most young people aspiring for these positions aim at studying in top management colleges. Many companies offer apprenticeships, and provide the necessary training. The larger companies are maintaining human resource development departments. The training material is related to the company needs. Promotions are often coupled with additional training.

Selling of specialized lines like engineering goods, chemicals, medical supplies and other such items require special knowledge of the company's products. It is also necessary to be well acquainted with competitor products. Such jobs are offered to those who are graduates in engineering, or hold a B.Pharm or B.V.Sc. degree, depending upon individual requirements. In such cases, the sales training is provided by the company through its own sales staff, or through special courses devised for the purpose. Many young people equip themselves better through postal courses, or through refresher courses on sales management, and finally emerge as good sales representatives/ supervisors.

Finding a Job

Jobs for counter attendants, sales attendants, sales assistants, etc. in general stores are not advertised normally. They are usually filled through personal negotiations only. However, jobs at higher levels in the field of selling are advertised in the national press. Positions in the export departments of companies are filled through advertisements in the press. Candidates are invited for interviews based on their qualifications, and selected on merit. Some training is provided to these candidates at the company office or plant to acquaint them with the different products, manufacturing processes and specialities, sales procedures, etc.

The training may last for two to three months, or sometimes

even longer, and may include working in different positions to be acquainted with different working procedures. Some on-the-job training is imparted by linking a new sales representative with one who is already well established in his territory. Senior positions in the sales departments are filled through promotions within the staff. Sometimes, they are filled directly. Such positions require a high level of experience and knowledge, and will of course not interest young people just setting out on a career in selling.

Income from Selling

At the lower levels, most people earn just enough to meet their basic requirements. However, one can expect to earn a reasonably good income from selling jobs as brokers, commission agents, retail shopowners, etc. The salary of a shop assistant is negotiable, and depends upon the individual's capabilities and the kind of work involved. Promotions come with experience. Some employers provide uniforms and incentives like commission on sales above a certain minimum, free tea, annual bonus and other similar benefits.

The salaries of sales representatives working for big companies are attractive with a basic salary, and a certain percentage of the sales made. Allowances for a scooter or a car and for stay in hotels, for entertainment of customers, telephones, courier, etc. are adequate to meet these needs comfortably. Handsome bonuses are offered to those who perform well. Promotions are linked to personal capabilities, making it possible for brilliant young people to rise quickly to the positions of sales supervisors, area managers, or even to become the sales manager or export manager of the company. The salaries at the higher levels are very attractive. They include many fringe benefits like free or subsidized housing, a company car, and other facilities.

The income of self-employed individuals is directly linked with their efforts. Many people engaged in selling as a career have made small fortunes from their work. They have been able to provide their families all the comforts of life.

Opportunities for Self-employment

There are innumerable opportunities for self-employment in a career in selling. Perhaps the largest number of self-employed people are engaged in the vocation of selling goods and services. For those who have some money to invest, there are opportunities for opening a retail store of a size proportionate to their means. Those who do not have anything to invest but their own hard work can begin by selling insurance, work as brokers, auction agents, order suppliers, or do some similar work. To be successful, it is necessary that besides being willing to put in hard work, one must be known for honest dealings. One must enjoy undisputed honour and integrity.

Service Providing

76

One of the oldest fields of vocations is providing of personal services. This may be as elementary as providing services as a domestic assistant, or as hi-tech as providing consultancy services to a corporate house. In the strict sense of the word a job too entails providing a service in return for remuneration. But in the present situation service providing is taken to mean a variety of services people are providing and are compensated for their effort by payment of a fee.

Through service providing individuals can provide their services through a variety of physical efforts. For instance, a gardener provides the services of looking after a garden, or a plumber provides the services of repairing toilets, or a TV mechanic provides the services of repairing TVs or electronic equipment. In the same way, a person may provide services that may not involve physical effort, but mental skills and abilities as are provided by a variety of consultants specialized in different fields of activities.

In the recent past a lot of new areas of service providing have created additional vocational opportunities. Many of these like Medical Transcription, Business Process Outsourcing, Call Centres, etc. are discussed in different parts of this book. Yet there are several other areas in this field that have been providing opportunities for work earlier, and will continue to provide useful openings for careers in different kinds of work.

Desirable Personal Qualities

To be successful in this field a person must:

- be well acquainted with the kind of service offered. The more intricate the kind of service offered the better the return.

- be honest and sincere in the work. Many of the services are sought for in good faith. Without honesty and sincerity one cannot last in this field.
- have good manners and etiquette. These ensure good and lasting relationships.
- have good public relations. This helps build a good clientele over a period of time.
- be observant to be able to recognize human needs that can be fulfilled.
- be willing to work hard at odd hours as required by clients sometimes.

Opportunities in Service Providing

Service providing aims at offering one's physical or mental abilities to individuals or groups in return for a fee or charge. We see this being done everyday from morning till night. The variety of services offered can be as simple as a youngster on the road offering to wash a car for a few rupees to the offer of an individual to suggest a good partner in marriage for a particular fee.

At the lower levels whereas there are individuals who are offering their personal services, those with entrepreneurial skills are offering services like providing domestic help, nursing staff, security staff and even technical staff for a charge. Home delivery services like providing milk, vegetables, provision items and even cooked food provide vocational opportunities to a lot of people. Many restaurants now have full-time delivery staff.

The providing of home maintenance services offers yet another large group of services in this field of vocations. People are offering plumbing services, electrical repairs, woodwork repairs and painting services. For the benefit of those who are busy at offices, there are services for the payment of municipal taxes, telephone and electricity bills.

The area of electronic repairs and services has grown tremendously over the years. Specialized services are now available for repair and maintenance of refrigerators and air conditioners, TVs, VCD and DVD players. Services are also available for repairs to computers and peripheral equipment. Inverters and electricity storage devices too have service providers.

With large corporate houses offering warranties for their products, it has become necessary for them to provide good follow-up service. This is being provided through authorised service centres being established in important cities around the country. Each centre caters to the need of the smaller towns around it through service engineers available on call.

The large number of cycles, scooters, motorcycles, three-wheelers, cars, buses and trucks need regular servicing and repairs. This area of service alone has provided opportunities of employment to a large number of people in every town. The more organized persons are operating well-equipped workshops.

Business consultants provide services in many areas of activity. Some do it on short-term basis for particular projects; others do it on long-term basis being available whenever necessary. Many consultants provide liaison services to international corporate houses to follow up their work on a commission basis. Financial consultancy and advising is yet another area where people seek the services to invest their savings.

Service providers have not ignored family needs either. We have consultants who help and facilitate the admission of children to school. There are others that provide marital counselling or suggest marital partners through Marriage Bureaus. There are now consultants and service providers who are willing to provide special services to parents and dependents of non-resident Indians settled abroad.

Human needs can be very complex. Service providers have an eye to look for these needs, and then reach out to fulfil it for a fee. These needs will continue to exist and provide opportunities for vocations for young people.

Educational Facilities

The field of providing services is very vast. For different areas of work a person will need different kinds of skills and abilities. In this field adaptation is important. If a person is clear on the kind of service that is to be provided, one can go in for training in that field. Most people learn special skills by joining established workers, and after some experience setting out individually, or as a group. Those who set up authorised service stations receive technical expertise through training with the principals.

Making a Beginning

In a country where a very large number of families are needy to the extent of not being able to send the children to school, many people have entered this field of work in their childhood and grown up into mature technicians and mechanics providing a variety of services.

The educated persons first qualify in their area of interest. After having qualified through appropriate education they join as assistants, or even take up free lance assignments gaining experience at work. They grow in the area of their work with time. Growth in this field is slow. Only the very capable people rise to high positions or gain a position of honour.

Income from Service Providing

Most people in this field are self-employed, charging a fee for the services offered. The income will be in proportion to the kind of clientele one can build over a period of time through good public relations. Those who provide regular service work on fixed charges that are negotiable. These are at par with the salary of a person possessing similar level of expertise.

Opportunities for Self-employment

Most of the people in this field of work are self-employed. Those who take up jobs receive salaries that are similar to those in similar fields.

Social Service

77

Most young people would not look at this field of work as offering any opportunities for a vocation. They feel that retired individuals or missionaries look after these organizations, and there is no place for younger people in search for a career.

Non-governmental organizations (NGOs) are not only doing great work, but are an important force in the development process of the country. Their role is likely to become even more important in the near future. There are organizations that are contributing significantly to the development of education, healthcare, care of orphans, mentally and physically challenged children, destitute women and to create awareness to causes like the degradation of the environment. New concerns will continue to emerge. There will be people and organizations to set them right.

It is true that at local level much social service is done through individual and group action when people contribute their skills and efforts to set problems right. With larger corporate contributions and an organized effort towards the development work, many organizations are now running full-fledged offices to follow-up their efforts. Young people interested in such areas of work can look forward to opportunities in this field.

Desirable Personal Qualities

To be successful in this field a person must:

- be endowed with a patriotic spirit. Patriotism is a great motivating force.
- have a missionary attitude towards life. Without a definite mission or aim one cannot achieve much.
- be compassionate towards the needy and the afflicted. One will need to deal with such people.

- feel deeply about the cause of concern. Without deep personal concern one cannot put in one's best.
- be willing to face opposition and hardships. Very few people in life are cooperative.
- be willing to work at odd times at difficult places.
- be persevering in all activities. One needs to keep going all the time.

Opportunities in Social Service

In a country that has seen hundreds of years of foreign rule there is no dearth of opportunities for social service. The problem is that the general public is not fully aware of their rights and responsibilities. This is particularly so because of lack of education. Only a few that are endowed with patriotic feelings are coming forth to seek relief against the atrocities against the poor and the needy.

Many organizations, both big and small, have set out to do whatever they can to create a better environment for the common man. Most organizations depend upon individual contributions by way of effort and personal skills to help the needy. A few that have greater resources by way of funds and influence are more organized and working in cooperation with the government and local agencies to fulfil their aim.

Many organizations belonging to different religious sects are running charitable institutions to provide education and healthcare at a nominal cost. They also provide other charitable facilities to people that follow their religion. These organizations have need for people to provide the services, some voluntarily and some on paid basis.

Many corporate bodies too have established organizations that provide different kinds of charitable and social service activities. Since these organizations are separate from the corporate bodies, their administration and services are looked after by a separate set of individuals employed for particular purposes.

To ensure that their funds and services are properly utilized many foreign charitable and social service organizations too have established offices in the country to oversee their work. Such organizations have need for employees to administer the office and the practical work of the organization like operating orphanages, educational institutions or providing scholarships for study abroad.

All these organizations are referred to as non-governmental organizations or NGOs in short. These provide services that can be clubbed together as social service. They have their need for good dedicated personnel to look after their work.

Educational Facilities

Since different organizations provide a variety of services, their need for help depends upon the kind of activity they support. Individuals seeking vocational activity in this field will need to be qualified in the field of their activity. There are no specialized courses available for charitable work, but people who prefer to serve in this field study Social Sciences and Public Relations. Some educational institutions are offering diploma courses in Community Development.

Making a Beginning

Depending upon the activities of the organization an individual can join as an assistant in the field the organization wishes to pursue. Sometimes, the work may require teamwork. Many times the individuals set out to work alone, reporting directly to their organization. The activity will depend upon the aims of the service organization.

Income from Social Service

Most people take up work in this field because of personal and patriotic reasons rather than for financial considerations. The salaries are negotiable and on the lower side. People work for intrinsic reasons. The work gives people great inner satisfaction and happiness. Many people in this field have other sources of income they can depend upon.

Opportunities for Self-employment

By the very nature of the work social service requires group activity. The purpose of such work is not personal income but the care of a particular concern. Paid personnel with a missionary zeal oversee the activities on behalf of bigger organizations that have the resources, but lack dedicated manpower.

Teaching

Although many people are working as teachers more because of personal circumstances than of choice, teaching continues to be a popular career amongst the educated people of our country. It keeps one in close touch with young people. All those who teach out of choice agree that it can be very satisfying and stimulating. It helps keep one well informed on a variety of subjects.

Until a few years ago, the lot of teachers was not too happy or encouraging. Presently, when teachers have organized themselves well, and the state governments have regulated the scale of salaries, established reasonable terms of service, and ensured that they are paid their salary regularly, teaching as a career is beginning to be attractive to many young people.

As incentives to teachers, the government has also instituted national awards based on their services, and offers merit scholarships, exemption from payment of tuition fees, rebates in bus and hostel fees, and similar benefits for their children. As a means of improving their position and status, teachers are permitted to appear for university examinations as private candidates without having to attend regular full-time classes.

Employment Pattern

A very large number of men and women are working as teachers in our country. Of these almost half are teaching in primary schools, a little over one-fourth teach in middle schools, and the rest in high/higher secondary schools and colleges. Since the majority of the primary and middle schools are in villages, almost 70 per cent of the teachers are working in the rural areas. The high/higher secondary schools and colleges are mostly based in urban areas. Whereas women teachers are preferred at the pre-primary and lower levels, men teachers dominate the scene at college and university level. About one-fourth of the teachers in primary, middle and high/higher secondary schools are women.

Working Conditions

In many states, the governments have regulated the conditions of work of the teachers. The pay scales have been regulated, and firm steps have been taken to ensure that they are paid their salaries regularly. On an average, a school teacher teaches 20 to 25 hours a week, and a college/university teacher about 10 hours a week. However, the teachers are expected to utilize the free hours for extra-curricular activities, for personal reading and preparation, correction of notebooks, evaluation of examination papers, preparation of periodical reports and such other activities. Many times the teachers need to carry some of their work home. Since schools and colleges close for the summer and winter vacations, mid-term holidays, etc., teachers are entitled to these holidays with pay, working for only 8 to 9 months in the year. There is now a provision for pension for teachers. Other laws have been enacted to ensure the security of service and a comfortable retirement.

Desirable Personal Qualities

To be successful in this field a person must:

- have a good knowledge of the subject one teaches.
- have a good all-round knowledge. To a student a teacher is a symbol of knowledge.
- have excellent communication skills. Unless a teacher can express thoughts in simple words, students find it hard to learn a subject.
- have clarity of thought. Students will ask all kinds of questions. Unless one is clear about the subject, it can be difficult to answer them.
- be able to speak audibly. Unless the students can hear, the teacher cannot hold their attention.
- have a neat handwriting. Teaching involves writing a lot on the blackboard.
- have a good knowledge of human nature. Students

will come from all kinds of homes and family backgrounds.

- be pleasant to talk to. All students look up to their teachers.
- be patient and tolerant. Dealing with students can be very exasperating at times.
- be a model person students can look up to as an ideal citizen.

Teaching in Pre-primary Schools

Teaching in pre-primary schools entails working with small children, 3 to 5 years old. Rather than possessing great academic ability, it requires a person to teach through the media of toys, drawings, playing, singing and dancing. For obvious reasons, women dominate this field of education. They are naturally endowed with the maternal instinct, and possess the tact and patience to handle little children. The teacher is expected to work with one group of children throughout the day. The teacher helps them to recite simple poems, read and write the alphabet, and numbers. Games and recreational activities help the children to develop muscular and manipulative skills. More than anything else, the teacher helps them learn to get along with other children of their age group.

Pre-primary schools are concentrated in urban areas. Although qualified teachers are preferred, young girls who have the ability to quickly become friendly with little children through story-telling, singing, dancing, a sense of humour, and lots of tact and patience find jobs in these institutions. Many of these teachers are untrained. Schools that are privately owned employ them. The salaries offered are meagre. Salaries in government institutions are better. However, they insist on qualified staff. The scope for promotions is not good unless one qualifies for other better teaching positions. Therefore, young girls who are waiting to be married and settle as housewives mostly fill these jobs.

For those interested in becoming qualified teachers for teaching in pre-primary schools, there are institutions all over the country offering one or two years' diploma courses. The basic qualification required for admission into these institutions is high school/higher secondary or 10+2. A list of schools offering this course can be obtained from the District Inspector of Schools. Jobs can be obtained through direct negotiation, or through the employment exchange. Those who are suitably qualified and have the necessary premises can become self-employed by starting a school particularly in the urban areas.

Teaching in Primary and Junior High Schools

Whereas the teaching responsibilities in the primary and junior high schools are similar, these schools are separately identified as Primary schools and Junior High Schools. Most of these schools are located in the rural areas. They lack the normal amenities desired for schools.

The teachers in a Primary School cater to the needs of children 5 to 11 years old, and teach reading, writing, arithmetic, etc. They also supervise games and group activities. The scope of teaching broadens in a Junior High School as subjects like History, Geography and the different sciences are added. The medium of instruction in these schools is the local mother tongue, or Hindi.

A teacher in these schools must have done higher secondary or 10+2, and must have received one or two years' training to qualify for a Junior Basic Teacher's Training Certificate, Basic Training Certificate, or Senior Basic Training Certificate. In the urban areas, it is common to find unemployed graduates offering their services for these positions. There are hundreds of institutions spread all over the country offering this training. One can obtain the address of an institution nearby by writing to the District Inspector of Schools.

Besides a few Primary/Junior High Schools run by private bodies in the urban areas, the majority are being run by the government, district boards, defence services, quasi-government institutions, etc. Although regulated by law, the salaries in these institutions are low. The prospects for promotion are not good unless one qualifies to move into better teaching positions. One can apply for jobs directly, or through an employment exchange. There is some possibility of additional income through part-time tuition.

Teaching in High and Higher Secondary Schools

A teacher in a high or higher secondary school teaches the ninth, tenth, eleventh and twelfth classes often divided into sections with as many as 40 students in a section, taking a definite number of periods in one or two subjects only every week. The teacher is designated as the Physics teacher, Biology teacher, English teacher, etc. Besides the conventional subjects, technical subjects have been introduced in some schools to make the education vocationally useful. Besides teaching, the teachers are expected to supervise sports and games, and other group activities, and also undertake responsibilities which include various aspects of running the school, like collecting school fees, managing the library, looking after the hostel, etc.

A high/higher secondary school teacher must have a university degree with high marks in the subject s/he proposes to teach. The teacher must have teachers' training degree like the B.Ed. or B.T., which requires one year's full-time study after graduation. Very often, the teachers hold postgraduate degrees like M.A., M.Sc. or M.Com. and even Ph.D.

Private bodies run the majority of the schools. Many are managed by the state governments, municipal boards, defence services, etc. Appointments are made by the selection committees appointed by the management committees as prescribed by law in different states. In some states where the government has taken over the responsibility of paying all the school staff, the District Inspector of Schools, or a person so authorized by the government is a member of the selection committee.

The scale of salaries has been regulated in almost all the states. The salaries are good. Teachers are entitled to other allowances and facilities also. There are prospects of rising through additional qualifications and added experience. One may rise to the position of principal of the school. Rules about taking private tuition vary in each state. A teacher can take up to two tuitions with the permission of the principal. Additional income is also possible through correcting Board examination papers.

Teaching Special Subjects in Schools

Besides conventional subjects like science, languages, economics, civics, etc., there is always the need for teaching subjects like physical education, art, music, dancing, handicrafts, etc. in schools. The qualifications of these teachers are different as of necessity they must specialize in the line of their teaching. Courses for such specialization may range from one to three years. Many teachers have received additional training to qualify as Career Masters who can provide the students with occupational and employment information in schools. They are entitled to an honorarium besides the salary. The pay scales for teachers of special subjects are similar to those for other teachers, but invariably they enjoy the privilege of being able to earn additional amounts through their efforts in off-hours.

Specialized Teaching

A career in teaching need not be restricted to teaching in the common schools and colleges only. It may be directed at teaching children and adults under unusual circumstances as, for instance, teaching the handicapped. This can include teaching the blind, the deaf and the dumb, and those who may be mentally retarded, or even physically handicapped. Besides a great storehouse of patience, understanding and sympathy, such teaching careers require specialized training, and are open to those who have passed high school and hold a teacher's diploma.

Career counselling is a very important field open to teachers with educational interest in vocational guidance, or a postgraduate degree in Psychology. A one-year's course leads to this specialization. Teachers so qualified can help guide individuals to select careers, and on other related problems.

Teaching in Colleges and Universities

Education facilities for higher education have expanded manifold over the years. Whereas three-fourth of our colleges provide facilities for higher education in art, science and commerce subjects, others provide education in subjects like medicine, engineering and technology, agriculture, veterinary science, management, teaching, music, fine arts and other similar subjects.

Lecturers and assistant lecturers constitute the bulk of the teaching staff in colleges and universities. An estimated 15 per cent of teachers in all categories are women. At the lowest level, there are tutors or demonstrators. Many of them work for only a part of the year. Therefore, they do not enjoy the benefits of the permanent staff. The salaries regulated by the governments in different states are good. The teachers in the universities enjoy a more favoured status as compared to their colleagues in the colleges.

Like other spheres of teaching, the responsibility of a teacher in a college or a university includes giving lectures in the subject of specialization, examining the work of the students, setting examination papers, evaluating answer books, and supervising extra-curricular activities like games and sports, dramatics, debates, etc. A very high level of academic education is required for a teaching career in colleges and universities. Most of the teachers are holding not only first class Master's degrees, but may also have done a Ph.D., D.Sc. or D.Litt. or similar academic work. When a person is dedicated to duty, there is the opportunity to rise to the position of principal in a college or the Dean of a faculty or Head of Department in a university. There are openings for well-qualified and brilliant people in all spheres of higher education, particularly in professional subjects.

Supplementing Income from Teaching

The pay scales of teachers in colleges and universities are comparable with pay scales in other professions. However, the pay scales of teachers at lower levels are not as attractive. Very often, the teachers find it necessary to supplement their incomes from teaching. Taking up private tuition is a common form of adding to one's income. In many states, there are restrictions on taking up more than two tuitions.

Part-time jobs like typing assignments, account keeping,

and such similar jobs have been useful to supplement the income in some cases. Those who are interested and qualified can earn additional sums through freelance journalism. They can write textbooks for schools or write articles and stories or illustrate books for children. They can also work part-time proof reading for presses or publishing houses, assessing manuscripts for publishers, writing advertising copy and a whole lot of similar work that can fit in with a career in teaching.

Self-employment for Teachers

Not satisfied with a job in teaching, or sometimes when a good job is not available, young people interested in a career in teaching have turned to self-employment by opening a school of their own. Many such schools and colleges are established throughout the country. They are providing education in a wide field of subjects like preparing students for university degrees, providing specialized coaching to students appearing for competitive examinations, technical coaching in computers and other subjects, and teaching languages.

Some aim at helping the tiny tots start on their educational career. The majority of these are for educating the very young. However, self-employment has given rise to schools for teaching art, embroidery or other crafts, cooking, baking, flower arrangements, etc. Since some subjects can be taught only through the written word, correspondence courses on many subjects have been prepared. This has given rise to teaching opportunities almost all over the world.

If you have specialized knowledge, know how to teach, and are interested in getting self-employed, you can turn your abilities into a fruitful effort to develop a full-time career for yourself. Study the needs of your community, and see how you can fulfil them with your personal capabilities and assets.

Telecommunications

Little did Michael Faraday who discovered electromagnetism and Alexander Graham Bell who invented the telephone using the earlier discovery ever imagine how their work will transform the way mankind will communicate with each other. They could have never realised that their work will pave the way for very swift worldwide communication revolutionizing the way people think, work or do business.

Telecommunications is the technology that makes it possible to communicate over distances through telephone, telegraph and cable and by other means. Over the years such rapid advances have taken place that the present generation that communicates through palm-sized mobile phones will never imagine how the original telephone worked, or messages were communicated through telegraph systems using the Morse key.

From the old crude telephone set to the modern mobile phone, and from the coded telegraph signals to the modern Integrated-Services Digital Network (ISDN) the way mankind communicates has undergone an unbelievable change. Keeping pace with the changes around the world, the field of Telecommunications has seen great developments in the country not only affecting the way people work, but at the same time providing innumerable opportunities for vocations for young people.

Desirable Personal Qualities

To be successful in this field a person must:

- be well acquainted with the modern day technology in this field.
- be fond of updating information in this field constantly. The changes are taking place at an unbelievable pace.

- be well acquainted with allied fields of engineering and technology.
- be willing to work as a team. The progress requires several people to pool in their knowledge to keep updated.

Opportunities in Telecommunications

The Telecom Regulatory Authority of India (TRAI) controls all the telecommunication activities in India. Bharat Sanchar Nigam Ltd. (BSNL) and Videsh Sanchar Nigam Ltd. (VSNL) along with MTNL operating in the metro cities provide the telecommunication facilities on behalf of the government. Mobile facilities are also offered by BSNL.

A few years earlier when mobile phones were first introduced into India, the responsibility was passed on to private corporate bodies. Two operators were licensed to work in each state of the country. This was to provide competitive service to the customers. To make this possible each operator installed its infrastructure in each state starting from the larger cities and gradually spreading to the smaller towns and the rural areas that could be included. The private operators in the states worked out mutual arrangements so that mobile connections sold by them could be used in other states also. This way, it became possible to move anywhere in the country and still be in touch through the mobile phone.

Reliance has now created its own infrastructure whereby it is now possible for one Reliance subscriber to speak to another Reliance subscriber anywhere as though it were a local call. One can speak across the country through other operators at additional cost.

The investment of large sums of money by different operators to create a vast infrastructure to connect almost every part of the country has resulted in rapid growth of telecommunications in the country. This rapid growth has provided innumerable opportunities for building and maintaining the infrastructure, the sale of telephone connections, instruments and accessories. With Internet facilities readily available on landlines and the mobile infrastructure other fields of activities have greatly benefited. There has been growth in other sectors.

With the increase in telephone and mobile connections an important problem that needs constant attention is that of maintaining correct records and the collection of bills in time. This requires good accounting services. New opportunities have emerged in this area.

A good telecommunications set-up has made it possible to keep in touch with people all the time. This has generated greater development. This has also meant the availability of increased opportunities for careers in this field.

Educational Facilities

For responsible positions in this field it is necessary to obtain a Bachelor's degree in Electronics and Telecommunications. Most engineering colleges are offering the facilities for such study. To specialize one can follow with a Master's degree in the field of one's choice. Admission requirements are similar to those for other engineering fields.

One does not need engineering skills to sell telephone connections, handsets or accessories. Individuals in the field of selling do most of this work. To succeed one must have selling skills. Good follow-up service is also essential. Marketing personnel supported by a chain of private distributors and retailers control this area of work. Personnel qualified in this area of work supervise the accounting work.

Making a Beginning

Technical personnel can join any of the companies depending upon their requirements for personnel. Once the infrastructure is ready maintenance is the primary concern.

With large-scale expansion of the infrastructure every company is interested in developing the market for the sale of its services. This is a field for marketing personnel who are devising a variety of ways to develop the market. The core marketing staff work through private distributors in each town who, in turn, appoint retailers. The retailers sell new connections and pre-paid recharge cards.

Since the openings at the company level are few, most of the work that is being generated is at the local level. Those who can invest larger sums can take up responsibilities as distributors. The majority of people join as retailers. Many people who are already in retail business have added this line as additional work.

Income from Telecommunications

The income in this field varies with the kind of work a person is doing. Engineers earn as much as they do in other fields of work. Similarly, the sales personnel too earn as much as they do in other areas of selling. The distributor and the retailers do the selling at the local level. Both work on commission. Their income is directly dependent upon the sales they can generate. With the rapid growth in this field, both have been earning steady incomes in this field.

Opportunities for Self-employment

The only opportunities for self-employment in this field are those in the area of selling new connections, recharge cards, instruments and accessories.

Transportation

80

We are living in an age where everyone is in a hurry to move from one place to another. Modern marketing too requires swift movement of goods from the area of supply to the area of consumption. This need has given rise to a big field of vocations in transportation. It is now possible to quickly move people and material by road, rail, sea or air. Each of these fields has developed into specialized lines of activity, offering different kinds of opportunities for careers for young people.

The opportunities for careers in transportation by rail, sea and air are discussed separately in the chapters on Railways, Merchant Navy and Civil Aviation. This chapter is devoted to the vast field of vocations offered because of opportunities in road transportation. This field is rapidly developing. It will continue to offer opportunities for careers for young people interested in this kind of work.

Desirable Personal Qualities

To be successful in this field a person must:

- be an extrovert fond of travelling around. Constant travelling is a part of careers in this field.
- be able to get along with a variety of people. One meets many kinds of people when travelling. Some of these people are good and cooperative. A few are not.
- enjoy good health. Constant travel can be strenuous and stressful.
- be able to live on different kinds of food. Food habits vary from one place to another.
- be willing to stay away from home for long periods. In this field it is not always possible to return home every evening.

- be willing to work at odd hours. It is not possible to have fixed working hours.
- be able to handle difficult situations and crises. If things can go wrong, they will. One must handle situations boldly.

Opportunities in Transportation

Next to Railways, road transportation is most important to move both men and materials from one place to another. The rapid development in this field has made it possible for truck operators to move goods to great distances quickly at most competitive prices, offering competition to the Railways. Besides, in many cases, the only mode of transportation available is through trucks.

To move passengers from one point to another, almost every state has developed its own road transportation system in the public sector. There is an effort to serve every nook and corner of the country. Bus operators in the private sector supplement this service. The transportation of goods is principally handled by the private sector.

Private operators handle the operation of taxis, three-wheel scooters, and similar transport vehicles almost exclusively. This has created opportunities for drivers, conductors, booking clerks, inspectors, maintenance staff, etc. To keep the vast fleet of trucks, buses, taxis, etc. moving, many people have found useful work to manufacture spare parts and retail them, to operate service stations, automobile garages, and offer similar services. The general insurance business gets substantial business from these vehicle operators to cover various kinds of risks on the road.

Transporters who have been able to organize themselves on modern lines are working as cargo couriers, offering delivery of goods quickly all over the country. Besides an efficient fleet of vehicles, both big and small, used for moving the goods, these transporters use modern business techniques to trace goods from one station to another. Their staff is specially trained for efficient operation and good public relations.

Educational Facilities

Most taxi and truck/bus drivers have learnt driving by practising with their friends. In the larger cities, there are driving schools where one can learn driving quickly under trained drivers. Conductors working on State Transport Undertaking buses are trained before being assigned their responsibilities. In the private sector, conductors learn as they work.

Making a Beginning

The requirements for joining a career in this field of transportation vary with the kind of work involved. To join a transport company/operator as a driver, one needs to have a driving licence for heavy vehicles. For working as a three-wheel scooter driver or a taxi driver, one needs a taxi driver's licence. These can be obtained from the appropriate transport authorities at the district level after qualifying in the driving test. There are many driving schools, particularly in the larger cities. These schools provide the necessary training, and help obtain licence after a driving test. On obtaining a driving licence, one can join a transport operator through personal negotiation, or when vacancies are required to be filled in one of the government transport undertakings. Advertisements for these posts are published in the press.

Conductors are employed through advertisements, or by inviting names through employment exchanges. After providing some training about the responsibilities involved, they are assigned to work on short routes. The ground staff required for maintenance work is hired based on their knowledge and experience. Maintenance staff working independently, and depending for work on the private operators, invariably has come up the harder way, learning the trade through apprenticeship. Technical jobs like checking of parts, reconditioning them, or doing similar repairs are done by repairmen specially trained by engineering business firms specializing in this kind of work.

Income from Transportation

Depending upon the kind of employer one is working for, a bus or truck conductor starts at the lowest level. The salary is negotiable. Drivers may get twice as much as a conductor. Again, the salary is negotiable, unless one is working for the government where the pay scales are fixed, and revised periodically. A taxi driver works under an individual employer. The salary is negotiable. Drivers who are knowledgeable, and can serve as guides draw better salaries, and a tip. Steady increments assure a reasonable income. Besides the salary, the drivers and conductors are entitled to allowances for food and outstation stay. Drivers who have been working for a long time earn well.

Opportunities for Self-employment

Many a persevering person in the transportation business has come up from the lowest position. Those who can manage to collect some capital to invest can get the balance from banks or finance companies at a reasonable rate of interest repayable in instalments. This way, enterprising young people have become self-employed by buying a three-wheel scooter, a taxi, a truck or even a bus.

Many farmers who own tractors have come into the transportation business by adding on a trolley, and transporting agricultural produce and other items. Many people have done it very successfully by not only operating a single vehicle, but through sheer perseverance, they have gone on to build fleets of vehicles to operate a full-fledged transport business.

Many car owners do not have full-time drivers. Sometimes, when they need a driver for a long trip, or to drive in difficult terrain as in hills, freelance drivers fulfil their need. These freelance drivers charge a higher rate. However, they do not get work round the year.

Travel and Tourism

81

Travel and tourism offer more opportunities than any other career. India is a vast country with an ancient history and culture, a variety of people, and richly blessed with bounties of nature. We have long stretches of plains, hills and mountains. There are deserts, rivers and lakes. There are religious destinations for all the major religions around the world. India has something of interest for everyone. As compared to other countries, it has more to offer to the international tourists. With growing education and development there is great scope for promoting tourism within the country.

During the recent past, there has been a rapid increase in tourism, both from within the country, and from abroad. With better facilities offered by the state and private transport companies, travelling has become easier. Air services have been extended into new areas. With India coming into greater political prominence, and with better publicity of our places of tourist interest in other countries, foreign tour operators are bringing in more tourists each year.

All the states have departments of tourism which are not only promoting places of tourist interest in the state, but are also setting up hotels, restaurants, bars, and are even conducting special tours to important places. This has resulted in growing opportunities for careers for young people interested in tourism. The prospects of future development appear to be even brighter.

Desirable Personal Qualities

To succeed in this field, a person must:

- have a pleasing personality. That helps win immediate attention.
- be an extrovert fond of moving about. Unless one is

fond of the great outdoors one cannot like the travelling involved.

- be service-minded. Good hospitality is always appreciated.
- appreciate the need for good manners and etiquette. They enhance an individual's personality.
- have a working knowledge of English and local languages. The tourists want all the details in a language they can understand.
- have good communication skills. It is a two-way communication that spells success in this field.
- know the area of specialization well. Many fields of specialization exist in this line of activity.
- know how to handle difficult situations and crises. If things can go wrong, they will. It is important that they are handled swiftly.
- be computer literate. Much work is now done swiftly through computers.
- be able to eat a variety of foods. People eat a variety of dishes in different parts of the world.
- be comfortable with a variety of people. One will need to adapt to their needs and habits.
- have knowledge of the history of the people and places one visits. It adds up to success in this field.

Opportunities in Travel and Tourism

Travel and tourism interest people around the world. More people are involved in this field than in any other. Yet opportunities continue to grow with newer destinations, more facilities and more people wanting to travel. Areas that were once distant and unknown have opened up to people. Man's desire for seeing the unknown continues to create newer opportunities. Whereas this trade had earlier been concentrating only on the foreign tourists, both inward and outward, the domestic market has opened up many opportunities. The field is gradually moving towards specialization of different activities.

At the lowest level in this vocation, many young people

are finding useful employment as tourist guides. Many of these young people work locally in a place of tourist interest. They possess only the most elementary knowledge, and depend upon personal experience gained through their work. Their fee is open to mutual negotiation. A trained tourist guide demands greater respect. He accompanies tourists, travellers and businessmen, and takes them to places of interest. He also guides them on preparing travel plans, making stay arrangements, and other related matters. Tourist guides who know foreign languages are always in great demand. They are paid extra for their additional knowledge.

At a higher level, many young people are finding ready employment as travel agents. Operating from an office, a travel agent provides the facilities of trained guides, arranging for tickets by rail, air or sea, taxis, hotel reservations, preparing travel itineraries, etc. Many travel agents conduct group tours by road, rail or air within the country at special rates. Some conduct group tours to other countries. Others conduct tours within the country in co-operation with foreign tour operators. Some of the bigger travel agents maintain branches in the larger cities, and have associates within the country and abroad. They maintain a big set-up with different departments looking after the various aspects of the business.

Many state governments have developed full-fledged Departments of Tourism which have promoted tourist complexes offering facilities for lodging, boarding, bar, sightseeing, etc. Besides, many of the rest houses in the states are now open to tourists. The addition of hotels, restaurants, snack bars, and tourist bungalows has all opened many opportunities for good careers. All state governments also maintain Tourist Bureau at important places where information of tourist interest is provided free of charge. In some states, conducted bus tours to important places are being organized regularly.

At the national level, the India Tourism Development Corporation is doing much to promote tourism all over the country, thereby opening up opportunities for interested young people in many fields of tourism.

Specialized Activities

The field of travel and tourism has grown to the extent of people specializing in particular activities. Those with more facilities may simultaneously handle several specialities. These are some of the popular activities:

- Local sightseeing.
- Making travel reservations—rail, road and by air. Airline reservations may include domestic and international travel.
- Hotel reservations around the world.
- Domestic group tours by road, rail and air.
- International group tours—both for inward and outward travel.
- Religious tourism that includes visits to places of religious interest—domestic and international.
- Adventure tourism that includes a variety of activities.
- Group tours for corporate houses—both domestic and international.
- Passport, visa and foreign exchange services.

Educational Facilities

A large number of people in this field learnt the work hands on. Many are still doing it. They begin with determination and work hard. Success follows. With great competition in this field it is desirable that formal education must be taken. Many private and government institutions are providing the necessary training in travel and tourism after 10+2. Some offer short-term diploma courses. Some institutions provide undergraduate and postgraduate courses also. Specialized courses in particular fields are also available. Practical training in established travel agencies follows many courses. It would be worthwhile to check the placement record of the institution you decide to study in.

Local tourist guides depend only upon their basic education and experience. Qualified guides are graduates who have studied subjects like English, History, Archaeology and

Psychology. Knowledge of foreign languages is an additional qualification. Many institutions offer courses in tourism.

The Andhra University, Waltair, offers a one-year course in tourism after graduation. The Department of History and Ancient Indian Culture, Marathwada University, Aurangabad, also offers similar courses. The College of Vocational Studies, New Delhi, offers a three-year BA course after 10+2. Sophia College and Basant Kumar Somani Polytechnic in Mumbai offer a Certificate in Travel Agency Work through a one-year course.

The Department of Tourism, Government of India, offers short-term courses for tourist guides. Several private institutions are offering similar courses leading to careers in tourism. Several hotels, government departments and correspondence schools also offer training in various aspects of the tourist trade. These courses are advertised in the national press from time to time.

Making a Beginning

Those joining this field can either begin work in an agency assisting in office work, or in the practical side by serving as travel guide. Those who have specialized in a particular area will need to join in that speciality as an assistant. One grows with experience, and moves into a particular line of specialization. This is a very competitive field and one will need to work very hard to prove one's abilities. The working hours can be very long and erratic. The clients can also be very demanding at times. Patience and tact are important in this field.

Young people interested in working as local guides can begin in a small way in their own towns by helping tourists to see places of interest. Qualified tourist guides can connect themselves with recognized travel agents or Government Tourist Bureau. They can pick up assignments as and when required. Many young people also start their careers by joining a department in a travel agency. After gaining valuable experience by working in different departments, they eventually rise to better positions. Many open their own travel agencies. Most of the positions have to be personally negotiated. Jobs offered by the government departments are usually advertised. Candidates are selected on merit to perform different duties.

Income from Travel and Tourism

The income at entry level is very much like that for other careers. However, as one gains experience and shows proven abilities, people rise quickly. The field being very competitive, few people rise to important positions. Growth is greatly dependent on one's ability to handle responsibility.

Rates for local untrained guides are negotiable. Since newcomers who are inexperienced fill the positions, they are happy to get what comes their way. Trained guides attached with recognized travel agencies and government departments receive payment at prescribed rates, depending upon the size of the group. Charges for outstation visits are higher. Besides the fees, the guide is entitled to free transportation, boarding and lodging. Guides knowing a foreign language get additional charges. A good experienced guide attached to a travel agency can earn well.

Travel agents do not charge anything for their advisory function. There are fixed charges for rail bookings, and ticket delivery charges. They get attractive commissions on air and sea bookings for travel by air or sea. The passengers pay the prescribed fares. Hotels pay commissions on bookings through travel agents. The income on group tours by road, rail, air or sea depends upon individual planning, goodwill and the kind of services offered. The salaries offered by the government departments vary with the kind of work. In general, they are at parity with positions of a similar kind in other government departments.

Opportunities for Self-employment

A large number of people in this field are self-employed. Most travel guides work independently. For a regular flow of work they register with established agencies on job basis. A very large number of people are running small businesses catering to travel and tourism. Many small operators have become big with time and experience.

Those with some capital and initiative have secured their positions by operating a taxi in which they take the tourists around, and act as guides. Many other facilities like booking seats, arranging for hotel accommodation, etc. can be conveniently provided even in the smaller towns. Young people are using these opportunities to build careers for themselves.

Group travelling by road, rail, air and sea is also becoming very popular. Many young people are using initiative and imagination to plan group tours within the country and abroad as a means to a career in tourism. With growing experience and knowledge of the trade, it should not be difficult for young people to start profitable travel agency work offering all kinds of services to tourists.

82 Veterinary Science

For those who love animals and are interested in a career that is related to medicine, veterinary science is a good option. India has a vast cattle wealth. However, it is not as productive as it should be. Serious efforts have been made in the recent past to develop the productivity of the country's animal wealth, opening opportunities for work in this field. Greater growth is yet to come.

The opening of large-scale poultry farms and piggeries has also opened many opportunities for careers in this field. Besides commercial applications for developing the animal wealth, the need for care of pets in the homes too has not restricted the availability of veterinary services only at government hospitals, but encouraged private veterinarians to operate private clinics. Dogs and cats are popular pets. Many also rear parrots and other kinds of birds.

With 70 per cent of the population living in villages and depending upon agriculture as the principal source of livelihood, with animal drawn ploughs and implements still very popular the vast scope for veterinarians can well be appreciated. The small landholdings do not permit mechanization on economic grounds. The animal wealth will continue to provide opportunities for careers in this field.

Desirable Personal Qualities

To be successful in this field a person must:

- have great love for animals. Without it one cannot succeed in this field.
- be observant to be able to appreciate an animal's problems. Unfortunately, animals cannot communicate through the spoken word.

- be gentle and caring. Even animals can sense a person's feelings.
- be well acquainted with modern medical techniques including surgery.
- be innovative to handle difficult cases often observed amongst animals.
- be willing to work at odd hours under difficult circumstances.

Opportunities in Veterinary Science

A few decades back the opportunities in veterinary science were restricted to government run veterinary hospitals. There has been a rapid growth in the recent past. The 'white revolution'—the spurt in milk production all over the country has been possible only due to upgrading of the quality of cattle, both cows and buffaloes. This has been possible with improved breeding techniques and better animal healthcare. Those involved with veterinary science have made this possible. While at one time we did not have enough milk to drink, today there is surplus to be converted into a wide range of milk products. This is only the beginning. A vast potential for growth exists.

Another area of growth is in the field of egg production and poultry for meat. Large-scale poultry farms have made this possible. If this growth is to be maintained there will be need for dedicated veterinarians to look after this work. The development of modern piggeries is waiting to be undertaken.

Hindus do not eat beef. They use goat meat. This is an area that needs development, as the production levels are less as compared to demand. In the cool hilly areas sheep are reared for wool. Angora rabbits too are being reared for a similar purpose. This area of work also offers opportunities in this field.

The vast desert area has needs for camels for transportation. Equally important, elephants too are used in certain forest areas to move timber and supplies. Horses are the conventional cart pullers, but with increase in mechanized transportation, their numbers are gradually dwindling.

The army needs mules to carry supplies in some difficult areas. To fulfil this need the army maintains breeding centres. These have a need for qualified veterinarians.

The population of pets is also on the increase. These pets need to be immunized against certain diseases and also taken care of in times of sickness. To fulfil this need there are private clinics for pets. Since it is not possible to carry pets along when travelling, there is need for kennels and shelters to provide temporary residence to the pets. The zoos too have their need for special medical care.

Educational Facilities

Veterinary science is taught along with other subjects as part of graduate studies in agriculture. However, those who are interested in veterinary science as a full-time career should opt for the Bachelor's degree in veterinary science in veterinary colleges spread all over the country. One can join after completing 10+2 with Physics, Chemistry and Biology. Admission requirements vary from one place to another and can be verified directly from the concerned college. Many offer to specialize in particular fields by opting for the Master's degree after graduation.

Making a Beginning

Soon after qualifying from a college a person joins an established veterinarian to gain valuable experience. There are openings in government veterinary hospitals and in private organizations. During the study period one can decide the particular kind of work one would like to do and gradually move into that field. Every district has a department of Animal Husbandry that oversees all the activities in the field. The private organizations hire veterinarians as assistants to existing staff. One gradually moves up with experience. Those interested in research in this field need to specialize in particular fields and join a research organization thereafter.

Income from Veterinary Science

The income from careers in veterinary science is similar to those in similar fields. The salaries in government jobs are regulated by rules made by the state government. The salaries in private organizations are negotiable according to need and the work involved. Research organizations pay well. In private practice the income grows with experience and increased clientele.

Opportunities for Self-employment

There are ample opportunities for self-employment in this field of careers. However, most people prefer to gain experience and build up contacts before going into private practice. That ensures regular work.

Uncommon Careers

83

There is a great variety in human needs. Each one of these is responsible for promoting different careers. When particular needs are common, more people get involved and those careers become popular. There are some fields that are not very popular, but to acquaint one of the career opportunities that are available, one must understand the uncommon careers also. A few are discussed in this chapter.

Meteorology

Meteorology is the study and scientific observation of the atmosphere with the purpose of forecasting the weather. With information regularly received from the satellites and observations made at meteorological stations spread all over the country, and with computerization making calculations easy, it is possible to forecast weather for several days.

Meteorology has made it possible to predict cyclones and hurricanes that can very often create havoc over vast areas causing loss to life and property. All predictions do not come out true as the weather depends upon several factors that can change suddenly. However, each time it helps meteorologists understand weather better through experience. In the normal course, predictions about dry or wet weather, excessive rains, and similar predictions help make important decisions.

Meteorology is not a pure science. It is rather an applied science drawing upon Physics, Chemistry, Mathematics and Biology. There are not many educational institutions that provide facilities for study of Meteorology. However, science graduates can pursue the subject at higher levels of study.

Opportunities exist in the government departments like the Indian Meteorological Department, Delhi, or the Indian

Institute of Tropical Meteorology, Pune. The Air Force and the Navy too have their need for meteorologists. Other government departments whose work is associated with Agriculture, Space Research, Pollution, Oceanography and Forests also seek meteorologists. TV channels that carry weather reporting too hire people as anchors and reporters.

Most young people join as assistants to those already established in the field and gradually specialize in a field of choice. It is hard work many times requiring one to be present around the clock to make observations. The salaries are good but the work is challenging. In this field there are no opportunities for self-employment.

Feng Shui

Feng Shui, pronounced *fung shway*, is an ancient Chinese system of designing buildings and positioning objects inside the buildings to ensure a favourable flow of energy. Its popularity can be evaluated by seeing the number of stores that stock and sell Feng Shui artifacts. The people's faith in the system can be seen from the artifacts that are visible in a large number of homes everywhere.

The purpose of Feng Shui is to create harmony between nature and the home or workplace. This way the residents benefit fully from the energy in the environment. One utilizes the positive energy and avoids the negative influences.

Contrary to what many believe one cannot master Feng Shui just by reading a few articles or books. To become a practitioner one must learn it from a teacher or Master in Feng Shui. There are no institutions offering courses in this field in India. Several exist in some South Asian countries. A few trained Masters do impart training, but one must be sure about the trainer's credentials.

Many young people claim to be experts and pass on suggestions and artifacts at high prices to gullible people. One needs to appreciate that Feng Shui is not a magical system that attracts good luck and wealth. It rather prepares individuals for efficiency and development through positive activities.

An Indian system that is similar to Feng Shui is 'Vastushastra'. It is now being widely adopted and practised by some architects.

Environment

With greater pressure on the land and natural resources due to increased population, a need that has been calling out loud for help is the environment. A few seek to help by making it their vocation.

Work in this field aims at finding solutions to problems that affect nature. These problems include air and water pollution, scarcity of ground water, solid waste management, industrial waste, etc. To find solutions to these problems creating awareness at all levels including the schools and colleges is important. Already people are becoming aware of increased air pollution particularly in the larger cities with a large number of petrol and diesel vehicles. The pollution of rivers is another area that is drawing great attention. Water shortage and the falling water table is yet another area of concern.

The problems have created vocational opportunities for young people who have specialized in Environment Management or Environment Engineering. To fulfil this need several universities are now offering postgraduate studies in Environmental Sciences. It is a multi-disciplinary subject that includes Biology, Mathematics, Engineering, Ethics and History. Young people who have studied Biology, Agriculture, Forestry or Microbiology at graduation level can specialize in this field.

The Central Pollution Control Board and several other organizations including those in the private sector oversee work in this field and offer opportunities for work. Planners are particularly aware of these problems when establishing new townships and industrial estates. Many agencies like the United Nations and the World Bank are also creating awareness in this field. Opportunities exist not only in areas like pollution control, but also in areas like water harvesting and management, land and soil management, ecological architecture and biodiversity mapping. Many NGOs are conducting research on the subject.

Besides technical expertise one needs the missionary spirit to work in this field. The beginning of a career in this field may be humble but the opportunities improve with experience and better understanding.

Career Counselling

A field that appears easy and attractive to everyone, and yet very difficult, is career counselling. Perhaps never before in the history of mankind did we have as many career choices as we have today? At the same time we never had more competition. Our schools and colleges are packed with young people looking for an appropriate career. The choice seems easy, but it is not. Since at this stage the young people are passing through adolescence when nature makes them somewhat confused the choice becomes difficult.

All good schools are looking for good career counsellors. They have two choices. The first to train a schoolteacher in the work of career counselling, but since it has become a specialized job with the need for continuous updating of knowledge, it is not practical. The second is to hire a part-time career counsellor. These are not readily available.

The work of a career counsellor aims at helping a student to understand one's feelings, abilities and circumstances and matching them with an appropriate career where one can find both a livelihood and fulfilment. This is not easy. To be able to do so the counsellor must have insight into human nature and also a vast knowledge of the many career options that are available. The opportunities for careers are forever growing into new specialized fields. One needs to update knowledge about these regularly.

To succeed in this field one must preferably do a Master's degree in Psychology and follow it with a diploma in counselling. It is important to have a good knowledge of the many career options that are available. It is also useful to understand the changing employment trends. Most people begin a career as an assistant to an established counsellor, and after gaining useful experience set out on their own.

Career counselling is a very satisfying vocation in that one finds happiness in helping young people build a good life. It appears to be good social service, and at the same time a good vocation.

Pet Training

People have always had a love for pets. The pet lovers would train the pets as they liked. Some would succeed in training them into obedient pets. But many failed to do so for lack of persistence, or wrong training techniques. This has given the opportunity for yet another uncommon vocation—pet training. With greater prosperity, those who can afford the cost of training are turning to professional pet trainers.

The purpose of training a pet is not only to make them do simple things like sitting down, greeting a guest, or be toilet-trained. The pet must become a part of the family and provide security. Those who like to take their pets to dog shows need training also. In the present-day when pet lovers are willing to go out not only to keep the pet vaccinated against diseases, but ensure that the pet gets special food, shampoo and deodorants, special training makes them the pride of the family.

Where does one learn to be a pet trainer? Although such schools exist in the developed world, there are none in India. It is said that anyone who loves animals and can understand them can become a trainer. Many of the trainers have either learnt the work through personal effort, or as part of the training team maintained by some police organizations that have trained dogs to trace criminals. Some have left their jobs and become freelance trainers.

Is the work remunerative and worth the effort? Most do it for the love of it. But it is also remunerative in that a dog trainer charges almost Rs. 2000 per month for five one-hour sessions every week. On an average the complete training takes about three months. A good trainer may be training as many as ten dogs at a time. At this rate the effort is well worth the while.

Pet boutiques and training schools are finding their way into the metro cities where people can afford these facilities. The trends indicate growth in this field. Pet lovers can look forward to better opportunities for a vocation.

SECTION THREE
Some Addresses

Some Addresses

84

This is not intended to be a directory of institutions of higher learning in India. Even if it were, it would not be possible to include the details of all the institutions for the simple reason that it would become too voluminous to handle. There are almost 1500 institutions that impart vocational education in the field of Medicine. More than 900 institutions impart education in the field of Management. Over 1000 institutions impart education in Engineering & Technology. If one were also to add the long lists of educational institutions that impart knowledge in the big variety of vocational courses that are available today, one would have a massive directory.

Every State has its own universities. Besides the many courses offered at different levels at the university, there are many colleges affiliated to each university. Besides these, there are several private universities recognized by the government. Many of the foreign universities too have their representatives and education centres providing a variety of courses. Many private institutions too provide vocational education recognized by the State Technical Education Boards. In the technical field many private institutions have franchise units spread out almost in every major town in the country. In the same way, to cope with the special coaching required to sit for the many competitive exams held each year there are well organized coaching centres with franchise units in major cities and towns.

Distance education is yet another field that has opened learning opportunities for young people in every part of the country. It is now possible to work and also study to improve one's prospects. When it has not been possible to attain one's educational potential, there are opportunities to learn through additional courses, studying at home. Studying through the Internet too has opened many opportunities for study. Individual circumstances will vary. Educational facilities available nearby too will vary from one place to another. One will need to adapt to suit personal convenience.

The addresses given in the following pages are only representative of the many fields that are open to the youth presently.

Accountancy

Institute of Cost & Works Accountants of India,
Kolkata-700016.

Institute of Chartered Accountants of India,
New Delhi.

Advertising

Apeejay Institute of Design
54, Tughlakabad Institutional Area, Mehrauli-Badarpur Road,
New Delhi-110062.

National Institute of Advertising
1, Deen Dayal Upadhaya Marg,
1st Floor, ITO,
New Delhi-110002.

National Institute of Advertising,
204/5, Lane W4D,
Sainik Farms (Western Avenue),
Khanpur, New Delhi-110062.

EMPI Professional Training & Development Academy,
Gargi College Campus,
Siri Fort Road,
New Delhi-110049.

Aeronautics

Institute of Aeronatics & Engineering,
Shahpur Road, Parvalia Thana,
NH-12, Bhopal-Jaipur Road,
Bhopal, M.P.

Indian Institute of Aeronautics,
House No. 18, Road No. 55,
Punjabi Bagh (West),
New Delhi-110026.

School of Aeronautics,
H-974 Palam Extension, Part I,
Sector 7, Dwarka,
New Delhi-110045.

Academy of Aerospace & Aviation,
M.P. Flying Club Ltd.,
Harshita Aviation Complex,
Aerodrome,
Pithampur By-pass, Nanand,
Indore-452112.

Hindustan Institute of Aeronautics,
5, Temple View,
Neori Mandir, Lal Gathi,
Bhopal, M.P.

Indian Institute of Aircraft Engineering,
A-191, Mahipalpur Extension,
Road No. 4, Lane No. 8,
New Delhi-110037.

Guru-Gram Institute of Aeronautical Engineering & Technology,
55, B.P. Near Escorts Hospital,
Neelam Bata Road,
Faridabad.

Agri-business Management

Indian Institute of Management
Ahmedabad.

College of Agribusiness Management,
G.B. Pant University of Agriculture,
Pantnagar-263145.

Agro-chemicals

Department of Agro-chemicals & Pest Management,
University of Delhi,
Delhi-110007.

Animation

Rtoonz Academy of Animation & Illustration,
708, Burari,
Delhi-110084.

Architecture

College of Architecture,
Goa University,
Campal Panaji, Goa.

School of Planning & Architecture,
New Delhi.

College of Architecture,
Punjab University,
Chandigarh.

Archival Studies

National Archives of India,
School of Archival Studies,
Janpath, New Delhi-110001.

Art

Shankar's Academy of Art & Book Publishing,
4, Bahadur Shah Zafar Marg,
New Delhi-110002.

Institute of Fine Arts,
Opp. State Bank of India,
Modinagar, U.P.

College of Art,
Tilak Marg,
New Delhi.

Faculty of Fine Arts,
Jamia Milia Islamia,
Jamia Nagar,
New Delhi.

J.J. Institute of Arts,
Mumbai.

Faculty of Fine Arts,
MS University,
Vadodara.

College of Arts & Crafts,
Chennai.

Astrology

Gurukul Kangri Vishwavidyalaya,
Hardwar.

Maharishi Mahesh Yogi Vedic Vishwavidyala,
Jabalpur.

Rajasthan Vidyapeeth,
Udaipur.

M.S. University,
Vadodara.

Banking

National School of Banking,
Indian Education Society Campus,
Babrekar Marg, Off Gokhale Road (North),
Dadar, Mumbai-400028.

Institute for Development & Research in Banking Technology,
Castle Hills, Road No. 1,
Masab Tank,
Hyderabad-500057.

National School of Banking,
Lucknow.

Biotechnology

Institute of Management Studies,
Lal Quan, G.T. Road,
Ghaziabad, U.P.

Bioinformatics Institute of India,
B-15, Sector 3,
Noida-201301.

G.B. Pant University of Agriculture & Technology,
Pantnagar-263145.

Banaras Hindu University,
Varanasi.

Goa University,
Taleigao Plateau,
Goa-403206.

Jawaharlal Nehru University,
New Delhi.

M.S. University of Baroda,
Vadodara-390002.

Book Publishing

National Book Trust,
A-5, Green Park,
New Delhi-110016.

College of Vocational Studies,
Sheikh Serai, Phase II,
New Delhi-110017.

Shankar's Academy of Art & Book Publishing,
4, Bahadur Shah Zafar Marg,
New Delhi-110002.

Call Centres

North Star Call Centre College,
B-109, Sector 5,
Noida-201301.

Careers for Women

Vidya Bhawan,
Connaught Place,
Bangla Sahib Road,
Opp. Kali Mandir,
New Delhi-110001.

Polytechnic for Women,
A-3, South Extension-I,
Ring Road,
New Delhi-110049.

Catering & Hotel Management

Bhartiya Vidya Bhawan,
Room No. 20,
Kasturba Gandhi Marg,
New Delhi-110001.

Indian Institute of Science & Management,
Pundag, Ranchi-834004.

Oriental School of Hotel Management,
29/924, Almaaz Building,
Kotooli, Calicut-673016.

Institute of Hotel Management, Catering Technology & Applied Nutrition,
Gangtok.

Hotel Management College,
Institute of Advanced Management,
AE-486, Salt Lake City,
Kolkata-700064.

Institute of Hotel Management, Catering Technology & Applied Nutrition,
11, R.A. Lines,
Dogra Mandir Lane,
The Mall,
Meerut Cantt.-250001.

Civil Aviation

Indian Institute of Engineering & Technology,
L-487, Shastri Nagar,
Meerut, U.P.

Asiatic International Aviation Academy,
201-B, Vidha Pati Building,
Race Course Road,
Indore-452001.

Air Hostess Training Institute,
K-86, Lajpat Nagar-II,
New Delhi.

Orient Flying School,
40, G.S.T. Road,
St. Thomas Mount,
Chennai-600016.

Orient Flying School,
Flat No. 2234, 1st Floor,
Sector-C, Pocket-2,
Vasant Kunj,
New Delhi-110070.

Air Technical Training Institute,
VIP Road,
P.O. Kolkata Airport,
Kolkata-700052.

Air Hostess Academy,
AHA House,
Nyayadeep Building,
'D' Wing, New Link Road,
Andheri (West), Mumbai.

Clinical Research

Institute of Clinical Research (India),
77, Karanpur Road,
Dehradun-248001.

Company Secretary

Institute of Company Secretaries of India,
ICSI House, 22 Institutional Area,
Lodhi Road,
New Delhi-110003.

Consultancy Service

Consultancy Development Centre,
Birla Institute of Technology & Science,
India Habitat Centre, Zone IV,
East Court, 2nd Floor,
Lodhi Road,
New Delhi-110003.

Cooking

Academy of Culinary Education,
Goa.

Foodcraft Institute,
18B, Ashoka Marg,
Lucknow.

Foodcraft Institute,
Sheshadri Road,
Bangalore.

Cottage Crafts

Shilpa Bharti Institute of Fine Arts & Crafts,
G-Building, South Patel Nagar Market,
New Delhi-110008.

Counselling

Indian Institute of Counselling,
S-13, Akarshan Bhawan,
23, Ansari Road,
New Delhi-110002.

Regional Institute of Education,
Bhopal.

St. Xavier's Institute of Counselling,
Mumbai.

Dairy Science

National Dairy Research Institute,
Karnal-132001.

Indira Gandhi Agricultural University,
Krishak Nagar,
Raipur-492006.

Dancing & Dramatics

National School of Drama,
Bahawalpur House,
Bhagwan Dass Road,
New Delhi-110001.

Padmini Kolhapure School of Acting,
New Delhi.

Imago School of Acting,
New Delhi.

The Sangeet Natak Akademi,
New Delhi.

Bhatkhande College of Hindustani Music,
Lucknow.

Rajasthan Sangeet Sangathan,
Jaipur.

College of Indian Music, Dance & Dramatics,
Vadodara.

Designing

Apeejay Institute of Design,
54, Tughlakabad Institutional Area,
Mehrauli-Badarpur Road,
New Delhi-110062.

VLSI Design & Research Centre,
Department of Electronics,
University of Pune,
Pune-411007.

Spectrum Institute of Design,
B-78, 3rd Floor,
Defence Colony,
New Delhi-110024.

Distance Education

Indra Gandhi National Open University,
Maidan Garhi,
New Delhi-110068.

Prof. G. Ram Reddy Centre for Distance Education,
Osmania University,
Hyderabad-500007.

Indian Institute of Ecology & Environment,
A-15 (HTH) Paryavaran Complex,
South of Saket,
New Delhi-110030.

National Open School,
B-31B, Kailash Colony,
New Delhi-110048.

Directorate of Correspondence Courses,
Kurukshetra University,
Kurukshetra.

Dress Making

South Delhi Polytechnic,
Lajpat Nagar,
New Delhi.

National Institute of Fashion Technology,
New Delhi.

Academy of Fashion Studies,
Greater Kailash-II,
New Delhi-110048.

Engineering & Technology

Malviya Regional Engineering College,
Jaipur-302017.

The ICFAI Institute of Science & Technology,
62, Nagarjuna Hills,
Punjagutta,
Hyderabad-500082.

National Council for Cement & Building Materials,
34 km Stone,
Delhi-Mathura Road,
Ballabhgarh-121004.

Indo Danish Tool Room,
M-4 (Part), Phase-VI,
Tata Kandra Road, Gamharia,
Jamshedpur-832108.

Entertainment

School of Audio Engineering,
Chennai & Bangalore.

Audio-Video Institute,
M-161/1A, 2nd Floor,
Behind Indian Oil Bhawan,
Gautam Nagar,
New Delhi-110049.

Entrepreneurship
A.K. Garg Engineering College,
27 km Stone,
Delhi-Hapur Road,
Adhyatmik Nagar,
Ghaziabad-201009.

Environment
Centre for Environmental Law,
Worldwide Fund for Nature-India,
172-B, Lodhi Estate,
New Delhi-110003.

Indian Institute of Quality Management,
STQC Directorate,
Malviya Industrial Area,
Jaipur-302017.

School of Environment Management,
Indraprastha University,
Delhi.

Indian Institute of Environment Management,
Navi Mumbai.

Event Management
Indian Events & Media Academy,
P/33, South Extension,
Part II, New Delhi

Fashion & Design
Senorita College of Fashion Design & Management,
20/3, Punjabi Bagh Extension,
New Delhi-110026.

Pearl Academy of Fashion,
A-21/13, Naraina Industrial Area, Phase II,
New Delhi-110028.

Academy of Fashion Studies,
B-37A, Gangotri Enclave,
Alaknanda, Near Greater Kailash II, New Delhi-110048.

Apparel Training & Design Centre,
A-223, Okhla Industrial Area, Phase I,
New Delhi-110020.

MB Institute of Fashion Technology,
37, Bungalow Road,
Kamla Nagar,
Delhi-110007.

Central Footwear Training Institute,
C-41/42, Site-C, Industrial Area,
Sikandra, Agra-282007.

Film & Serial Making
Indian Film & Theatre Academy,
C-317, Saket,
New Delhi-110017.

Asian Academy of Film & TV,
Marwah Studios Complex,
FC 14/15, Film City,
Sector 16-A, Noida-201301.

BAG Films Ltd., SOMES,
F-23, Sector 16A, Film City,
Noida-201301.

Apeejay Institute of Design,
54, Tughlakabad Institutional Area,
Mehrauli-Badarpur Road,
New Delhi-110062.

Foundation Institute for Learning Media,
D-48, Kalkaji,
New Delhi-110019.

Director IMS, New Delhi YMCA,
4th Floor, Cultural Centre Building,
1, Jai Singh Road,
New Delhi-110001.

Imago Acting School,
1st Floor, Sudhan Bhawan,
37, Saidulajab
(Opp. CISF Camp-Saket)
Mehrauli-Badarpur Road,
New Delhi-110030.

AVI Institute of Media Studies,
M-161/1A, 2nd Floor,
Gautam Nagar,
New Delhi-110049.

Hindustan College of Arts & Science,
40, G.S.T. Road,
St. Thomas Mount,
Chennai-600016.

Fortune Institute of Communication & Television,
G-17D, South Extension-II,
New Delhi-110049.

Film & Media School,
Institute for Integrated Learning in Management,
3, Lodhi Institutional Area,
New Delhi-110003.

Finance

International College of Financial Planning,
5th Floor, Bajaj House,
97, Nehru Place,
New Delhi.

Fishery

G.B. Pant University of Agriculture,
Pant Nagar (UA).

College of Fishery Sciences,
West Bengal University,
Kolkata.

Osmania University,
Hyderabad (A.P.)

College of Fisheries,
Gujarat Agricultural University,
Krushinagar.

Fitness & Beauty Business

Pearl Academy of Fashion,
Naraina Industrial Area,
Phase II, New Delhi-110028.

National Vocational Training Institute for Women,
Sector-1, Noida-201301.

Forensic Science

National Institute of Criminology and Forensic Sciences,
GGS Indraprastha University,
New Delhi.

Punjabi University,
Patiala.

Harisingh Gour University,
Sagar.

Forestry

Indian Forest Research Institute,
Dehradun.

Indian Institute of Forest Management,
357, Nehru Nagar,
Bhopal-462003.

Gemology

Indian Institute of Gemology,
10980, East Park Road,
Karol Bagh,
(Opp. Model Basti P.O.),
New Delhi-110005.

Gems & Jewellery Export Promotion Council,
Mumbai.

The Gemological Institute of India,
29, Gurukul Chambers,
187-189, Mumbadevi Road,
Mumbai-400002.

Jewellery Product Development Centre,
New Delhi.

Jewellery Design & Technology Institute,
F-11, South Extension Part I,
New Delhi-110049.

Jewellery Design & Technology Institute,
A-89, Sector 2,
Noida-201301.

Indian Diamond Institute,
Surat.

Gemstones Artisans Training School,
Jaipur-302017.

SG Jhaveri Centre for Diamond Technology,
Mumbai.

National Institute of Fashion Technology,
New Delhi.

Jasani Department of Jewellery Design & Manufacture,
3rd Floor, P.V. Polytechnic,
S.N.D.T. Women's University,
Juhu Campus,
Santa Cruz (West),
Mumbai-400049.

South Delhi Polytechnic for Women,
New Delhi.

Government Service
Local Coaching Institutes.

Grooming
Pivot Point India,
J-1, 1st floor, Kailash Colony,
New Delhi-110048.

Hair Styling
Habib's Hair Academy,
F-38, South Extension Part-I,
New Delhi-110049.

Homoeopathy
Nehru Homoeopathic Medical College & Hospital,
Faculty of Unani & Ayurvedic Medicines,
V.P. Chest Institute Building,
7th Floor, University of Delhi,
Delhi-110007.

Solan Homoeopathic Medical College & Hospital,
Chamba Ghat,
Solan-173212.

Horticulture & Floriculture
Narendra Deva University of Agriculture and Technology,
Faizabad, U.P.

Hospital Management
Delhi Institute of Paramedical & Technical Education,
RZ-C-117, Gopal Nagar,
Najafgarh,
New Delhi-110043.

All India Institute of Local Self Government,
22-23, Institutional Area,
'D' Block, Pankha Road,
Janakpuri,
New Delhi-110058.

Human Rights
Indian Institute of Human Rights,
Green Gate,
A14-16, Paryavaran Complex,
South Saket,
New Delhi-110030.

Society for Upliftment of Masses,
E-7/16, Vasant Vihar,
New Delhi-110057.

I.A.S. & Allied Services
Local Coaching Institutes.

Information Technology

Jawahar Lal Nehru University,
Computer Centre, Hall No. 8,
Lecture Halls Complex,
New Delhi-110067.

Vishwesharaiya College of Engineering & Technology,
CB-152, Main Ring Road,
Naraina, New Delhi-110028.

Regional Institute of Technology,
Jamshedpur-831014.

Apeejay Institute of Management & Information,
Sector-8, Institutional Area,
Dwarka, Papankalan,
New Delhi-110045.

Instrumentation

University Science Instrumentation Centre,
Kurukshetra University,
Kurukshetra, Haryana.

Insurance

Amity School of Insurance & Actuarial Management,
RB Education Foundation,
E-27, Defence Colony,
New Delhi-110024.

Insurance Institute of India,
Universal Insurance Building,
Sir P.S. Mehta Road,
Mumbai-400001.

Delhi Insurance Institute,
78, Janpath, 1st Floor,
New Delhi-110001.

University of Madras,
Centenary Buildings Chepauk,
Triplicane, Chennai-600005.

Kalyani University,
Kalyani-741235.

HRD Foundation,
Vanita Samaj, Building No. 13,
Institutional Area, Lodhi Road,
New Delhi-110003.

Interior Designing

Exterior-Interiors Pvt. Ltd.,
F-12, Kalkaji,
New Delhi-110019.

International Trade

Indian Institute of Commerce & Trade,
5/28, Vikas Nagar,
Lucknow-226022.

Delhi Institute of Foreign Trade Management,
B-4/59, Safdarjang Enclave,
New Delhi-110020.

Foreign Trade Development Centre,
N-5, South Extension, Part I,
New Delhi-110049.

Indian Institute of Export Management,
1953 (B1) 9th Cross,
4th Main,
New Thippasandra,
Bangalore-560075.

Indian Institute of Commerce & Trade,
5/28, Vikas Nagar,
Lucknow-226022.

Investigation Services

National Institute of Private Investigation,
S-2, Paradise Plaza,
Alaknanda Commercial Complex,
New Delhi.

Globe Detective Agency Pvt. Ltd.,
New Delhi.

The CBI Academy,
Ghaziabad.

Lancers Network Ltd.,
New Delhi.

All India Private Detectives Association,
New Delhi.

Journalism

Delhi School of Communication,
Chinmaya Building,
Near Indian Airlines Colony,
Vasant Vihar,
New Delhi-110057.

DB College of Mass Communication,
A-35, Sector-19,
Noida-201301.

IAAN School of Mass Communication,
IAAN House,
Opp. C-765,
New Friends Colony,
New Delhi-110065.

AJK Mass Communication Research Centre,
Jamia Millia Islamia,
New Delhi-110025.

MG School of Communications Management,
E-14, East of Kailash,
New Delhi-110065.

Janki Devi Memorial College,
Sir Ganga Ram Hospital Marg,
New Delhi-110060.

S.P. College of Communication & Management,
Bharatiya Vidya Bhawan,
Kasturba Gandhi Marg,
New Delhi-110001.

Languages

Department of English & Modern European Languages,
Jamia Millia Islamia,
New Delhi.

Jawaharlal Nehru Academy of Languages,
Bhartiya Vidya Bhawan,
Kasturba Gandhi Marg,
New Delhi-110001.

Japanese Cultural & Information Centre,
32, Ferozeshah Road,
New Delhi.

Central Institute of English & Foreign Languages,
Orient Longman Pvt. Ltd.,
248/B/31/A, Road No. 3,
Banjara Hills,
Hyderabad-500034.

British Council's English Language Teaching Centre,
17, Kasturba Gandhi Road,
New Delhi-110001.

Alliance Francaise,
D-13, South Extension-II,
New Delhi.

Law

Nalser, University of Law,
City Office:3-4-761, Barkatpura,
Hyderabad-500027.

Law College,
Abhishek Tower,
15, Subhash Road,
Dehradun-248001.

National Law University,
JNU University (New Campus),
Bhagat ki Kothi,
Jodhpur-342005.

Librarian

Department of Library & Information Science,
2nd Floor, Tutorial Building,
University of Delhi,
Delhi-110007.

GLA Institute of Technology & Management,
Mathura.

Management

DPC Institute of Management,
IE/10, Jhandewalan Extension,
Delhi-110055.

Bharti Vidyapeeth's Institute of Management & Research,
A-4, Paschim Vihar,
Rohtak Road,
New Delhi-110063.

Advanced Management Institute,
B-294, Sector-20,
Noida-201301.

Skyline Business School,
Hauz Khas Enclave,
New Delhi-110016.

Symbiosis Centre for Distance Learning,
SCDI Building 4, Wing A-2,
First Floor, New Ajanta Avenue,
Paud Road, Pune-411038.

Jagannath International Management School,
E-289, Greater Kailash-II,
New Delhi-110048.

NIMT,
G.T. Road, Opp. Indira Priyadarshini Park,
Near Hindon River Bridge,
Ghaziabad.

International Institute of Management Sciences,
CF-151, Salt Lake City,
Sector-1,
Kolkata-700064.

The Indian Institute of Planning & Management,
11 PM Tower,
C-10, Qutab Institutional Area,
New Delhi-110016.

College of Business Studies,
Vivek Vihar, Phase II,
Delhi.

Marine Engineering

T.S. Chanakya,
Mumbai.

Tolani Marine Institute,
Pune.

International Maritime Institute,
New Delhi.

Materials Management

Indian Institute of Materials Management,
Plot 102 & 104, Sector 15,
Institutional Area, CBD, Belapur,
Navi Mumbai.

College of Materials Management,
Jabalpur.

Medical Transcription

Pan American Institute of Medical Transcription,
E-986, C.R. Park,
New Delhi-110019.

Indo-American Academy of Medical Transcription,
D-133, Okhla Industrial Area,
Phase I, New Delhi-110020.

Medical Transcription Institute of India,
3rd Floor, Herman Plaza,
2, West Patel Nagar,
New Delhi.

Janki Devi Vocational Centre,
JD Memorial College,
Sir Ganga Ram Hospital Marg,
New Delhi-110060.

Indian Institute of Medical Transcription,
E-17, 3rd Floor,
South Extension Part-I,
New Delhi-110049.

Medicine

Delhi Institute of Paramedical & Technical Education,
RZ-C-117, Gopal Nagar,
Najafgarh, New Delhi-110043.

National Institute of Immunology,
Aruna Asaf Ali Marg,
New Delhi-110067.

Merchant Navy

Maharashtra Academy of Naval Education & Training,
S.No. 124, Kothrud,
Paud Road, Pune-411038.

Academy of Maritime Education & Training,
BIT Extension Centre,
3/4/5, Ambedkar Street,
Gandhi Nagar, Saligramam,
Chennai-600093.

Sea Horse Academy of Merchant Navy,
70-7-68/9,
Thota Subbarao Nagar,
Kakinada-533003.

Meteorology

Punjabi University,
Patiala.

Centre for Atmospheric and Oceanic Sciences,
Indian Institute of Science,
Bangalore.

Shivaji University,
Kolhapur.

Modelling

Le Modelle,
A-54, 1st Floor, Naraina Vihar,
New Delhi-110028.

Multi-level Marketing

Modicare Ltd.,
4, Community Centre,
New Friends Colony,
New Delhi-110065.

Multimedia

Arena Multimedia,
Ask for the nearest centre at Aptech.

Maya Academy of Advanced Cinematics,
New Delhi.

Apeejay Institute of Design,
New Delhi.

Centre for Electronics Design & Technology of India,
A-34, Phase VIII, Industrial Area,
Mohali-160059.

Nursing

Kailash Institute of Nursing,
G-29, Sector 27,
Noida-201301.

Goutham College,
Manjunathanagar, WOC Road,
Rajaji Nagar,
Bangalore-560010.

R.R. School of Nursing,
888, Sector 14,
Gurgaon.

BHRC School of Nursing,
Bhandari Hospital & Research Centre,
21-22 GF. Sc. No. 54,
Vijay Nagar,
Indore, Madhya Pradesh

Optometry

SNDT Women's University,
Juhu, Santa Cruz (West),
Mumbai.

College of Optometry & Ophthalmic Sciences,
Nasik.

Bausch & Lomb International School of Optometry,
Hyderabad.

Elite School of Optometry,
Chennai.

Lotus College of Optometry,
Mumbai.

All India Institute of Optometrical Sciences,
Kolkata.

Personality Development

Tuff Trak International,
Pearl Academy Building,
A-21/13, Naraina Industrial Area, Phase II,
New Delhi-110028.

Petroleum Engineering

University of Petroleum & Energy Studies,
Building No. 7, Street No. 1,
Vasant Vihar Enclave,
Dehradun-248006.

Pharmacy

National Institute of Pharmaceutical Education & Research
67, S.A.S. Nagar,
Mohali-160062.

Sardar Bhagwan Singh PG Institute of Biomedical Sciences,
Balawala,
Dehradun-248161.

Photography

Academy of Photography,
Rabindra Bharati University,
Kolkata-700050.

Sri Venkateshwara University,
Tirupati, Chittoor-517502.

JJ School of Art,
Mahatma Gandhi Road, Fort,
Mumbai-400032.

Bhartiya Vidya Bhawan,
Kasturba Gandhi Marg,
New Delhi-110001.

National Institute of Design,
Paldi, Ahmedabad-380007.

Jawahar Lal Nehru Technological University,
Mahaveer Marg, Masab Tank,
Hyderabad-500028.

Triveni Kala Sangam,
New Delhi.

Physiotherapy

Ayushman Hospital & College,
C-Sector, Shahpura,
Bhopal, M.P.

Institute of Applied Medicine & Research,
117, Navyug Market,
Ghaziabad-201001.

Printing

School of Printing Technology,
Jadavpur, Kolkata-700032.

School of Printing Technology,
Dr. D. Naoroji Road,
Mumbai-400001.

Regional School of Printing Technology,
Allahabad.

Real Estate

Hermann Business School,
S-Block, Rock Garden,
Greater Kailash-II,
New Delhi-110048.

Rehabilitation

All India Institute of Physical Medicine & Rehabilitation,
Haji Ali Marg,
K. Khadya Marg, Mahalaxmi,
Mumbai-400034.

Religious Services

Vedanta Academy,
Malavli, Maharashtra.

University of Vedic Sciences,
Plot No. 56, Road No. 8,
Jubilee Hills,
Hyderabad-500033.

Retail Selling

Elite School,
B-55, Greater Kailash Part-I,
New Delhi-110048.

Self-employment

Society for Self-employment,
E-26-29,
Flatted Factories Complex,
Jhandewalan,
New Delhi-110055.

Selling

Indian Institute of Pharmaceuticals Marketing,
5/28, Vikas Nagar,
Lucknow-226022.

TKWS Skill Development Centre,
10/23, East Patel Nagar,
New Delhi-110008.

Social Service

Indian Institute of Rural Development,
IIRM Campus, Tagore Marg,
Mansarovar, Jaipur-302020.

Teaching

Institute of Education,
University of Bundelkhand,
Kanpur Road,
Jhansi-284128

Department of Education,
Delhi University,
33, Chhabra Marg,
Delhi-110057.

National College of Education,
National House, Bhandari Bagh,
Dehradun-248001.

Manava Bharati Teachers Training Institute,
Angaila Hills, Ghanghora,
Dehradun-248141.

Tool Manufacturing

Central Tool Room & Training Centre,
B-36, Chandaka Industrial Area,
Bhubaneshwar-751024.

Central Institute of Tool Design,
Ministry of SSI, Balanagar,
Hyderabad-500037.

Total Quality Management

Quality Institute of India,
Harit Dwar (Gunvatta Entry),
A 14-16, Paryavaran Complex,
Saket, Maidan Garhi Marg,
New Delhi-110030.

Transportation

Local Driving Schools.

Travel & Tourism

Institute of Labour Development,
6/2, Near Keshav Vidya Peeth,
Jaipur-302003.

Indian Institute of Travel & Tourism,
Govindpuri, Gwalior-474011.

Benaras Hindu University,
Varanasi.

Institute of Tourism Studies,
Lucknow University,
Lucknow-226007.

Centre for Vocational Studies,
DA University, R.N.T. Marg,
Indore-452001.

Institute for Career Studies,
YMCA, Jai Singh Road,
New Delhi-110001.

Kuoni Academy of Travel,
M-14, South Extension Part II,
New Delhi-110049.

The Academy of Travel Management & Training,
E-4 Defence Colony, Ring Road,
New Delhi-110024.

Institute of Tourism Management,
Moti Mahal,
2, Rana Pratap Marg,
Lucknow-226001.

Veterinary Science

Central Veterinary Research Institute,
Izatnagar.

Narendra Deva University of Agriculture & Technology,
Faizabad (U.P.).

Tamil Nadu Veterinary & Animal Science University,
Tuticorin.

Wood Industry Technology

Indian Plywood Industries Research & Training Institute,
2273, Tumkur Road,
Bangalore.